Prayer Is a Place

Other Books by the Author

NONFICTION

The Shaping of a Life
The Divine Hours (Volumes 1, 2, and 3)
Christmastide: Prayers for Advent Through Epiphany from
"The Divine Hours"
Eastertide: Prayers for Lent and Easter from "The Divine Hours"
Greed
God-Talk in America
A Stitch and a Prayer
Re-Discovering the Sacred — Spirituality in America
The Tickle Papers
Wisdom in the Waiting
The Graces We Remember
What the Land Already Knows
The City Essays

LITURGICAL DRAMA

Tobias and the Angel
Children of Her Name
Figs and Fury

GENERAL EDITOR

Home Works — A Book of Tennessee Writers
Confessing Conscience — Churched Women on Abortion

Prayer Is a Place

America's Religious
Landscape Observed

PHYLLIS TICKLE

Doubleday

New York   London   Toronto   Sydney   Auckland

PUBLISHED BY DOUBLEDAY
a division of Random House, Inc.

DOUBLEDAY and the portrayal of an anchor with a dolphin are registered
trademarks of Random House, Inc.

Book design by Patrice Sheridan

Library of Congress Cataloging-in-Publication Data

Tickle, Phyllis.
Prayer is a place : America's religious landscape observed / Phyllis Tickle. —1st ed.
p. cm.
1. United States—Religion—1960— 2. Tickle, Phyllis. I. Title.

BL2525.T525 2005
200'.973'09049—dc22
2004061859

ISBN 0-385-50440-3

PRINTED IN THE UNITED STATES OF AMERICA

July 2005

First Edition

1 3 5 7 9 10 8 6 4 2

For Sam, in whom everything has always begun and ended for me,
and for our sons and sons-in-law

John Crockett Tickle II
Philip Wade Tickle (dec.)
Samuel Milton Tickle, Jr.
Devereaux Dunlap Cannon
Emmett Vincent Ballard
Leon Angelo Palermo
Donald Lester Wolters

Because of them, I live each day in the wisdom and comfort of good men.

The story of my participation at a private mass celebrated by Archbishop Desmond Tutu has been told once before in a slightly different form in *Re-Discovering the Sacred: Spirituality in America* and is adapted here with the permission of Crossroad Publishing.

Prologue

. . .

I will be seventy years old on my next birthday and well past that mark by the time you begin to read what I have written here. What surprises me most about that accumulation of years is how light a thing they are, how much less impressive in reality than in the weighty sound of their summing. Seventy years and over should make a lifetime, should arrive at some kind of conclusion or constitute some kind of a whole. They should, but mine at least have not.

Please don't misunderstand me. I can look back from here and say of my life, "Had it not been for that, then this would never have been." Most of us have to arrive at no more than a third of seventy before we begin to discern a cause-and-effect relationship between single days and the years they make. Some of us—the lucky ones, perhaps, though I am not sure of that—even come fairly early to a kind of belief in the overall integrity of life. That is, we (for I am among this group) begin to trust the principle that the confusing, the painful, even the unbearable and destructive in life are movement within a pattern and toward some final end that is either good or nothing.

It is not so much, then, that I think my seventy-odd years have lacked continuity. Instead, my concern is with accurately describing the nature of their continuity; for my seventy have been more analogous to a string of knotted beads than to the flow of a river. That is to say that over the years there were choices made that unquestionably became "me" as well as the integrating thread for all the other choices, but the experience itself has been all about the beads.

I said something to this effect to an acquaintance a year or so ago, and he looked at me with more animus than I could ever have imagined his being capable of. "You damned married women," he said. "You have no idea how lucky you are, able to flop like that from one thing to another wherever your fancy takes you." With that he walked away, shoulders sharply erect and face glowering. I was so stunned by the resentment in his words that I was temporarily baffled by their logic. Later, of course, I began to appreciate the valid distinction that was buried in the rubble of his rage. I was, and for fifty years have been, married to Sam Tickle. We have had seven children together. We have buried one of them and long since reared the other six to adulthood. Over those years I have indeed moved from the domestic to the professional and back again as the need arose and, in my later years, from one occupation to another within the book industry, as the opportunity arose. In answer to my accuser, to whom I could not respond at the time, most of those early moves, if not the later ones, were occasioned by the circumstances and needs of a greater unit called "Sam and Phyllis and the children." However worthy and natural a cause that may have been at the time, though, the end result has still been one of variousness and catenated segments.

I say all of this here because what follows is the story of one segment. It is the autobiography more of one of the beads—the last one—than of me. Admittedly, the circumstances of any story—the strange way of its coming to be—must always be told as well. This one is no different from any other story in that regard. The tale itself, however, begins in late 1992 and ends in

2004, a dozen years in which I found what was happening to me much less interesting than the amazing show I was watching and recording.

The years from 1992 to 2004 were the closing ones of a near half century in which American religion effected a reconfiguration and cultural repositioning that history will, I wager, see as having been more comparable to the upheavals of Europe during the Christian Reformation and preliminary to Counter-Reformation than to anything else. By the grace of God or, perhaps, by appointment—who knows?—I was standing on the street corner, pad and pencil in hand, paid to count the traffic as that animated and sometimes raucous parade went by. What follows here, then, is not a spiritual memoir. Rather, it is a first-person account of religion in those twelve years of passionate upheaval. It is a description of the landscape, both rural and urban, which was and became the grounding of all their activity. Of necessity, of course, the painting reveals the painter and the writing, the writer. So be it.

Lucy, Tennessee

Chapter 1

• • •

All stories, even "Once upon a decade" ones, must continue with "and in a certain place" if they are to tell themselves completely. For this story, the place is Lucy, Tennessee . . . Lucy, where all things begin now and where, pray God, they will also arrive someday at their natural ending.

Lucy, when Sam and I brought our children here in 1977, was a clapboard, cinder-block, and tin-roofed village of no more than two dozen houses. It was surrounded by sparsely populated farmland and possessed of one aging general store, one magnificent old county school larger than the township, a railroad track with a spur, a Baptist church, a United Methodist church, two A.M.E. churches, and—incongruous as it may seem at first blush—a genuinely Anglican one. The school was testimony to the stature that Lucy once had enjoyed; the railroad with its spur was the explanation behind that stature.

Lucy had once been a bustling railroad stop for passengers and cargo on their way south and west toward Memphis. The general store had been both way station and café, while the village's shade trees had functioned like oases in the midst of the

desiccating heat of West Tennessee summers. But as with much
of rural America, the coming of affordable cars, then of good
roads, and finally of huge trucks had obviated the railroad and,
thereby, the town, long before our arrival.

When Sam and I first moved to Lucy, we and such neighbors
as we then had used to quip that Lucy was only twenty miles but
over a hundred years removed from Memphis. The twenty miles
have held constant since 1977, but the number of years has
shrunk considerably. We old-timers are forced now to admit—
with unstinting regret—that we live only about thirty years away
from the city these days. We still operate off septic tanks, in other
words, but by order of the Shelby County Health Department
we all had to have our wells closed off and cemented up a few
years ago, lest our use of them somehow contaminate Memphis's
aquifers. We still keep coal-oil lamps—or at least the Tickles
do—handily placed about, though we lose power no more than
twice or three times a year now. There is no television cable
strung in to us and there are few fancy telephone wires, but satellites and cell phones have more or less obviated them as well. The
old general store withered first into shut-down gas pumps and
then into only a few shelves of staples before it finally closed; but
it has been replaced by a thriving operation where the older men
still gather every day for checkers and where the shelves bulge
with every kind of tool or supply needed for restoring old houses
to meet suburban expectations and for building new ones to meet
a bludgeoning suburban demand. Most of us still grow our produce, but few of us still preserve it for winter. Instead, there's a
Wal-Mart just a few miles up the highway that sells us our winter provender handily as well as cheaper. Besides, for Sam and
me at least, there is no longer any need . . . no need, that is, to
prove a point.

He and I came to Lucy not to be villagers but to be a pair of
her surrounding farmers. Sam is a physician—a pulmonologist,
or specialist in diseases of the lung. For sixteen years, while he
was building his career and I mine, we lived in Memphis in a kind
of conclave of doctors and professionals that was, literally, almost
within the shadow of the University of Tennessee Medical Center

and the major hospitals that are its teaching as well as its healing hub. There was nothing wrong with that settled, tree-lined, well-maintained area. It still goes, in fact, by the name of Central Gardens, primarily because that is exactly what it is—central and as chock-full of pleasant gardens as of pleasant people.

Our concern in the mid-1970s, then, was not with the place where we were, but with who we were. If this, however, is to be an accurate record of things as they were then, I must qualify the "we." In the long months before our leaving the city, the concerns Sam and I expressed to each other were all about who and what our children were becoming, not about us or ourselves. Only years later and in retrospect did I perceive that, as is often the way of parents, we were projecting onto the children shortcomings and lapses we ourselves were also suffering from, albeit ours were more negative than positive. That is, had the two of us had time to be more self-scrutinizing in those days of diapers and mayhem, I would like to think now that Sam and I would have also been concerned about who we as adults were not and about who we were not becoming in the midst of the affluence we found to be so limiting for our youngsters.

It was the time of America's bicentennial, the time when patriotism was studied—too studied, one felt somehow, and not quite as naturally come by as once it had been. The dust of Vietnam was always on the mirror we looked at ourselves in; and there was the keening sigh, audible even in the city, of an earth being used, not tended. Sam and I sat down to supper each night with five children (Nora, our oldest, was a bride in 1976) who, being bright, knew exactly how much each dish on our table had cost at the market. We sat down as well with five children who had no more than a vague intellectual knowledge of where that food had come from prior to its arrival at the market. More disturbing than that, however, was that we sat down each night with children who had no knowledge, academic or otherwise, of what that food, that table, those eating implements, the walls around us, the clothes we wore, and the napkins we were using had cost in terms other than ones of money.

Because they were indeed bright children, good students and

much-loved citizens of their world as well as southern in rearing, they understood the end worth of some things in terms of their utility and of many other things in terms of sentiment and familial heritage. They just did not—could not—grasp the initial cost of those things in nonfiscal terms. And because the stuff of life as they acquired it was being recorded in dollars, life itself was slowly but perceptibly coming likewise to be reported in dollars.

Sam and I watched with growing alarm even as, at the same time, we began to take long drives and scour the real estate listings. We were looking for that improbable thing: a farm big enough to sustain us, small enough to be run by people already working full-time, and near enough to the hospitals for him to be able to get to a patient in distress within a matter of a few minutes. We were looking for Lucy. When we found her—when we pulled across that cattle guard and I walked for the first time on the land that would become our farm—I was so sure, so blindingly, painfully, burningly sure, that I wept as I have rarely wept before or since. We were home.

The children, in the way of children, would call that place "the Loosey, Goosey Farm" while they were growing up here. Now, in the way of adults scorning the infantile in their own background, they call it the farm in Lucy, except they both say and write it as "The Farm In Lucy," which I suppose is how it shall stay as long as there are Tickles living here either in time or in memory.

And so it was that we seven, ranging in age from two to forty-five, set about the business of joining our lives more immediately to the land's. We still bought our staples—our sugar and flour, butter and coffee, etc. but I made our bread, and the girls and I canned, froze, or dried our produce. We bought our cloth and yarn and, except for uniforms, we made most of our own clothes out of them. Sam discovered and rescued an ancient orchard that had been lost under vines for years and gone fallow. He trimmed and watered it back to fertility, and we made our own sweets. The jellies came from the apples and peaches, the honey from the hives he and the boys tended near the tree line, and the jams from the blackberry brambles we cultivated as breaks to protect the gardens and orchard.

We put in a herd of twenty-some head and grew the hay and fodder to sustain them. The children—the boys more than the girls—despised tending cattle, but we all enjoyed eating the roasts and steaks and stews that were a portion of the end result. We pumped water and hauled off garbage. We buried the calves that didn't make it and shot the coyotes and wolves that wanted to strike those that did. We laughed a lot and complained a lot, saw stars in a sky so dark at night that theirs was the only light, learned to chop wood and repair tractors, make do and . . . and, inevitably, become different.

Different had been the point, of course, the stated purpose behind our coming; but different tends to become a total, rather than a partial, thing. Within a matter of no more than five or six months, both our sons and our daughters could calculate the cost of their breakfast eggs in terms of how many times the rooster had flogged them as they'd gathered the things and, even worse—"Yucky!" I believe was their word—how many times they had had to empty, clean, and reline the soiled nests in the henhouse in order to get any eggs in the first place. Within a matter of less than a year, all of them over five could absolutely and painfully calculate what the okra on the supper table had cost in terms of itch and rash from its picking, or what the corn had cost in terms of stings from the saddleback caterpillars that inhabited the rows and mimicked the coloration of their stalks. Within two years they could calculate the cost of a hamburger in terms of a cow they had watched birthing, a calf they had fattened, and a yearling they had helped slaughter and butcher. Such things are graphic experiences. They command the attention and then, fairly quickly, they also command the conversation.

Sam and I went in and out of the city to our professional responsibilities, and the children in and out each week day to the parochial schools where they were still enrolled. But slowly, slyly almost, the locus of the days began to shift for each of us. Occupied in town, we still were restless to get home, to get back to the chores that had to happen if we and the animals were to eat, to reassume as soon as possible the ease of a common jargon and deeply physical experience, eager as well to move again, like water to its level, into that paradoxical expansion and diminishment of self that occurs in open space.

So it was that the Tickles—old and young alike—became the owners of two lives. We learned, each of us, to play both the role of City Mouse and the role of Country Mouse, the highway north toward Lucy or south toward Memphis becoming the symbolic portal between the two . . . which process was also how The Farm In Lucy became a state of mind as well as a plat of acreage on the Farm Bureau's maps.

Chapter 2

. . .

During our city years, I had taught, first as a visiting lecturer at Rhodes College in Memphis and then, for almost a decade, as Dean of Humanities at its sister institution, the Memphis College of Art. The years of teaching were good ones professionally as well as personally. In those days, a female academic dean was so rare a thing that no one, at least in our part of the world, had yet developed any kind of protocols and standards governing the consequences thereof. As a result, I taught and administered right up until the fourth Tickle was born in 1970, going immediately back to teaching and administering within a few days afterward. The new baby and his siblings were simply part of the college family as well as of its foyers and hallways. Many of my colleagues became avuncular playmates to the lot of them; and those connections have held as emotional anchors ever since, not just for me, but also for the now fully adult children who were their original source.

Beyond the fullness of range and derring-do that come from working in a receiving and sustaining place, the years at the College of Art gave me as well the education of eye and ear that are necessary parts of the writer's craft. No one can give a writer—or for that matter a painter or a dancer or any other creative artist—the twist of personality or the skew of interpretation that are his or her fundamental content. The ability to see and hear the resonance between one's content and one's medium, on the other hand, can be taught. More to the point, they can be taught across the apparent, but ephemeral, barriers of aesthetic disciplines.

For young writers in those days, however, and especially for young writers living outside the northeast corridor, the opportunities for publication were limited. In the South, they were primarily limited in form and shape to poetry and to short, irregular, and usually poignant first-person essays. In outlet, the limitation was almost always to largely regional, usually newsprint journals. How many young writers were mowed down in those days by such circumstances no one will ever know. Only a romantic or a naïf, though, could have ever been benighted enough to think that talent alone would out, that the gift will always find its way. Not so then, and not so now. It was and is, rather, the lucky, the fortunate, the ones blessed by an apparently capricious circumstance in whom the talent will out. In all the others, the gift simply crumbles back into the dark from which it came.

How much of all this I actually could or did articulate to myself in my mid-thirties is unclear to me now. My suspicion is that I simply intuited most of it. But I most certainly understood enough of it to be prodded into action; and it was the professional artists around me who showed me how, whether they intended to or not.

Anyone who teaches in a professional school of art learns fairly quickly that the studio trash bins are the most relevant appointments on the whole campus. Into them go small gems and massive heartbreaks, class exercises that are more than what they are but still are exercises, sketches and fragments no longer of use to their creator but nonetheless still a pleasure to another's observing eye. Sam and I have a farmhouse full of such refugee treasures, for in the mid- and late 1960s I excelled at trash-bin patrol. What I was scouring for, however, was not just the abandoned canvases or half-realized sculptures that drew the rest of the staff to scavenger there, but also the poetry. We human beings speak too often in hyperbole to always be taken literally by our friends and families. I know that. But in this one thing at least, I would like to be heard as speaking absolute truth: There was, in the 1960s, in the trash bins of the Memphis College of Art, more raw, visceral, compelling poetry than I have ever found, before or since, in any other single place.

Sometimes the throwaways of the students (and sometimes, I finally realized, the throwaways of the faculty) were only two- or three-line images. More often the work was a scrap or palimpsest of several lines, a sustained and orchestrated juxtaposing of voices or images. Occasionally I would come upon a fully realized construction that, once resolved, had lost its interest for its creator. In whatever category they fell, however, few if any of my finds were as accomplished in their craft as they were in their conception; yet their sheer clarity almost justified their jagged edges and roughly textured music.

Within a semester or two of becoming dean, I was hooked . . . hooked not just by the beauty being thrown away all around me, but even more perhaps by its origins. Why could youngsters no more than eighteen and nineteen years of age perceive their world with such surgical precision and awful beauty? How, given almost no prior training in verbal art, could they so economically grasp and then render the patterns and harmonies of what they perceived? And, the biggie: What would happen if we taught them?

It was the last question, mixed with a kind of philosophic fascination and a kind of moral mourning for the beauty being hauled off, unread, to the city dump, that would not let me go. At first, it was merely an issue on a list of many issues, but within a matter of a year or so, the question grew to be a cause. I cannot claim it as a private cause, however. Rather, in record time and with essentially no resistance, at least not as resistance is usually measured in academic or institutional affairs, a cadre of five of us on the faculty were seduced enough to begin working together on a plan. We would teach poetry, writing, and editing in the academic division; we would teach the art of the book as a physical object as part of the sculpture program; we would teach book design in the design departments, and book production in the advertising and printmaking ones. In short, we would establish a college press. How simple. Problem solved.

Looking back now, I don't know whether I am more amazed by our naïveté or by our passion, especially by my own. From childhood I had loved—maybe even revered—words. I had snatched the time, a bit here and a bit there over the years, to produce a respectable number of those de rigueur newsprint-published pieces, and I was proud of them as well as grateful and encouraged by them. But the work being lost beneath my very nose to the local dump, the talent not being trained, the cycle and craft of production not being realized . . . Dear Lord in Heaven! These seemed to me so overwhelmingly prior (and fixing them so beautiful a thing) just then that I don't think I ever once even doubted or hesitated. What those youngsters could natively do was much stronger, more vital, more laden than anything I could do at that point. Beyond that, what a college press could do for them was so much more empowering and enabling than any other outlet available to them that I plowed ahead in what was probably the only act of complete abandon in my entire life.

Saint Luke, though he is popularly celebrated as the patron saint of physicians, is also the patron saint of artists; and it was his benediction that four of us sought to invoke one spring day in 1971 when, standing in the printmaking department of the Memphis College of Art in front of two brand-new, top-of-the-line printing presses, we christened our idea, naming it St. Luke's Press . . .

But St. Luke's Press was not to be. Not there, anyway. Not at the college. And not for the five of us as a team.

What followed that giddy day of pipe dreams and self-congratulation in the printmaking department was six months of such destructive tragedy that not one of us would be left standing afterward. One personal disaster would follow another until we all were leveled. For me, near the end of that May, tragedy was the death of Philip Wade Tickle . . . Wade, the fifth of our children and the second of our sons. He died at two weeks of age, almost before we could know him, but not before I could love him with all the fierceness of every hope and purpose I had ever known.

In almost anesthesizing grief, I resigned, as had the others before me, and sank into myself and the husband and children I had. St. Luke's lay a decayed dream, and any passion I might once have had was so stilled as to be completely forgotten. In the end, though, the idea of a publishing house would not let me be. In fact, as I began to heal, it was the memory of our excitement and of the possibilities we five had seen that became a rope of salvation for me, a route of escape from myself back into a world of meaningful activity.

My father, for whom Wade had been named, had left me a modest amount of money when he'd died in 1969. What, I wondered, what would happen if I were to gamble that money on establishing a publishing house independent of the College? Sam and I talked. I approached the College. Without the five of us who had been the structure of the thing, the school had neither the desire nor the staff with which to continue. St. Luke's Press as a name and an idea was mine, if I wanted it. I called the two out of the original five colleagues who were still in Memphis and asked if they would like to go back to work for no money and out of sheer stubbornness. Being themselves as crazed as the idea was, they both said yes. Shortly thereafter, St. Luke's Press became a legal entity, complete with a tax number and no offices. We brought out our first two books—one using work from the College and one I wrote about Wade's death—in 1975; and for the next thirteen years I never looked back

The mid-1970s was the golden age of southern publishing; and even a cursory look at the record will show that most of the successful publishing houses in the South today had their origins around that time. For us, St. Luke's began to take on life and influence almost from the first, though once again the "we" changed as staff came and went and as my own commitment and responsibilities increased. By 1982 St. Luke's had become only one part of a corporation doing business as the Tickle Publishing Group. Sam, still working full-time as a physician and as a farmer, began to work full-time as group publisher as well. He and I were overseeing not only St. Luke's, but also a book-production division (Shelby House), a medical imprint (Osler House), a belles lettres house (Iris Press) that we had bought from members of the faculty at the State University of New York in Binghamton, and our interest in a poetry house (raccoon books).

We were surprisingly successful. If we were not making any great amount of money, we weren't losing any either. The day we made a front-page mention and an accompanying "The Arts" section feature in the *New York Times* for having discovered and published the original, precensored edition of Upton Sinclair's *The Jungle*, we had to admit even to ourselves that we had probably more or less arrived. We also had to admit that we were dog tired . . . hound dog tired, in fact, to use an inelegant, but graphically southern, expression.

Everywhere I looked, there was St. Luke's or Iris or Shelby House or Osler or raccoon. The farm's dining room had long since become our conference room. Half of the house's big kitchen was now my office. The sitting room had been emptied out by 1979 or '80 to make room for sales and marketing staff. What once had been a spacious garage for storing cars and farm equipment was now a cramped and inefficiently crowded editorial office. Shipping was up the road and across the highway in space we had rented in an old school building. Warehousing was in other rented space in Memphis. In a protective move to try to preserve some semblance of dignity to all of this, we had opened another office, attached to Sam's medical suite in the city, where I met authors and publicity people and industry folk, hoping every minute of the time that none of them would ever ask to see the guts of the thing they were there to discuss. It was absurd . . .

successful, but absurd. Beyond that, it was no longer an occupation of joy.

One wintry evening in early 1988, I was standing in our kitchen talking after-hours business on the phone while, at the same time, watching Sam try to cook something or other on a stove that was no more than twelve feet from my desk and five feet from a counter-high stack of book cartons. The man I was talking business with was Wayne Elliot, publisher of Peachtree Publishers in Atlanta. Suddenly, like a kind of madness or maybe just a wave of health, I was awash in the ludicrousness of the whole thing. "Wayne," I heard myself saying, "do you want to buy a publishing house, because I'm through with this one."

Sam dropped the spatula he was holding and turned to me with an expression of pain and astonishment that I still cannot manage to forget. There was also astonishment on Wayne's end of things, apparently, because he didn't say anything at all for a good thirty seconds. Then he said, rather tentatively, "You're serious, aren't you?"

I looked at Sam, I suspect with real pleading in my eyes, for I suddenly knew I had to be free. "Yes," I said into the phone, and Sam nodded his head. "Yes, I'm serious."

"What do you want for it?"

I said, "Just a minute," turned to Sam and said, "How much?" He named a figure, I repeated it into the phone, and Wayne shot back, "Fair enough. It's a done deal."

Four months later, St. Luke's and its sibling imprints became divisions of Peachtree. The merger was a big enough event in import, if not in dollars, to merit coverage in *Publishers Weekly*, the international trade journal of the book industry. Somewhat to the surprise of all three of us, in fact, *PW* ran not only a picture of us shaking hands over the signed paperwork, but also a sizable article outlining the terms of the deal. For the second time, we realized that St. Luke's had arrived, so to speak.

As is usual in publishing mergers and buyouts, Sam joined Peachtree's board of directors and I, by contract, agreed to continue to work and maintain the Memphis office for at least two more years. Even if I was not entirely free, I was at least liberated from the ubiquity of manuscripts and galleys and spec sheets. The fiscal burden was gone; the farm was restored to something like a home; and my professional day was back to the traditional eight hours. I could even think again, for the first time in years, of reveling in words as well as of packaging them.

Our eighteen or so months with Peachtree were happy ones, companiable and productive. They were also short. In 1990, a Memphis-based publisher of cookbooks, The Wimmer Companies, wanted to purchase an established, general-trade, book-publishing division to complement and advance its line of cookbooks. Peachtree was made an offer none of us could refuse; and once again Sam and I were attached to the deal. The difference was that this time I had an office completely removed not only from my domestic space, but also from Sam's medical offices. I also had a secretary who was basically an executive assistant, and good at it, to boot. And I had just enough free time to begin to think about things I would like to write myself, or compile, or edit.

Such thoughts are dangerous ones for an inveterate wordsmith to entertain. It was not long before some of them began to morph into writing assignments and publishing contracts of my own. By mid-1991, in fact, I had five contracts in my hand, or at least I had them filed under a paperweight on my writing desk in Lucy. Each and every one of the five had seemed both exhilarating and possible at the time I had committed to it. In aggregate, however, they were beginning to edge me toward something close to panic. I was much too old to panic attractively, I discovered, but I was not too old to be spared the debilitating feel of it. The Wimmer Companies wanted to take St. Luke's in a new direction, and they certainly did not need me any longer in order to do that. What I, on the other hand, needed was to be out at last, truly out. At the end of August, I came home to The Farm In Lucy. I was fifty-eight and a half years old, officially and honorably retired with a business card that said "Director Emerita of The Wimmer Companies Trade Division," and I was free to be just a writer and a lover of words at last.

And I was. For fifteen bucolic months, I lived the life of the retired publisher and thoroughly preoccupied author. In the course of those months, I discovered a number of things, the first of which was that I cannot write fiction. As a result, I had to cancel one of my five contracts. Three of the others I finished within the first twelve months; and I was happily chipping away at the last of them when the phone on my desk ran one morning in early November 1992. "Hello," I said.

"Hello," my caller said back. "This is Daisy Maryles at *Publishers Weekly.* I think you and I need to talk. Do you have a minute?"

I did, and that is where this story really begins.

New York City

Chapter 3

• • •

The people of the Chickasaw Nation were the original citizens of my part of the world; and their language, the source of its unusual name. *Loosahatchie* is a Chickasaw term meaning "beautiful river." As a phrase, it has been shortened over three centuries of white, English-speaking settlement to "Lucy," but only when one is referring to the township or its environs. When, on the other hand, one is talking about the river that once was the southern boundary of those environs and that still is a sizable tributary of the Mississippi, one always says, "the Loosahatchie River," though generally nowadays with little awareness of the redundancy implicit in that usage.

Some five or six miles up the highway north of the Loosahatchie River, Amhurst Road turns off west and then, in another mile or so, curves back north again past the old school, becoming, without so much as a by-your-leave, Main Street. A wooden sign—the brainchild of some of our Johnny-come-lately and more citified neighbors—now sits in the northwest corner of the crossroad where Amhurst leaves the highway. It says, in modest blue letters on a tasteful white background, "Welcome to Lucy."

The intention is hospitable, I assume, and even I have to confess that the sign has made giving directions to visitors somewhat less taxing; but the sign is still a lie. Lucy . . . Lucy in my heart . . . begins the minute the front tires of the car clear the bridge going north over the Loosahatchie River. Even after all these many years, I never make that crossing without perceiving a kind of benevolence settling across my shoulders and containing me. Home.

There is a place, when one flies from Memphis International into La Guardia, where as he brings the plane lower, the pilot banks slightly and turns just enough west by northwest for Manhattan to materialize, like some kind of shimmering forest, out of nowhere . . . and at just that moment, it is there again, that sense of benevolent arriving. Even after all these years, it is always there . . . the catch in the breath, the lifting of the heart, the lover's ache to embrace.

Lucy and New York, the Farm and Manhattan from midtown to Battery Park, these are the antipodes of my life, the havens I swing between and the states of mind that I inhabit even when my body is not in either of them. Lucy is my village, New York my city. Country Mouse and City Mouse with nary a space of my own in between. Or at least there was none until 1997, but more of that later. It is 1992 that concerns me at the moment.

It was hazy, almost cloudy, just before noon on December 4, 1992, when the pilot banked, made his turn, and laid out the Chrysler Building and all its kith and kin in panorama before me. I suspect that in that moment I knew I was going to say yes; but I am very sure that I did not dare acknowledge such yet, even to myself. Somehow the whole idea of running a religion department for Daisy Maryles and *Publishers Weekly* was too exhilarating to handle in theory. I had to see for myself in faces and body language and arrangements what we were talking about before I could let myself move into that kind of space and try it out for feel and size.

By 1992, I had known Daisy Maryles by sight and by reputation for a number of years, but only as one knows the leaders of one's industry. That is to say, I knew her with respect, but also with no small amount of awe; for she was and is a powerful woman whose genius and opinion are formative players in the shaping of American book publishing. From the beginning, I, like every other small publisher I knew, had held *Publishers Weekly* itself in something close to groveling fear; its approval and goodwill could make all the difference in a crowded and primogenitured business. A part of the Reed Elsevier conglomerate, *PW* is to the book industry what its sister journal, *Variety,* is to the entertainment industry and wields about the same heft of critical influence. We did, however — Daisy, *PW,* and I — have one small bit of prior history.

Once, in the mid-1980s, I had written an Op-Ed essay for Daisy, though at the time doing so seemed like one of those out-of-nowhere events that one never quite grasps the why and whence of. At the time, St. Luke's was about to publish a biography, *The Angel of Beale Street.* It is the story of Julia Ann Hooks, who, among other things, was grandmother to, and formative influence upon, Dr. Benjamin Hooks, who, for most of the years of the civil rights movement, was the firm-handed executive director of the NAACP. Like her famous grandson's, Julia's, too, had been a dramatic and politically powerful life. The granddaughter of Captain Tom Marshall of the Marshalls of Virginia and a consummate concert pianist as well as politician, Julia was the first black faculty member at Berea College; Julia taught William Handy to play; Julia was confidante and adviser to Ida B. Wells and Robert Church, Sr. A good story, in other words, and an important one.

As St. Luke's moved nearer and nearer to the publication date for *Angel,* though, the sales staff racked up more and more merchants across the entire nation who declined to stock the book. I finally got on the phones myself to see what the problem was; and the answer was a kind of mantra, repeated word for word over and over again in my ear: You can't sell through the brown curtain.

Finally, after numerous phone calls, I demanded of one luckless merchant that she define exactly what she meant by that phrase. "Blacks don't read and whites don't care," she said. I was livid.

I was so livid, in fact, that I forgot my own temerity, picked up the phone, and called the executive offices of my trade journal. Within less than a minute my anger had projected me through the usual barricades and straight to Daisy Maryles. I ranted . . . actually I remember with some amusement now just how impassionedly I did rant. She let me have my head for a minute or two before she interrupted to ask the shrewd questions that are one of her hallmarks. Was I sure that that particular wording had been the wording used? Yes. Was I sure the reaction was not just southern? Yes, I was damned sure, thank you very much, and, plus that, I resented the implication of the question since the worst racism I ever saw was in the north and, plus that . . .

I remember her calm interruption that none of that was the point. What mattered was whether I was sure it was national. Yes. Could I cite, if challenged, the names and stores of those who had articulated such reasoning. Yes. Then: "Are you willing to say so in print?"

It stopped me dead, that question that Daisy Maryles asked me in 1986. What she was really asking . . . what we both understood she was asking . . . was "Do you care enough to risk it all for this particular cause?" I hesitated. "Think about it," she said, and waited.

"Yes, I'm willing," I finally said, with a cold, clamping sense of what could happen to us as a result. Then that firm voice said back to me, "You write it, and I'll most surely run it." So I wrote and she published.

But that had been almost the whole sum of our contact with each other. As it turned out, the Op-Ed evoked some supportive comments, but only time was going to achieve the difference in attitudes that, in my decision to write, I had hoped for. Yet all of those emotions of passion, anxiety, and seductive possibilities were playing inside my head again like mice in a laboratory cage when the intercom announced, "Ladies and gentlemen, North-West Airlines would like to be the first to welcome you to New York's La Guardia airport, where the local time is . . ." whatever the local time was. I was oblivious to the details by that point.

Chapter 4

• • •

When I am asked to name the twentieth-century events that caused the tectonic upheavals in American religion in whose wake we in the twenty-first century are now living, I always thrash about for a minute or so in a sea of excess. Once, in the process of beginning a new book on the subject, I actually sat down and made a list of such causative factors. It came in at three dozen and counting before I finally gave up on list making and went to writing.

In such an extensive catalog of causes, there always are certain items of greater, and others of lesser, importance. In this particular case, though, even the number of central determinants is fairly unwieldy in its scope. The one thing that seems to me to have been prior to them all, however, the contemporaneous force that enabled all the other causal changes and the key to their being incorporated into the culture, is the democratization of information and, by extension, the consequent democratization of theological and religion information. Every day of our lives, we Americans chug—and for at least five decades have chugged—like good little tugboats through a veritable ocean of information;

and every one of us ships some water as we do so . . . which nautical metaphor means that none of us can escape the wash of facts, theories, and opinions that unceasingly rock and support us.

Nowadays, what the radio does not insert into our waking time the television does, while the computer and/or the Web not only override both of them, but even help us determine which parts of their offerings we will attend to. Lest, God forbid, we should lose some part of what we have discovered or enjoyed, there are tapes and CDs and DVDs and disks that let us own and, at will, reenter any of those experiences again and again. The magazines that come our way are augmented by the free infomercial catalogs and proselytizing pamphlets that join them in most American mailboxes. Billboards instruct us as we move about; and the cinema teaches us in images and audible dialogue what our newspapers may have failed to convey in printed words. And above them all, holding primacy of place as credible source and final authority, sits the book . . . the book now easily and cheaply owned or publicly available or hearable on tape. In a society of ever-increasing literacy, the whole lot of them put together could not help but result in the democratization of all information, both sacred and profane.

Religion and the book have always had a symbiotic relationship rather like that of inoperatively joined Siamese twins. Since the day Moses first came down from Mount Sinai with two tablets inscribed by the finger of God, Western culture in particular has been composed almost exclusively by "the people of the Book," to use the prophet Muhammad's phrase. For Americans, whose pilgrim antecedents were primarily protestant in both social theory and religion, the Book (and by another extension, the book) has for almost five centuries been subordinate only to God Himself in authority and in reverence due.

As a position, such homage is neither as benighted nor as antique as I may seem to have just insinuated. The truth, rather, is that during the last half of the twentieth century, under the onslaught of many media, especially electronic, the nature of the book's primacy, like the nature of the book itself, changed from that of having once been the sole medium of mass communication to the more marketable one of being the most trusted "first among equals."

With that shift from one to many sources, from restricted to mass access to information, from privileged to inexpensive ownership of expertise, more changed than the book's singular role in religion. America's national conversation about religion changed as well. It changed in its syntax from theology to god-talk, in its venue from ecclesial space to bars, kitchen klatsches, and chat rooms, in its source for points of reference from academic or learned to popular culture, and in its general attitude from reverently compliant to openly participatory. God and god, both upper- and lowercase, were big business in America—big in scope, big in public fervor, and big in the making of books.

It was into this foment of excitement and near chaos that I was moving as I picked up my luggage, queued up for a cab, and said to the driver, "Two forty-nine West Seventeenth, please." Within less time than I could have either imagined or dreamed, I would be printing out letters on stationery that had both my name and that address on it. As Caesar once observed "The die was cast and the Rubicon already crossed." I just seem to have been the only one who did not know it yet.

Chapter 5

• • •

People in the book business are astute observers of the larger culture in which they operate for two very good reasons. The first is money; the second is an irrevocable passion for ideas and the role of ideas in the moral and aesthetic well-being of any culture. Even if one renders that principle more colloquially, the truth still is that it takes both dirty hands and a golden heart to be a book publisher . . . or, for that matter, to oversee the content of the industry's weekly trade journal.

It was not, in other words, as if any of us in the business had failed to observe and even to discuss, prior to 1992, the growing obsession with religion and spirituality in America's public discourse and common life. We had. As early as 1987, I had observed in print that books were changing in their role, that more and more they were becoming what I called then (and have ever since) "portable pastors." No, what we lacked, in the late 1980s and opening 1990s, was not insight. Rather, we lacked the hard figures that could give quantitative support to our qualitative observations. Those figures, as I found out within the first twenty minutes of being in Daisy Maryles's office that Friday morning, were what she now had.

During most of the last century, Baker & Taylor was the largest supplier of books to America's libraries. For that reason the annual reports of B&T's fiscal and product statistics were always analyzed with considerable care by the rest of the industry. When Baker & Taylor finally released the data for its fiscal 1991, however, the most telling news required no such close scrutiny for its discovery; the report showed quite clearly that Baker & Taylor had enjoyed a 92.3 percent increase in fiscal 1991 over fiscal 1990 in its movement of religion product to the country's libraries. That was all it took. That was the missing piece and all the undergirding Daisy had needed to justify expanding *PW*'s religion coverage in preparation for the onslaught . . . and it was to be an onslaught. A lesser word would fail to convey the tumultuous burgeoning of religion that would soon overtake American publishing.

Within two years or so of the Baker & Taylor figures, the Ingram Book Company, the nation's largest distributor of books to the retail trade, would report a 246 percent increase within one fiscal year in its movement of religion books to America's bookstores. It was an expansion that would continue, though at a less malignant pace, for the entire closing decade of the twentieth century. During most of those years, religion would continue to be the fastest-growing segment either of American trade publishing in general or of American adult trade publishing, depending on the vigor of the children's market, with which it ran neck and neck for one or two of those years. As a category, religion would continue its pattern of growth into the new century, still laying claim intermittently to the number one position in genre growth, the difference over the years having become one of perceived impact more than anything else. By 2002, publishers, and we who covered them, had learned how to accommodate a bit better to such rates of expansion, as well as to the pervasive popular interest of which they were proof positive.

Even in December 1992, however, it didn't take quite twenty full minutes of conversation in Daisy's office for the figures to convey their initial impact: This thing was coming, *PW* had to be ready to cover it, did I want to establish and run a department to do that job. It was that simple, except for one thing. I needed, Daisy said, to meet for a few minutes with *PW*'s Group Publisher, a man named Fred Ciporen, whom I had merely heard of before but never met. Devious soul that she is when she has made up her mind that she is going to do something, Daisy trotted me down the hall from her office to his much larger one with a line of light chatter and no indication of this being anything other than a courtesy call.

Daisy knocked on an opened office door, said, "Do you have a minute?," thrust me ahead of her, and immediately drifted back almost into the hall. The man behind the desk was balding and only about half the size of the collection of disarray he was sitting behind. He looked blankly at me, at my toes first and then slowly all the way up to my face.

"Hmmmpf" was all he said. Daisy cleared her throat. He looked at a piece of paper on his desk and then back at me. "You're Phyllis Tickle." It was a statement that required no answer, so I gave none, while he continued to look dead ahead at my midsection. Then he looked up with what has to have been one of the most piercing scrutinies to which I have ever been subjected.

"So tell me," he said. "Why do you want to work for me?"

That did it. This was an interview, and it had been years since I had been subjected to an interview. What most would call my natural arrogance and my mother more charitably used to call my Irish was tripped beyond my control. Without even thinking, I shot back, "I have no idea. You are the ones who called me."

The Ciporen eyes picked up their famous twinkle. I could see the smile gathering up all the little wrinkles around his face and lips into some kind of Jewish Santa Claus laugh. "Well, that's clear enough," he said. "Sit down." Behind me, the malevolent and scheming Daisy chuckled. She still denies it, but I heard her. She chuckled.

From that "Sit down" until Fred's being promoted ten years later to head the corporation's newly established book division, I remained something of a Fred fan. Charming, yes, but as astute as he was direct and one of the most supportive and loyal employers I have ever worked for, albeit at a considerable remove. We have laughed from time to time about my "interview," and he simply shrugs his shoulders. "You don't know unless you ask," he says. He also says the same thing about his last question, delivered just as I got up to leave.

"You Jewish?"

"No, Christian."

He shrugged his shoulders that time, too. "Mazel tov anyway."

"To all of us," I responded.

"To all of us," he nodded, the bright eyes suddenly deadly serious. "To all of us, as we do this thing."

Thus it was determined that, commencing at nine o'clock on Monday morning, December 7, 1992, I would officially become a line item on the payroll of *Publishers Weekly*. The seventh was also Pearl Harbor Day, of course, but I doubt that I would ever have forgotten the date even if the day had not been a memorialized one. I, who for almost sixty years had thought I understood religion rather completely and very well, was about to discover how dangerously superficial and confined not only my intellectual grasp, but also my private understanding of it had really been.

Reared from infancy as an observant Christian, I had never had what Evangelical Christians call a "conversion experience." That is, I had not (and, for that matter, still have not), assuming that I understand correctly the full meaning of those two words. Quite the contrary. Having lived for fifty years with a steady conviction that could claim no particular moment of grand beginning, I had entered my sixth decade with no understanding at all of sacred excitement. Religion and well-tutored passion made sense to me, and always had. Faith and unfettered thrill, on the other hand, were too far removed from each other to even be regarded as incompatible, much less placed in the same sentence. Today, I no longer deny any of these things — or a myriad more — as authentic phenomena, nor do I disparage the efficacy of what they name.

There were, on Pearl Harbor Day 1992, in other words, whole worlds of faith out there just waiting for me, worlds, Christian and otherwise, that I would never in my Anglican provincialism have suspected, much less engaged, had it not been for two good Jews—Daisy Maryles and Fred Ciporen—who took me on as educatable.

And so, as at least one of them would most surely say just about now, "Mazel tov to all who go beyond this point."

Chapter 6

• • •

Saturday morning in New York, alone and with the whole city laid out before me to enjoy. Delicious!

Traveling people routinely grouse in a de rigueur kind of way about the sharp difference in round-trip airfares if one flies home on Friday afternoon instead of laying over through a Saturday night. I am remarkably silent during those conversations simply because the wanderer in me has always counted free Saturdays in a hotel in somebody else's hometown and on somebody else's coin as one of the serious joys of the traveling life. This is especially true when New York is the town. Life doesn't get any richer or more diverting than Union Square on a Saturday morning, unless maybe it's the Village on a crisp, sunny Saturday afternoon in early December when the delis and bakeries are full and redolent with food odors and human laughter. But not that first Saturday. Not that December 5.

I lay abed until even I was ashamed of myself. Then I moved to a chair by the window and watched desultory pigeons with all the disinterest of someone who lives in the country and sees snow-white egrets, soaring eagles, and carnivorous buzzards on a daily basis. I finally put on some clothes in midafternoon and wandered around Times Square, thinking that the gathering theater crowd would distract me. It didn't. Defeated, I went back to the hotel, had a glass of wine and an early—very early—supper.

At first blush, an amateur psychologist might say I was depressed, but nothing could have been further from the truth. The truth was that all of me was busy, frantically busy, inside my head. My attention was riveted on what had happened and on what, as a result, now had to happen, not to mention the sequencing in which it had to do so. None of me was free at the moment to come out and play.

Once my time before the mast in Fred's office was done, Daisy and I had spent almost the entire remainder of Friday in hers, even ordering lunch in so we would not be interrupted. For many, many years, *PW* had run one page of religion copy per month. That coverage was called "Religious News"; and truth told, I suspect there were some months during the sixties, seventies, and even early eighties when the gleanings were few and one page hard to fill up. My first battle, however, had been not the frequency of our intended new and expanded coverage, but its titling. News, I argued, is not "religious," at least not when it is commercial in nature. Books most certainly are not "religious." They are "religion" books and the news, "religion" news. To speak of either as "religious" is by implication to ghettoize to a remove and to demean by grammatical inflection. It's not "childish" publishing or "fictional" publishing, I said. By the same token, it is not "religious" but "religion" publishing.

The argument seems so obvious now, but it was counter to universal practice at the time in both the media and among publishing houses themselves. Those of us on *PW*'s religion staff— we call ourselves "Team Religion" these days and are now six in number—have laughed from time to time over the years as yet another professional organization, media outlet, or publishing house has changed its choice of words. But in 1992, it was serious business to effect such a change, because it struck at the very heart of every newsroom's comfort level, *PW*'s included.

Religion is messy and it is highly flammable. For that reason, conventional wisdom held, it is best left to its own communions and its own outlets. To bring it and its multitudinous, often anti-thetical, and mutually hostile expressions into an open forum on an equal footing with every other segment of national life was, and sometimes still is, a risky business. Certainly, prima facie, changing the rhetoric about any deep-rooted prejudice in order to change its public presence is a fool's or a zealot's mission. I obviously was both, but having discovered myself to be so bothered me considerably more on Saturday in retrospect than it had on Friday in the heat of conversation.

Daisy, from her first call to me, had been quite clear that what she was building was a department within the journal. What that translated to in application was several related, but different things. First it meant making an immediate jump from one page of whatever each month to a major feature every month. It also meant assuming an active presence, for the first time, within the news department's pages, with coverage of significant changes and events in religion publishing, including financial reports and personnel shifts. Beyond that, she and I would have to generate additional and broader reportage by being present at, and covering, every convention and books show of any significance within religion book publishing. In addition to the continuation and expansion of the journal's annual Bible issue, edited lists of forthcoming titles in religion would have to be prepared for inclusion in the magazine's semiannual, prepublication listing for booksellers and librarians of the more significant books to be released over the next six months. Perhaps even more significantly, we would have to institute, as soon as possible, a prepublication reviewing system that would offer critical reviews of religion titles on the same basis and with the same rigor as that applied by the magazine to every other genre of book. All I had to do was figure out how to make all of these things happen immediately and simultaneously. Piece of cake . . .

If I were not depressed, I certainly was, at the very least, overwhelmed. I knew writers. Thank God, I knew writers who knew religion and who could produce journalistic as well as feature copy. As I wandered Times Square that Saturday afternoon, that one bit of surety anchored me; and I counted the names of potential department writers over in my head like a woman counting her prayer beads. Trying to appear as if I were crowd gazing, I really was calculating, first here and then there, how to begin the process of getting a stable of writers in place where none had been before, and how to do it in less than a month.

In many ways, however, the logistical issues had been the more superficial, albeit still exhilarating, parts of our conversation, Daisy's and mine, on Friday. There had also been the dear parts . . . the flash of intimacy, the moments of candor. It had been midafternoon and we were both exhausted when she stopped talking and looked at me with a shift in intensity that signaled the seriousness of where the conversation was to go next.

"What do you know about Islam?" she asked.

"Almost nothing personally. I mean, what I know is almost all from books, not experience; but I have to tell you up front that I'm not overly fond of what I do know."

She nodded and was quiet for just a second or two. "Nor am I," she said. "But, Tickle . . ."

It was to be how she would address me for the rest of our lives together. Tickle. And her unconscious choice of surname over given name lent not only energy and drama, but also camaraderie to the instant.

"But, Tickle, if you—if we—do this, it's going to have to be all religions equally."

It had never occurred to me that the case might be otherwise, and I'm sure my surprise showed on my face. "Of course, and that means everything from Wicca and paganism to Orthodox Judaism," I said.

She nodded and then chuckled. "All of them together in one heap inside one set of covers. We have to be crazy."

Chapter 7

• • •

Two or three of the potential problems that Daisy and I had begun to talk about on Friday would prove themselves easier to resolve than we had initially thought possible. The first hurdle was to persuade the industry that we were serious; and that would take time as well as work. The second problem we had discussed looked even tougher, at least on paper. The magazine's sales force had to be racheted up to speed almost immediately. More plainly put, for our grand scheme to work at all, *PW*'s sales representatives had to become instantly knowledgeable enough about religion and comfortable enough with what we were doing to generate a flow of ad revenue sufficient to support such a dramatic leap in editorial costs.

During almost my entire career as a book publisher in the South, my primary contact with the industry in general, and certainly with its trade journal in particular, had been a woman named Robin Mays. A brash, big-boned, loud North Carolinian who was smarter than most in a notoriously smart industry and with a streak of native generosity as wide as the Mississippi River, Robin was for years *PW*'s sales manager for the Southeast, though she almost never stayed within the confines of that role for very long. Somehow, through some form of charisma known only to her, Robin became a friend whether you thought you needed one or not. I loved her, though for the life of me I could not tell you exactly when I perceived that truth or by what means we arrived at that level of personal relationship. I can tell you that my state of deep affection and almost unconditional regard was shared by at least two hundred other of Robin's dearest and nearest friends, people whom I still know and whose devotion to her memory is still the basis for our common conversation.

Robin died on Palm Sunday 1999, after what was the most anguished and pain-racked battle with breast cancer that I have ever watched with any immediacy. Before she died, though, she and I traveled the globe together, or at least the Euro-American part of it. In 1994, she took me as her guest, for my first time abroad, on a company-sponsored trip she had won for herself and a companion as *PW*'s sales rep of the year. Then two years later, in the summer of 1996 and just before she knew she was ill, she and I were the guests of the Italian government in Rome to attend the first capital-based, national *fiera* for religion books and products. Robin, you see, had managed to get Fred Ciporen to create, and then to let her occupy, the position of national sales manager in Religion.

Actually, to tell the truth about the thing, Robin had achieved this bit of legerdemain in late 1990; for it was Robin at the magazine who, like Daisy and me, saw the religion tsunami coming and who pushed most earnestly for *PW*'s early preparedness. It was also Robin, I now know, who first pushed Daisy as well . . . pushed her to call a woman named Phyllis Tickle as part of their preparedness campaign. *Requiescat in pace.*

I never quite knew where Robin was in her own religious convictions. Externally, she was an Episcopalian of sometime practice and indifferent commitment, though she had our southern virtue of wanting all the junctures and intersections of life blessed on holy ground and memorialized by holy words. But intellectually, she knew her stuff when it came to religion; and as is sometimes true of the casually observant, she was without prejudice of any kind. All religion was equally exciting to her, and equally absorbing; and when Robin was absorbed, she was as hard to move as a bulldozer without an operator.

Within three weeks of my taking the job as *PW*'s religion editor, Robin somehow persuaded Fred that he should assemble the whole sales force for a day-long meeting in our offices in New York in January to talk about religion sales. At that meeting, she said, I would overview everything there was to know about religion in a half-day morning session. Then we would all spend the afternoon together going over a multipaged document (which I was to write, she also said) that outlined for each rep's greater convenience everything I had told them that morning about all there was to know about religion.

Only Robin could have so blithely dreamed up such idiocy, and probably only Robin could have persuaded Fred Ciporen to spend a fair amount of money on actualizing it. Certainly only Robin could have pulled the bloody thing off; but she did, and it worked. To this day I do not know how I found the time, much less the information, to gin out a kind of crude "Sales Rep's Guide to Religion." The best memory serves, I don't even think Robin offered to help beyond saying, "Just the facts. Tell 'em where the bodies are buried. That's all they need to know, just the raw facts." I do remember that she sent Sam and me a lovely and embarrassingly excessive fruit basket for Christmas that year in Lucy and that I took it as a peace offering even as I sent less-than-peaceful thoughts winging their way back to her. But shortly thereafter, of course, Robin and I were winging our own way back to Manhattan. Even as we shared a taxi in from La Guardia to the office, we both acknowledged—she nonchalantly and I begrudgingly—that her idea had been a sound one.

There is, in every news organ of integrity in this country, an impenetrable wall between the ad or sales division and the editorial department. It's the periodicals industry's permutation of the golden-heart syndrome. Editorial does what editorial has to do to report fairly and accurately. Sales does what it has to do to pay the bills and perpetuate the exercise of such freedom. One must not in-fluence or prejudice the other much beyond the realities—black hands—of issue page count and ratio of copy to advertisement.

That having been said, however, it is equally true that sales-people are thinking people. Beyond that, in the trade magazine business they are, like Robin, usually smart folk in a notoriously smart industry. Nor do they suffer vague theories and diffuse maybes lightly. Their native wit is honed by and around three questions and an addendum: What is it? What should it generate in dollars? How do I sell it? And the addendum, which is the killer: Do I believe what I just heard?

As I tried to tell her on our cab ride into the city, what Robin had done by throwing me into the midst of a sales training day, like a Christian among so many lions, was to force me to hone myself against their questions. There had been a certain "holy cause" excitement or energy to what Daisy and I had talked so animatedly about in early December. In the innumerable phone conferences that had followed, a sense of purpose and the tease of beginning to effect the patently impossible had sustained me, kept me focused, lent me both courage and the rush of all its pleasures. How long I could have, or would have, run on those emotions, had Robin not intervened, I do not know. What I know is that getting ready for her sales meeting brought the ex-hilarating theories out of the stratosphere by reducing them to a few sheets of paper and to "The facts. Just the raw facts."

That early translation, I shall always think, was pivotal not only to the program at *PW,* but also to me. I learned—or began the process of learning—in those three tense weeks of prepara-tion to see religion as a construct as well as a system of personal belief. How it grew for me, in the course of what was ostensibly a purely secular exercise, would become the subtext (or maybe the whole text. I'm not sure) of the next ten years of my life. How religion has gone, for me, from what I must defend to what I am hourly compelled to amazement by . . . from what I once held as private to what I now engage as the most public of forces . . . from what I had been reluctant to analyze to something so magnificently huge and vital that it demands my and every other thinking person's analysis . . . how all these things happened began with Robin Mays and a sales meeting.

When that day Fred Ciporen said to a group of twelve or fifteen people sitting around a conference table, "You all know why we're here. So, this is Phyllis Tickle, and she's going to tell you what you need to know to do what you have to do," he waved his hand in blessing over us all and sat down. He knew, as well as I did, that it was the addendum of "Do I believe what I just heard?" that would tell the tale here. He also, by his own admission, thought, just as I did, that such would be a hard sell. That is, we both thought that I was about to try to sell one of New York's most agnostic and sophisticated subgroups on the joys of talking religion . . . talking it, in fact, not only to people at denominational publishing houses that were small and by definition religion-obsessed, but also to people in the magazine's most prestigious, commercial accounts, like Harper, Doubleday, Simon & Schuster, Putnam, Random House, and so on. Done wrong, the loss of face there could be not only personally, but also fiscally compromising. Or that's how things had looked going into that meeting.

I began with the Baker & Taylor figures, statistics always being a good way to get the attention of salespeople. Then I gave them the new philosophy of all-inclusiveness. I had now played the only two sure cards in my deck. Innocuous and safe were all used up, and dangerous was the only thing left. I took the marker in my hand and drew a line down the newsprint flip chart, putting "Institutionalized Religions" on one side of the line and "Noninstitutionalized Religions" on the other. Suddenly the electricity in the room was palpable. Even Fred leaned forward and rested his arms on the table in front of him.

"These divisions and lists are on the cheat sheet Robin and I will go over with you after lunch," I said with more confidence than I actually felt. "But she thought you needed the whole overview before we begin to work the sheets." Robin nodded as if to assume, however belatedly, some responsibility for whatever was to happen.

Then I began the uncanny process of dicing and slicing religion in 1993 America into all its multitudinous parts, separating each major column into pieces and parts not in terms of faith, but in terms of each entity's distinctive practices and each entity's probable proportion of impact on the book market. How large demographically was each piece? How literate? How likely to be driving which part of the current surge? Black hands maybe, but notebooks had begun to appear from somewhere under the table, and even Fred had relaxed back into his chair.

I added religion houses to the faiths and communions they were particular to and then worked my way through the editorial track record of each of the major commercial houses in terms of which faiths and communions each seemed to be inclined toward and appeared to be publishing to most frequently . . .

It went on and on. At some point, I remember looking at Robin and realizing that she was having fun. Then I realized that I was, too. This thing was going to work, by the grace of God and without any other possible explanation.

Coming out of the meeting for the lunch break, I stopped, more from habit than need, by the ladies' room on my way over to Daisy's office to pick up my coat. I was hardly inside the washroom door when one of the sharpest of the female reps grabbed me by the sleeve. "Thanks," she said, and I was briefly stunned to see tears lining the lower lids of her eyes. "It's hard to talk about it, until somebody gives you permission, you know. My husband and I . . . we go to services every Sabbath, but I've always been shy of saying so in there."

Like the process of bringing theory to fact and vague belief to observable surety, that minute and a half in a women's lounge was to be pivotal. It was also to become my first experience with a substantial, if carefully shielded force in American urban religion. Later that afternoon, as I was leaving the office for drinks with Daisy and Robin, one of the secretaries slipped me a note. Folded over several times to prevent accidental access, it said, "I heard what you talked about in there this morning. I go to a Pentecostal church. Can I write you sometime? Thanks." The next morning, I went in by way of her desk. "Yes" was all I said, but she nodded; and though she has long since left the magazine for an administrative job in banking, we have maintained an e-mail conversation ever since.

The theologian Paul Tillich once wrote, "Hear this one important warning! Never consider the secular realm Godless just because it does not speak of God."

It is a telling observation, and a humbling one. I have it written on the front of the "April" divider in my Day-Timer as the only quote I keep always at hand when I am working. I keep it there lest I forget its great truth, of course, but also lest I ever fail to remember that only working as part of the American press could have given me the chance to understand it so fully.

Chapter 8

• • •

If getting a sales force quickly up to speed had proved less awkward and, in the final analysis, considerably less difficult than I had envisioned, our other immediate and complementary task of persuading the industry that we were serious about expanding our coverage of religion was to prove more wearying than I had at first understood. I suffer from a chronic, low-grade wanderlust. For whatever reasons, whether of restlessness or simply a slack self-discipline, I am, and always have been, ever at the ready to board the next plane for the next new thing.

Thirty years of motherhood had obviously put some temporary restraints upon my natural inclinations toward traveling, but by 1993 the children were more or less gone. Certainly not one of them was a child any longer. As a result, Daisy's concern about our being not only present, but also very visible at religion and industry gatherings had seemed at first to me like the carrot at the end of the donkey's stick. All over the country for days at a time, life in a hotel two or three times a month, a new city and new faces every other whipstitch . . . what could be better than that?

Well, actually nothing. I still live, and love, that kind of life, though I find that the cities are all more familiar now and that the faces tend more and more to belong to friends rather than strangers. Yet natural to me or not, and appealing or not, traveling presents its own peculiar set of burdens. Not the least of them is the fact that the work of editing a magazine department for a weekly periodical tends to be fairly omnipresent work. It is also considerably more difficult to accomplish on the road than it is in an office that has files and Rolodexes and a proper P.C., not to mention direct phone lines and fax machines within easy reach.

As a result of the juggling act implicit in all of this, the first eleven months of 1993 went by me in what I am sure must have been, even at the time, a blur of suitcases and twelve-hour days. They certainly remain as a largely indecipherable memory now. I can remember some parts of them, though most of what I remember has to do with the speeches.

I love to talk to audiences. I especially love to talk to them about things I myself am passionate about in the way that I was, and still am, passionate about religion and the interface between it and popular culture. I jest now with audiences—primarily in self-defense—about being a recovering academic; but like most quips, that one too has its roots in reality. I *am* a recovering academic; and in my veins course all the chemical thrills of a good exposition well developed or an astute observation clearly delivered. That's basically what teachers are and do under any set of circumstances. My father, who was one and therefore could appreciate the same proclivities in me, was wont to remind me on a frequent basis that a good teacher was just like a good actor, 98 percent ham and 2 percent information, most of it not of his own making.

I never quite figured out whether this observation was a slam of criticism or just a cautionary bit of wit lest I begin to think too well of myself. Either way, I have long had to honor the truth of the thing. But I had also discovered, by November 1993, that I was talked out. I was ready for one meeting or convention where

I did not speak and did not have to be "on" all day and half the night. Daisy either sensed my weariness or was herself feeling the same ennui.

The final essential, professional event of the calendar year for religionists is the annual meeting of the American Academy of Religion and the Society of Biblical Literature. Composed in large part of academics and teaching clergy, the two groups in those days always held their annual meetings jointly and on the weekend immediately preceding the Thanksgiving holiday, when classes are either already dismissed or can be more gracefully canceled. Publishers, who can smell a serious reader a mile away, flock to AAR/SBL as to a feeding frenzy; and as is not always true at other meetings, they are reluctant to leave the exhibition hall's selling floor for anything short of death.

Because it is basically academic in tone, AAR/SBL was, and still is, one of my favorite shows each year. By its very nature, it evokes something like a holiday spirit in me. Beyond that, in 1993, AAR/SBL was held in Washington, itself a place that evokes more exhilaration than do most big cities. Daisy and I arrived on the Friday before Thanksgiving and began our now familiar round of lunch with one group, a coffee break with another, early cocktails with a third. She, being Orthodox and observant, retired to her room at sunset to keep Shabbat, while I went out to supper with yet a fourth gathering. On Saturday, with Daisy in seclusion, I played hooky long enough to hear a paper or two and attend the discussion afterward. By Sunday, however, the two of us were back at it, working the floor, watching what was being bought in the bookstalls, talking to academics about what they thought was coming next in religion studies and research, talking to publishers and editors about which of those ideas they thought might impact the general reading public, and so on. By midafternoon on Tuesday, things were in winddown and, more dangerously, she and I were beginning to chatter instead of meaningfully converse with people.

"I quit," she said. "Enough is enough, and I've given this magazine more than that already this week."

I was more relieved than I was willing to let on, but I was immediately recharged when she looked at her watch and said, "The new Holocaust museum is still open. I've not been yet. Want to grab a cab and go see it?"

A chance to see that in company with an Orthodox Jew whom I loved? You better believe I wanted to go. So we did.

The museum, as we walked in, still looked as austere as new, not yet landscaped or fully occupied buildings tend to do . . . or that was how I first interpreted its starkness. There was little signage beyond a single arrow that pointed to the ticket desk; and at the ticket desk there was no surface clutter or homey commercialism. We asked for two tickets, we got two tickets. After that, there was nowhere to go, so far as I could see, except back out the door we had come in or across a high but strangely inhuman lobby to some elevators. We punched the Up button on the wall beside one of the elevators, the doors opened, we went inside, the doors closed. No choices that I remember. The thing was a box . . . not exactly a cage, but a box. Its walls were metal, industrial, and, when I caught myself in mid-misstep, cold to the touch. Then the sounds of a railroad car moving at half throttle began to fill the box. After that, first the voices, and then the screams, began to filter in as well.

I have no idea what I had expected. Probably, I had simply anticipated being talked to or shown things . . . things in cases that had accompanying and informative narratives in well-lit frames beside each of them. I certainly had never foreseen this, not this demand that both anguish and horror be in some small but all-intrusive way experienced for the price of a ticket. I cannot remember now what I said, if anything, to Daisy as we stumbled out of our steel holding cell and onto the museum's top floor. I certainly said nothing—I couldn't—once we began working our way back down through one experiential set after another. Kristallnacht here, a ghetto reconstructed there. Heaps of trashed suitcases and piles of confiscated shoes. Gold rings and once-loved bits and pieces of kitchens and dining rooms and parlors forever interrupted. Film clips of Roosevelt saying it really wasn't so bad and tear sheets from the *New York Times* saying it really was. The rebuilt hull of a desperately small fishing boat that had been used by the Danes to spirit their Jewish fellow citizens across the Channel in the fog and after dark. The ovens . . .

And just when I thought I could not bear another room of it, the route took us into a long, narrow space where the walls and ceiling were papered with family photographs rescued from a Lithuanian shtetl before its occupants were murdered by the Einsatzgruppen. The floor of that dreadful space was paved in carved stones, as had been the road into Auschwitz—paved with the tombstones from Jewish cemeteries that had been scavenged and then desecrated. That corridor would have been impassable for me, I think, had it not had at its far end another corridor or skybridge filled, even at that late hour, with natural light. The walls there were of a thick glass onto which had been etched, by country, the names of all the Jewish towns and villages that had been torched and then sown with salt by the Germans.

Unable to read either Hungarian or Polish and not conversant in any way with the geography of midcentury eastern Europe, I passed through the Lucite corridor and on to a space where I could at last look down to the lobby below us. It was over. The elevator, complete with a comfortable button for pushing "Down," was straight ahead of me. Unable to sort out the cacophony of what I was feeling, I leaned against the pleasantly plastered wall and tried to deal with the irrefutable actuality of what I had just walked through. Holocaust—Shoah—had never gone any farther into me than my head before. Now I could not get it to return to my head for a moment, much less remain there. At some point, I also realized that I had lost Daisy.

Since it was almost closing time and since there had not been more than two or three other people in the rooms to start with, I couldn't understand. She could not have passed me without my knowing it, not even as deeply abstracted as I was. The only explanation was that she had gone back for some reason. I walked back the way I had come, and there she was, still almost in the stone-paved chamber of photographs, but studying the Lucite wall with its census of obliterated villages. She had her glasses off, as she does when she is reading intently, and was moving her finger down the column of names nearest her.

"What in the world are you doing?" I asked. It simply had never occurred to me until that very moment that she might be able to read the wall, and I was more amazed than curious.

"Looking for my father's village," she said, as easily as if I had asked her about some bit of copy on a computer screen. Then, stopping her finger in midlist, she pointed to a column just beyond me. "I already found my mother's over there," she said, and went back to moving her finger down the column she was working on.

"I had no idea." It was all I could have said at that moment, for it tumbled out of me with the confusion of a world upended. She stopped reading and walked closer to me. "I thought you knew," she said, almost as if she were apologizing. "My father was nineteen and my mother seventeen when the camps were liberated. They met a few weeks later in a Displaced Persons camp and fell in love. They stayed, though, because they thought one of my father's cousins might have survived. It turns out that she hadn't, but I was born in the D.P. camp. I was almost three when we finally got to this country."

There were no tears, there was no self-pity. Just a deadly quiet in the empty museum. "And that," she said, laying her right hand on my left forearm, "and that, Tickle, is why you and I cannot . . . must not . . . fail in what we have set out to do."

There are ordinations in this world that forever mark those upon whom holy hands are laid. You have just read the story of mine.

Chicago — That Toddlin' Town

Chapter 9

• • •

No one speaks of ordination lightly, for it is not a light thing to bear. From the very beginning—probably even from Daisy's first phone call—I had had a sense of purpose about the work to be done at *PW.* The book professional in me was excited just by the knowledge that a substantive shift in industry focus and emphasis was taking place right before my eyes. The notion that I might not only be part of recording such a reconfiguration, but also might in some way help to shape it had, from the first, added fervor to that excitement.

The erstwhile administrator in me was also ambitious enough to want to wrestle, and presumably conquer, the dozens and dozens of problems inherent in preparing to cover the realignment of a large industry. My fingers—both mental and digital—had quite literally itched when, back at The Farm In Lucy, I first began digging into the work.

Beyond that, the observant believer in me had been, as I remain, consciously grateful that the work was to be in religion. In age, the work of God, however commercialized, takes on a benignity and a centeredness that it often lacks in youth. Sam, an observant believer who had already lived with the professional and the administrator for four decades, was himself aging into grace. As a result, he had been content not only to let me have my head, but also to facilitate my being able to run with it. These things, however, are not ordination. They are purpose and circumstance.

 Ordination, by contrast, is "purposeful" and intransigent. It points beyond its own ends and records allegiance to a worth so much beyond the ordinand's as to evoke submissiveness—the kind of submissiveness that cannot act against itself. Ordination emanates from past pain and a tradition of sacrifice, its exercise being always restrained by story. The act of ordination, moreover, is always preceded by a time of theological study and, frequently, of theological confusion. Only in retrospect did I come to understand just how completely this last aspect of ordination had preceded and characterized my own.

I had gone into the annual meeting of the American Academy of Religion in Washington not only weary of speech-making and networking, but even more . . . what shall I say? moved? unresolved? unsettled? None of these words is sufficient, yet all of them together might overstate the case. Perhaps better to say that I went into the AAR/SBL convocation in November still caught up in an amazement which, at that point, had already been part of me for some ten or twelve weeks.

Based on preliminary contact and early press releases, the Parliament of the World's Religions, to be held from August 28 through September 4, 1993, in Chicago at the Palmer Hilton Hotel and Convention Center had not seemed to me to be nearly so compelling religiously as it was professionally and culturally. Joel Beversluis, the Parliament Council's factotum with many roles, had begun bombarding us with information in January. Over the months after that, it had become very apparent to both Daisy and me that the Parliament itself was going to generate a solid, if small, number of publishing projects. Beyond that, there was going to be a sizable presence at the parliament by some of our larger publishers as well as by a myriad of smaller ones, both domestic and foreign. We needed to report this kind of industry activity and, as Daisy said, "show up for work alongside them." Joel had issued us our press passes, and we had packed our bags.

Theoretically, for that was how I had primarily engaged the thing in the beginning, the 1993, or second, Parliament of the World's Religions was the centenary of a major event in earlier American religion. The original Parliament, convened at the 1893 Columbian Exposition, Chicago World's Fair, was history's first formal convocation of Eastern and Western spiritual traditions and, as such, had had global as well as domestic ramifications for decades. Julia Ward Howe had in no way exaggerated the public perception and general tenor of that first Parliament when, in her address to its assembly, she said:

> The voyage of so many valorous souls into the unknown infinite of thought, into the deep questions of the soul between men and God—O, what a voyage is that! O, what a sea to sail! And I thought, coming to this Parliament of Religions, we shall have found a port at last; after many wanderings we shall have come to the one great harbor where all the fleets can ride, where all the banners can be displayed.

Howe was, indeed, prophetic as well as accurate. The 1893 Parliament proved central to the public acceptance of the practices and schemata of Eastern religions, especially of Hinduism, within our American conversation. Through the influence at and after the Parliament, of leaders like Swami Vivekananda, what had been a kind of pervasive "spiritualism" in this country began to take on a greater rootedness not only in terms of its acceptability but also of its self-understanding, discipline, and organization.

Nineteenth-century America was one of the most fertile centuries, religiously speaking, in Euro-American history. It was rife with new faiths, most of them Christocentric, but all of them still heterodox and heavily influenced by the surrounding culture's concerns with gender and gender-equality, extramedical healing of the body, and the engagement of the spirit world. In particular, Seventh-Day Adventism, Christian Science, Transcendental-ism, New Thought, Unity, Divine Science, Theosophy—some would even say Mormonism—have their origins in this kind of nineteenth-century religious restlessness. Each of them, with the possible exception of Mormonism, was effected by the Parlia-ment and its sequelae.

Together with the Parliament and its residual influence, these movements became an early but seminal force behind the ram-pant "I'm spiritual but not religious" mantra that, by the summer of 1993, was driving the book industry, hell-bent for leather, into overdrive and was thrusting the last decade of the American twentieth century into cataclysmic reformation.

Chapter 10

• • •

The 1993 Parliament differed from the 1893 Parliament not so much in its intention and structure as in the world from which it drew and which it sought to address. The ten decades from 1893 to 1993 had quite literally translated our species from human race to human family. A globe that once had been benignly vast, partitioned by its own natural barriers and subdivided by its climates, no longer was. Like the trembling in all its parts of a spider web when it is touched in any one of them, so the globe now was threatened when any of its parts was afflicted. The century intervening between the two Parliaments had also been the bloodiest, most war torn, most inhumane and torturous one that history had ever recorded.

Beyond the political ambition, greed, and, in some cases, sheer madness that underlay that hell of human creation, there was another stimulus to twentieth-century terror: religion and the hegemony of religions. God only knows how many Buddhists, Sikhs, and Hindus did not die, but were instead martyred, in that hundred years; but by 1993 we knew how many Jews had been sacrificed. By decade's end we would know as well what we already suspected, namely that forty million Christians likewise did not die, but were martyred, in that twentieth and most accursed century of Western time.

What the Second Parliament of the World's Religions sought first and foremost, then, was to achieve a safe space where all humanity's faiths could converse without fear of human reprisal, a space that would, in fact, be safe not only for eight days in North America, but also for years thereafter in human thinking everywhere. Hans Kung, the great German theologian, was, as Julia Howe had been before him, a central voice in sounding the tone of the convocation when he observed to the second Parliament that its work would of necessity have to be one more of ethics than religion, but that it would also have to be ethical rather than political—a distinction of such nicety that almost it fools the eye until the mind catches it and says, "Oh!"

Kung was speaking not so much from prescience, however, as from months of hard work; for it was he who had been assigned the task by the Parliament's Council of drafting for the consideration of the full assembly "A Declaration of the Religions for a Global Ethic." Daisy and I, going into Chicago, had already been privy to that initial draft as well as to Kung's almost heartrending recitation of the difficulties that had attended its creation. Most affecting . . . most preordination unsettling for me . . . were these words of his:

> There were suggestions to make the Declaration more "religious." However, new difficulties would result from this. If we, for example, were to speak "in the name of God," we would a priori exclude the Buddhists. Moreover, there is no consensus on a definition of what "religion" is. Nevertheless, I have clearly addressed the dimension of transcendence without forcing the compliance of the nonreligious whom this Declaration should include.

On the last day of the Parliament at the last convocation and after many preliminary conversations, some of them bitter and aflame with harsh rhetoric, Kung's "Declaration" would be accepted. Though my belief in the efficacy of declarations veers toward cynicism, I do believe in the residual worth of the process. In this case, however, I believed in both. So too must a great number of other people; for the Kung "Declaration" has been central to much of the work in global ethics in the years since its adoption in Chicago.

None of my premeeting research and preparatory reading had fortified me, however, against the assault on my religious equilibrium—or stasis, if you prefer—that commenced the minute Daisy and I walked into the Palmer Hilton in Chicago on Friday, August 27. The time from our entering that place until our leaving it was destined to compose nine of the most instructive and threatening days of my life. They were also nine of the most self-contained or self-referencing days of my adulthood.

Daisy and I had arranged to join forces with a writer named F. Lynne Bachleda. A dear friend of many years standing, Lynne was, and is, a professional researcher, something of an expert on religion with a particular affinity for Eastern and natural spiritualities, as well as being herself an all-around good heart. Perceiving my considerable need, she had been among the first who had agreed to write and review for us, at least for a while and to the extent that her other commitments permitted. Because Daisy had never met Lynne and because being in the same place at the same time seemed the perfect opportunity to strategize together about upcoming coverage, we three had arranged to have lunch on Monday. I remember that meeting because it was business and required a part of my brain that was used to functioning clearly and remembering more or less carefully. I also know that that lunch meeting is one of the few clear memories I have of either Lynne or Daisy during the entire Parliament. It was as if, with that one interruption, I was alone in my experiencing, as if they and their presence had somehow been driven out of mind by the press of activity around me. I was alone in a carnival . . . alone in a carnival of souls.

There were over eight thousand of us souls, in fact, and almost all of us dressed in the costumes of faith. The Victorian grandeur of the Palmer House lobby, restored and probably exaggerated by Hilton when they had taken it over, was the quintessentially perfect midway for what was happening. Thousands of colors and fabrics and intonations pushed their way through that lobby, back and forth between a beleaguered and confused Chicago outside and hot, crowded lecture halls and convention spaces inside. Wherever I went those nine days, short of my room itself, orange robes floated like buoys in a sea of yarmulkes and cassocks of every hue.

Turbans and brilliantly batiked dashikis bobbed along beside multicolored silk saris and protective veils, while the sacred eye of the *tilak* mark watched over us all from the center of several hundred foreheads. Almost naked sadhus engaged in deep, if somewhat more signed than said conversation with purple-shirted Roman prelates; and shamans with feathers in their tunics chanted to hypnotic drumbeats for Shinto priests in black, high-topped hats.

At one point, there was a shouting match between a group of Sikhs from the Punjab and Indians of other faiths over past persecutions. At another point, the Host Committee of Orthodox Christians walked out to protest the fact that neopagan and Wiccan practitioners were in attendance; and four Jewish groups withdrew in midcareen to protest the appearance of Louis Farrakhan, who was representing the Nation of Islam. It was a carnival of passion as well as color, and I would not for a moment have had it otherwise.

The sights and sounds, even the contradictions and arguments, alternated for me between being intriguing and being a serious reason for hope. They also evoked in me a pervasive gratitude that by some miracle of unknown intention I should be able to witness such a thing. All of these are good—or at least clearly defined and easily controlled—emotions. What was chaotic in experience and transporting in consequence for me, however, were the workshops, the lectures, and, in particular, the demonstrations of praxis.

Chapter 11

• • •

Since I was either alone or simply had somehow managed to isolate my attentive presence from Daisy and Lynne, I wandered more or less at will among the dozens of plenary sessions, worship services, lectures, practical demonstrations, and discussions. Three or four of them I shall not easily forget.

As Daisy and I had confessed to each other on that first Friday of my career with *PW,* Islam in 1993 was not a faith familiar to either of us at any experiential level. That lacuna would have disturbed me more—in terms of editorial integrity, if nothing else—had it not been for the fact that Islam, in 1993, was unfamiliar experientially to most Americans. Still largely a religion of immigrant practice, it was bound unto itself by the other restraints of cultural and ethnic differences. Yet I was mildly surprised—at least surprised enough to remember being so—that, by costume anyway, there appeared to be fewer Near Eastern imans and mullahs in the churning crowds than Buddhist monks. The notion that eight days in the United States might not be an attractive prospect, much less an imperative, for Arab clerics had simply not penetrated my thinking at that point.

Because any near experience I had ever had before 1993 of Islam as a practiced faith had been limited to indigenous expressions like the Nation of Islam and some few African-American converts of my acquaintance, I rather suspect now that I had gone into Chicago expecting to see, hear, and touch a bit of Islam in a more paradigmatic state. Certainly, it was the desire to do so that drew me into the one thing on the schedule that looked even remotely instructive of Islamic praxis: a demonstration by a group of Muslim Mevlevis, or whirling dervishes.

Even in my relative ignorance, I knew that Sufism is or is not Islam according to whom you ask. That same principle is operative in every major faith. Ask a Latter-Day Saint if he or she is Christian, and the answer will be a resounding yes. Ask a Southern Baptist if that same Latter-Day Saint is a Christian, and the answer will be a resounding no. Ask a scholar the question, and he or she will say, "Well, it depends on how you define 'Christian.' " It is always and ever thus with religion, so much so, in fact, that I canceled out on my list of concerns any issues of disagreements internal to Islam; showed up early in the appointed place; and claimed the most front-and-center seat in the house.

A small crowd began to gather . . . small, but remarkably subdued. Or else they were reverent, as if entering sacred space. Though there were still plenty of seats in the hall, an attractive younger woman sat down next to me. "Have you ever seen dervishes before," she whispered. I shook my head no in answer. She simply smiled and whispered, "Good luck," before she moved over a few seats to my right and settled in. In thinking to myself that her departure was curious, if not peculiar, I came to realize that few of the people near me were sitting next to anybody else either. I turned around to look behind me. There, too, people were scattered, some of them already engaged in some kind of abstraction or absorption that looked, for all the world, like private prayer or meditation. But then the drum started, not intrusively, but soft and seductively. Without meaning to, I let it carry me wherever it was we were going to go.

They came on to the stage so quietly and so "unphysically" as to have more collected like dew than arrived. They were in white, some eight or ten of them, and they moved about, not like dancers in a learned or practiced ballet, but like separate creatures consciously part of one another. The effect was more ghostly or diaphanous than corporeal or even aesthetic. At some point so fluidly achieved that I did not note it, they began to run their hands up and out from the sides of their bodies, and that was when they began to spin. Around and around and around with not a muscle moving. Like tops without string or child any longer attached, they spun. They spun until I spun with them. Until the young woman a few seats to my right spun. Until we all spun into ecstasy. Then they stopped. As abruptly as if by common signal, they stopped, and they disappeared.

When I had started to cry, I do not know. It didn't matter. I had never seen ecstatic worship before, never understood before that the human body is light and its God a consuming fire from which it emanates and to which it returns with erotic ferocity when it frees itself to know itself.

Oh, God . . . God . . . God. It is all about God. That's all any of it has ever been about and all it ever will be. They're not religions, they're ways to the center where the body flames up and the dervishes whirl.

I have seen dervishes a time or two since the Parliament. Once, in 1998, while a guest at The Fetzer Institute, I even sat in a quasi lecture by the Sufi dancer Zuleikha. I remember listening intently to all of her explanations, to her demonstration of the various drum tempos, to all of the commentary she offered. But none of it mattered, because then she began to spin, like the Mevlevis at the Parliament, so subtly that she went into the place of luminous fire without my knowing how, though she took me there with her.

Islam, by whatever name, was no longer a theory.

Chapter 12

• • •

One could not walk the hallways of the Palmer Hilton, especially alone, without overhearing both the ambient conversations and some drifts and murmurs from the adjacent meeting rooms. Within two days of such wandering, I began to realize that beneath the costumes and the faith-specific practices around me, there was an overriding sensibility informing almost all of them. Over and over again, there were exhortations—both conversational and formal—to a greater concern about the earth and our human environment.

Part of the stimulus to such a pronounced emphasis was, I am sure, due to the same point Hans Kung had made originally, namely that the Parliament of necessity would discover its most visible result in its ethical, rather than its religious, work. But this was more than an ethical issue. If for no other reason, I would have reached that conclusion just on the basis of the emotional tenor surrounding it. While people can indeed become emotionally involved with ethical questions, rarely do any of us become quietly reverential about them. Ethics are to be argued and explored. Ecology—for "ecology" was the word I had first tried to apply to what I was hearing—ecology as a matter of ethical concern can certainly be argued and explored; but what was being voiced around me was something quieter and more supple than moral rectitude.

"Ecotheology," Lynne said to me on Monday at that one lunch meeting I remember. Her eyes laughed at me in a kind of gentle "Do you still not get it?" way. "It's ecotheology. It's what I've been trying to tell you for the last four or five months. It may not fit in any of your boxes, babe, but that doesn't keep it from being real."

Ecotheology. I still cannot define the word with precision; but Lord knows that since the Parliament, I have used it often enough, primarily as an umbrella word and almost entirely because the English language and I lack any other term that would work as well.

The Orthodox Christian hosting committee, which had, at the last minute, withdrawn its support from the Parliament because of the presence of the The Covenant of the Goddess and of the Wiccan and neopagan clergy in attendance, was right about the fact that the earth religions were participants. What they were wrong about was the assumption—or what I took to be their assumption—that reverent involvement with the spiritual aspects of the physical world could be so easily exorcised, or even so openly and neatly identified.

The space between worshipping Nature and worshiping the Great Spirit is a relatively narrow one. The space between reverent acknowledgment of the Great Spirit and affixing liturgical practice to the physical flow of the earth's seasons, while definitely a space, is still arguably not a great one. The space between finding transcendence in the flow of earth time and consciously calling it to mind as a matter of one's worship of the God of creation is much smaller. And the space between the doctrinal assertion of God as Creator and the active, God-fearing, God-honoring assumption of care for the earth as religious obligation is downright minute.

Where along that sliding scale one chooses to draw the line

between the religiously acceptable and the religiously unacceptable is a matter of one's own convictions or those of one's faith community. Drawing a line in matters of religion, however, is a lot like deciding which of the two hundred first, second, and third cousins at a family reunion one is willing to claim as kin. I can say that now and know I mean it; but it took me one Parliament, a fellow writer, and several years to get there. (I have probably been assisted as well by the fact that I personally have a number of third cousins, and even one or two first cousins, whom I deplore . . . or, at best, regard as having failed to realize the full magnitude of our common DNA.)

DNA is wily stuff, a fact I was also forced to face at the Parliament. It tends to operate from associative bases and innate affinities that we human beings are not yet clever enough to describe, much less account for. When Fred Ciporen had asked me if I was Jewish, I had answered truthfully in saying, "No, Christian." I had come home from New York, however, still amused by his question and had told Sam about it. More than amused, perhaps, I was also flattered. Otherwise, I would not have thought the moment significant enough to include in a long list of things about my trip that wanted sharing.

I am Christian and gentile . . . or a goy, if one prefers . . . but I don't look like it, a circumstance that I discovered years ago through the process of being told so over and over again. Having adult children, at least four of whom look more Jewish than Fred Ciporen ever will, has only reenforced that bit of self-perception. The complete truth is that while I am gentile, my father's mother was of Jewish extraction. It is, in me and mine, as if the genes remember what laws of descent and the circumstances of environment deny. Fred's question, innocently asked and coming well after any pretense of an interview was over, had pleased me because it meant, once again, that he had recognized — or thought he recognized — something in a southern demeanor that he could not otherwise identify. DNA. God be praised for the signatures of our ancestors upon the tablets of our hearts.

But while I might have a Jewish countenance, it would be

fair to say that in 1993 I had never had any significant amount of exposure to Jewish worship. I had had a tribe of Levi roommate in college who probably did more for my Yiddish than for my soul, this being especially true because of the general tenor of the Yiddish she employed and then shared. In addition, for years, while Sam and I lived in the city, we had had intimate ties with our Orthodox next-door neighbors; but those years had taught me more about daily domestic customs, child rearing, and interfaith good manners than about synagogue and what happened in shul. Yet I had been content.

What I mean by that is, while I might have been pleasured over the years by the notion of some truncated physical associations with Judaism, I do not think it had ever once occurred to me to consider the possibility of any kind of shared religious sensibilities. Christianity was here, Judaism was there. Between them there was not a relative space, but "a great gulf fixed," to put the matter biblically. That gulf was not an instrument of antagonism, God knows, nor was it a reason for rejoicing. Rather, it was a sad fact, an impassable reality of differentness that, within my southern Protestant experience at least, was sanctified by both faiths because for centuries each had seen it as having been established by God.

At the Parliament, it was this state of approved, but very functional distancing that, with no malice of aforethought, allowed me for several days to navigate around dozens of obviously Jewish conversations without eavesdropping, and to walk quite dispassionately past the lectures and discussions labeled as "Jewish" or about "Judaism" in my program. But then there came that late afternoon . . . after four o'clock but not quite happy hour on a day I can otherwise not remember . . . when I was tired; and the door nearest me was opened onto a meeting room that was invitingly quiet, half lit, and empty of people on its back two rows of seats. If I had looked at the signage outside the door—which I did not—I would have seen that there was to be a demonstration performance by a prominent cantor. All things being equal, that probably would have attracted me.

Things were not equal, however. I was simply tired, and I entered the meeting room innocent of what I was about to hear.

I do not know who he was, but I do know he looked like a dark-haired edition of a Greek god—arrestingly handsome with a speaking voice that more cavorted with my ears than commanded them. The modulation was incredible, and the dark-suited body, fluid and easy. He had my attention even before he began to speak of the cantor's role, of his own rabbinic studies in preparation for this work, of his synagogue and of others like it. Then he began to sing or chant or whatever aesthetic cantillating it is that combines the two. The holy words of the millennia rose visibly, like angels, from the book before him. He moved effortlessly from chanting a section of the Torah to the music of the prayer book, the siddur in his hand no longer a needed text for so beloved an exercise as this. . . . And a space opened.

In the years since 1993, I have written and spoken often on the subject of prayer. I write and speak, however, with progressively less and less belief in my own competence to do so . . . or in much of anybody else's, for that matter. There are far too many words about prayer these days. It is as if, in our starving, we think a cookbook rather than a meal will feed us. That having been said, there are a few things . . . almost descriptive principles, if you will . . . that I do know about prayer. The first is that prayer is a place.

Prayer is a nonlocative, nongeographic space that one enters at one's own peril, for it houses God during those few moments of one's presence there, and what is there will most surely change everything that comes into it. Prayer, its opal walls polished to transparency by the centuries of hands that have touched them, is the Tabernacle realized and the wayside chapel utilized. Ever traveling as we travel, moving as we move, prayer grips like home, until the heart belongs nowhere else and the body can scarcely function apart from them both. Prayer is dangerous and the entrance way to wholeness. And if the cantor did not—indeed could not—teach me that in a single afternoon, he slid open a door and showed me where it was I should begin to look.

What the cantor also did . . . or, more correctly, what my hour of listening to the Holy Writ and prayers that were the cantor's singing did . . . was more immediately unsettling. An appreciation of prayer as place took, and yet will take, years of contemplation and practice. Perceiving that the cantor's words were also my words did not. That recognition was immediate, and it was visceral.

My laying claim that afternoon to the holy words of Hebrew worship was not a matter of biology; nor was it some half-romanticized delight in something I thought of as part of an attenuated family heritage. Certainly it was not any kind of silly claim to linguistic agility, as if undergraduate or neighborly experience had somehow left a familiarity of sound or cadence in their wake. This possession of the presence in the cantor's words was a religious one. Those chanted and sung phrases were as natural to me as the cadences and intonations of my own worship. They were my belief, my passion, my exercise of reverence being released in words that I understood and perceived that I understood even while also perceiving that my intelligence had no idea where in either the Torah or the Psalter we were at any given moment during the whole hour. Religious DNA.

One may wince at so flip a label, but here too I have not yet managed to contrive a more dignified but still descriptively adequate wording. The cantor and I? We were and are of the same cloth and from the same source. We are Abrahamics. The stuff of our souls is of a common stock; and ours, thus, the affinity of religious DNA. All of which is to say that the cantor had not so much transported me in the usual, often trite sense of that word, as he had released his angels to lift me just high enough above history to see. What had looked, from the ground, like a gulf was, from above, the bed of a deep river that watered the plains on either side of its coursing. Shalom. Amen.

Chapter 13

• • •

My nine days of Parliament gazing were not as freewheeling an assignment as I perhaps have made them sound. Some work must have gotten done, for Daisy and I came out of Chicago with a healthy amount of reportage. Several publishers also expressed their pleasure—a few even appreciation—that their industry journal was on-site as part of the working press. That all says to me that we did more concrete journalism than I can now remember the mechanics of. The one piece of journalism that I do remember, however, was also the only firm appointment that I had made before going into Chicago.

The Dalai Lama was to give the keynote address at the Parliament's closing session on Saturday. He would arrive in Chicago on Friday and, at four that afternoon, hold a session that was to be somewhere between an audience and a press conference. One hundred and twenty-five people—some press, but more, I suspect, supporters and admirers—were to be allowed in. Lynne and I were to be among them.

Once more, I had that sense of impossible good fortune or beneficence. There was no other explanation for my being in that

place at that time. At a practical level, the senior editor of a religion publisher and herself an American Buddhist had invited us
to use two of her passes; but that is not an explanation so much
as it is merely a description of the means by which the end was
accomplished.

Going into that room at a quarter to four on that Friday afternoon, I was as near to humble as I can usually ever get. Mine
was not a case of being starstruck by the presence of the Dalai
Lama, but it was an almost overwhelming awareness of the awful power of the press . . . what it could accomplish in the shaping of opinion and thereby of functional reality, what it could
barter its influence for, what a limited and chipped lens one person's mind is for reflecting the world to itself.

My own restlessness was surrounded by a whole room of
restlessness. We were seated in straight chairs that had been
arranged in fairly generous rows with an aisle down the center of
them for His Holiness to enter. In front of us was a U-shaped
arrangement of three tables. Those to our left were to be occupied by the Dalai Lama and his entourage; those to our right, by
Christian monks, among them Brother Wayne Teasdale, who
were friends and colleagues of His Holiness as well as supporters of his struggle to gain freedom for Tibet. At four, the doors
were locked, and the guards—pleasant, nicely suited, nonthreat-
ening, but still wired and probably armed—began to pass among
us down those generous aisles. In 1993 being questioned or
searched was an almost unheard of thing, and I was as much fascinated as offended.

Having been cleared to stay, we waited. The Christian monks
came and went, up and down the aisle, between the back door
and their side of the U. The imp in me noted . . . and remembers
noting . . . that their cowls and scapulars actually did fly and
bounce a bit, meaning they were not nearly as calm and detached
as popular perception would have had them be. As the minutes
ticked on and nothing happened, Brother Wayne spoke briefly
about the obvious: The Dalai Lama was not yet in the hotel.
More restlessness. Finally, the casual beginning of a few conver-

sations up and down and across the rows, when abruptly the back doors snapped open, and like a tide rising, every row from back to front began to stand.

As part of a press corp, I have seen the Pope two or three times since 1993 and have been in audience with religion leaders from the Chief Mullah of Jerusalem to Orthodox archbishops, as well as a panoply of religious in between; but I have never seen anything that comes near in veneration to the passage that afternoon of the Dalai Lama from the rear to the front of that meeting hall. Obeisance is not a Western practice, certainly. It is definitely antithetical to protestant Christianity and, more or less, to the Anglo-Catholic Christianity out of which I come. As a result, I have had to wonder a thousand times since that Friday if my sense of disgust was a matter of cultural distaste or of religious conviction. Either way, I was not any happier with my own reaction to all the bobbing heads and bending bodies than I was with appearing to be the only person in the room who, albeit standing in respect, was not worshipping . . . for that is what was happening.

What the Dalai Lama said once he got to his place in the U I could not, for the life of me, relate without going back to some other reporter's coverage. Truth told, I do not remember any of his words or any of my own notes, assuming I took some. What I remember instead was watching him with total absorption: the glorious orange robe, the magnificent Rolex watch that kept catching the light and flashing it out toward us, the eyeglasses in designer frames. What I kept wondering, basically, was "How could he?" How could any human being permit, allow, endure what he had just permitted and endured—had empowered even, and apparently enjoyed . . .

. . . he could, only if that human being were divine and knew it. Or, barring that, he could only if he were a very skillful and informed opportunist playing on the gullibility of crowd mentality. Those at least seemed to me to be the only options that appertained. The only ones, I concluded, that could appertain to a triumphal entry . . .

Oh, God!

Had the doors not been locked, I am sure I would have fled out of that place, half drunk for air. I have no idea how my understanding of Buddhism has been affected over the years since by that single minute of epiphany, but I've got a fairly sound notion of how my perception of Christianity has, for it took on a messy but vivid historicity for me at that exact moment. Real people had done this same thing once in Jerusalem, and it had been permitted then too, permitted by the one whom I worship as God. Either He is and knew Himself to be, or . . .

In either case, "Oh, God!"

In either case, "This is no game we play. This is."

The minute the doors were unlocked, I was through them without so much as a by-your-leave or a thank-you. I literally ran, I think, away from the crowd and toward a pair of what I took to be service elevators. I punched, one opened, I got in. We were almost to his floor when I realized the man in the other corner was Arlo Guthrie, who apparently had managed to get out of the meeting more quickly even than I had. "That was something, wasn't it?" I said. Inane, but the best I could do at the moment. "Yep," he said. I have no idea where Arlo Guthrie was religiously at that point in his life, but I thought he looked about as drained as I felt when he got off the elevator.

Chapter 14

• • •

The private discoveries that overtook me at the World Parliament were neither mine nor private, of course. Each of them—Islam, Judaism, ecotheology, Buddhism—had been able to slap me to attention because all of them were ubiquitous in Chicago, pervasive in the way that scent is subtly everywhere in one's experiencing of a place.

Having said that, I think it not quite correct to say that the roiling leitmotifs themselves were pervasive. What was pervasive, rather—what the scent was—actually came from the aggregate of all of them together. It was in their congress with one another that they exuded the fresh, alien sweetness of the wind that immediately precedes a change in the sea. Yet separately, they would also prove to be four of the dozen or so major forces that would fuel the engine of religion book publishing for the rest of the twentieth century. In fact, they would not only fuel that engine, but they would shove it into overdrive.

My suspicion is that even without Gulf Wars and Twin Towers, our shrinking globe and expanding media still would have thrust Islam into the general American conversation before too many more years went by. Beyond the stimulus in that direction from broadcast information and constricting geography, there was also the fact that Islam's physical presence in urban America had increased significantly in the decades preceding 2000. There were, by the millennium's end, as many Muslims as Jews—some figures actually show considerably more than, in fact—in this country. The major difference, at a political and cultural level, was that in the years since World War II, Judaism had shifted, over two and a half generations, from seeing itself as an expatriate community to seeing itself as composed of American Jews who were formative participants in a dynamic culture. Muslims, present in significant numbers in this country for a much shorter time, are just now beginning to effect that shift in self-definition; but as a change, it was already in process in 1993.

Within a year, KAZI Publications, an Islamic publisher (also located in Chicago), would emerge as a recognized force in religion book publishing. A professional organization, the Islamic Publishers Association, would be founded and become instrumental in merging its member houses more and more into the larger industry. While Islamic bookstores would also open in some major American cities, including Chicago, somewhat more telling was the fact that more and more general bookstores, both chains and independents, would establish Islamic sections as part of their religion stock. Just as significant culturally and/or religiously, non-Islamic publishers would begin, with considered but obvious haste, to publish books about Islam for the general reader. Some of those books would step beyond religion per se— or at least beyond its facts and theories—to begin addressing the human, the everyday, the practically appealing in another's faith. Regardless of thrust or origin or venue, though, almost all of these efforts did well in the marketplace, earning their publishers and retailers a tidy financial return and the surrounding culture, a certain amount of early benediction.

The growth in both reader interest and publisher output in Islamic materials was contemporaneous enough with the Parliament so that in May 1994, *PW* ran its first ever coverage of Islamic publishing in this country. In fact, what we ran that May was more than coverage; it was a full-fledged feature. Bob Summer, another old friend and fellow writer, had—and has—a great respect for, and considerable intimacy with, Islam, holding it in something very close to a religious affection. His was the perfect combination of information and sensibilities to write the magazine's first feature. After that, Bob continued to give counsel, review books for the department, and even do another feature or two, all in terms of Islam and our coverage of it. Bob was invaluable in another way, too. Along with his other work, he had for years been *PW*'s southeastern correspondent. As a result, he not only knew the book publishing industry like the back of his hand in the dark, but he also knew all the ins and outs of *PW*. There is, I have long since concluded, just no accounting for good fortune sometimes, especially when it comes in the form of charitable polymaths.

My having decided at the Parliament to ignore the dichotomy between Islam per se and Sufism did not mean, of course, that the distinction is not there. It is. But I am also enough of a realist to know that had terrorism and imperialistic wars not overtaken contemporary history, America's engagement of Islam would have been a more constructive, welcoming, accepting one than it presently is and that, in no small part, Sufism would have lain at the root of that difference. My suspicion, in fact, is that what most Americans during the early to mid-1990s saw as the religion of Islam (as opposed to Muslim culture and politics) was far more Sufi than Shiite or Sunni Mohammedanism. Certainly the dervishes—now well publicized, documented, and popularized—have provided a very sympathetic presentation of one Islamic way of worship. It is, however, the poetry of their founder that has truly fired the popular religious imagination.

Rumi—his full name was Jalal al-Din Rumi, but few of us ever use it—Rumi was the thirteenth-century Persian mystic whose poetry (over three thousand pieces of it) and discourses (seventy-two in sum) became the aesthetic and theological foundation for the Mevlevi, or order of dervishes. One of the more arresting isolated facts about American book publishing in the 1990s is that Rumi was—and still is—the best-selling poet in this country. While to those who share the proverbial Yankee disdain for poetry that may seem of small consequence, the truth is otherwise; or at least my informed guess is that it is otherwise.

I accept as hard fact the premise that the people reading Rumi in this country are doing so because of his content. Even artful translators like Coleman Barks, the preeminent one for Rumi's work, cannot entirely obliterate the fact that translation is translation and sometimes a bumpy, less than melodious road. There is little possibility, as a result, that Rumi's meter and verse schemes, already culturally alien as well as translated, are the reasons for his success in gaining an American audience. Rather, it is his images, all of which speak to, or in terms of, the transcendent, the mystically spiritual, an erotic beauty so far beyond dogma as to be Beauty.

Because of this shimmering luminescence, Rumi's work has served as a source of reassurance and as an object of meditation and transport for many religiously animated Americans. In order to exercise and mature their life with God, late-twentieth-century seekers after truth have often found it necessary to disavow the established religious institutions of the late-twentieth-century West. To the extent that that process of reforming and regrouping was the central thrust of late-twentieth-century Euro-American religion—and it was—I must conclude that Rumi's audience was almost entirely disenfranchised believers. Given the staying power of Rumi's sales, I must secondly conclude that his influence has been disproportionately present in the places where it mattered, namely in the hustings, where reformation has been the order of the day for some time now. But if Rumi may be said to have become the beloved mystic of the "I'm spiritual, but not religious" seekers, Buddhism by 1993 had already, and at a far more informing level, become their disciplinarian, their instructor, and the gold standard they used for all things spiritual.

Chapter 15

Buddhism has at least two characteristics, neither of them
enjoyed by the monotheistic faiths, that have functioned to
its advantage in its migrations westward. The very nature of
Buddhism, however, requires that at least one caveat be offered
before any discussion of its characteristics goes very far. The
caveat is this: There is no such thing as "Buddhism" in the first
place. There is no such thing, that is, if in using the word one pre-
sumes the existence of some kind of monolithic whole.

While it is popular (and pleasantly easy) to speak of the
divisions in Buddhism as being similar to the divisions of Orthodoxy, Roman Catholicism, and Protestantism within Christianity, or to think of the schools within Buddhism's divisions as
similar to denominations within, for example, Christian Protestantism, both analogies are more handy than accurate. A more
nearly accurate image might be that of the relationships that exist within the family of Abraham among Judaism, Christianity,
and Islam or, in the case of Buddhist schools internal to its divisions, as somewhat analogous to the relationships in subset
among Christianity, Christian Science, and Mormonism.

To the extent, then, that one can even speak of "Buddhism" without first employing a whole string of qualifiers, one can speak of its defining characteristics. The first of the two that are pertinent here has to do with sacred texts. Although Buddhism, worldwide, has a huge canon of sacred writings from which to draw its principles and wisdom, it does not have a single or exclusionary scripture composed in one language and forming a closed canon from which, and through the application of which, it must draw its governance. Among other things, this means that Buddhism has no dogma, either certifying or confining, that appertains across all of its divisions, schools, and observant cultures. Such is the kind of flexibility that monotheists would at times die for. God knows, many have certainly died from the lack of it over the centuries.

Secondly, Buddhism is not inherently theistic. Even in Mahayana Buddhism, the grand division out of whose Avalokiteshvara school the Dalai Lama descends, there is worship not of a holy creator and judge, but of bodhisattvas as the ideal; that is, as human beings who live as the Buddha lived while simultaneously living as celestial beings whose function is, in part, to receive petitions and veneration. The bodhisattva's exquisite compassion comes from his great wisdom, which in turn has come from his understanding that there is no enduring self and no reality beyond the assemblage of stimuli present in any particular moment of time.

When this essential fluidity and broad provision for nontheistic belief systems entered America, it seemed at first blush that it was perfectly possible for a spiritual or religious seeker to be an adherent of any of the monotheistic faiths and a Buddhist all at the same time. In a way, that is true. Even if it were erroneous, though, the greater truth would still be that some part of Buddhist thought or practice has been assimilated at some greater or lesser level into every major faith system in the United States, be that faith system an established or nonestablished one.

Interestingly enough, the American engagement with Buddhism has not only influenced the thinking and experiences of other faith groups in this country, but it also has created a new one. Somewhere around 1998 or 1999, I began to see manuscripts and attend meetings where the central theme was the emergence of what could only be called "American Buddhism." That is, the emergence of something that is Buddhism, but that differs from its Oriental counterparts as sharply and cleanly as does a second-generation Japanese-American stockbroker on Wall Street from hers. Assimilation is the American way, but it has also always been the way of Buddhism as well, thus twice blessed.

The roar of Buddhism across the North American continent had its origins, certainly, in some of the nineteenth century's fascination with what was then called Spiritualism or Orientalism, both of which were more campfires than conflagrations. The match of conflagration was struck in our mid-twentieth century when three wars took American young people into eastern theaters of war and, as a result, into intimate contact for the first time with Oriental culture and religious sensibilities. Many of those young men and women found the latter to be both attractive and sympathetic. It was 1965, however, when the match's flare truly caught.

In 1965 Congress changed the immigration laws, allowing people of Asian descent to enter this country for the first time in over half a century; and they came in droves. They came, as had every other wave of immigration since before the Pilgrim Fathers, bringing with them an enviable work ethic, a resiliency of intellect and body, a simplicity of needs, a fierce loyalty to one another . . . and Buddhism. Buddhism the adaptable, Buddhism the fluid, Buddhism the serene way of seeing and, thereby, of being. For a country like this one, which had had almost no mysticism in its national experience . . . the Pilgrims were remarkably short of supply in that area . . . and whose citizens had for three centuries lived the hardtack life of those who conquer objective, not subjective, continents, Buddhism was like a road map to an unknown country, and not just any unknown country. It was a map into El Dorado.

Even though I had been an amateur religion watcher for many years before *PW* started paying me to do so, and even though I was most certainly fully mature and aware by 1965, it is still hard now to relay with sufficient poignancy and force the extent of yearning that characterized the decades of the 1960s and '70s. Nuclear war had taught us that we could now slaughter each other and ourselves with efficiency. There had to be more than that to our being here. The pill had freed us from the threat of pregnancy, and freedom had become license. The body had ceased to be a temple of the ecstatic and had become, instead, a place of social exchange. Recreational drugs and drug experimentation had shown us that there were indeed whole continents inside each of us that were their own reality. Terror, ironically mixed with a deep human need to feel something—anything—made the possibilities of another world contiguous with this one seem not only actual but necessary. Now, if only we could get to it.

Mainline, Caucasian-American Protestantism had none of the "smells and bells" needed for transport into that new space. Roman Catholicism, by heritage, had them; but the meditative tools of the Roman tradition, including its smells and bells, were almost entirely confined to Roman naves by Protestant fears. Either that, or they were socially scorned as the hallmarks of bead-fingering, working-class, often pathetic middle-aged women. Jewish mysticism was just awaking from a long Enlightenment slumber, and "Kabbalah" was several years from becoming a comfortably American word. But Buddhism . . .

. . . Ah, there was cloth of a different stripe. Buddhism had the words—a whole lexicon of them, in fact—for talking about the interior world of the psyche and about the exterior, contiguous one of the spirit. Buddhism had the practices that told one how to engage them both and how to experience their unity. In addition, Buddhism had the golden glow of two and a half millennia of safe travel and happy result. Buddhism.

When Daisy had decided *PW* needed to establish a religion department, Buddhism was already present in the supporting data she used in making her case. By 1994, however, only two or three years later, Buddhism had become a principal factor in everybody's set of book-publishing figures. Books about it were everywhere, the bulk of them admittedly more about Buddhist meditation practices than about Buddhism per se. Likewise, many other of the more successful ones taught the hungry how to combine Buddhist principles and meditation practices with those of other faiths: how to be a Jewish Buddhist, for instance, or a Buddhist Christian or some permutation thereof. Some of those books were not only instructive, but also quite lovely in both their words and their precepts. Others were bone-out silly.

The day I was shown a manuscript (which, fortunately, never went any further) about how to be a Buddhist Jew with Christocentric affinities, I knew we had probably pushed this particular envelope as far as it could go without some kind of course correction—which, predictably enough, did come, course correction being the way of human affairs in religion as in everything else. Buddhism slowed down as a conflagration and, by 1997 or '98, had become a comforting but robust fire by which many faiths warmed their American hands. It also, of course, had settled in and begun to make itself at home, becoming the Americanized edition that was the subject of all those late-twentieth-century books and meetings I have already mentioned.

As for ecotheology and the shock of recognition in seeing Judaism as complementary forebear, they would not only stay the course as well, but they would continue to grow and, by century's end, to assume a major role in the drama of American religion. I would have to go to a different part of the country, however, to begin to more fully understand their genesis.

California Dreaming

Chapter 16

• • •

No one can work very long as a paid observer of religion without having to come to grips with the question of just exactly what religion is. At some point the phenomena being watched cease to present as individual matters of faith and begin to coalesce into a larger whole that is, like it or not, a human construct. There is, in the course of that shift in point of view, a disconcerting, almost threatening time of internal examination; or there was for me anyway. I can laugh now about having had to organize my schizophrenia to survive my job, but the process of getting to that point was anything but amusing.

As one part of its belief structure, Christianity has a pair of theological precepts called the "offense of particularity" and/or "Christian triumphalism." Either boils down to a doctrine which holds that only in Christ can there be salvation. All other systems and their adherents operate in error and, for their own good, all are to be enticed to correction by whatever means possible. While the matter may not always be so bald-facedly stated as that, the "offense" principle is built into Christianity and has been for at least seventeen hundred years. Much of the bloodshed of Western history since the fourth century, in fact, has had both its impetus and its justification in the offense of particularity.

Equally intrinsic and cogent to Christianity, however, is the possibility it provides for more than one interpretation of how it is that one can move through Christ to salvation. There is, in other words, a considerable list of scriptural citations that seem to teach that one does not have to be a confessing Christian to be rescued from meaninglessness and the descent of one's soul into horror. As a result of God's mercy and God's unknowable, unfathomable wisdom, one can be included in the plan of Christian salvation through Christ's salvific presence in other venues and manifestations. All of which is to say, if you were reading carefully, that Christianity is itself a little schizophrenic, likewise not an amusing fact. It is especially unamusing if one is a traditionalist Christian. It becomes even less amusing when, twenty-four hours a day, six days a week, one is looking down on Christianity as only one cluster of pieces in a far larger jigsaw puzzle.

In my own maturing, I had moved in my head from the "one way only" dogma of my rearing to the "mercy of God and many manifestations" position with little or no difficulty, primarily because the New Testament seems to me not only to leave that door wide open, but also to point earnestly in its direction. There came that inevitable day, however—a nice spring day in 1993, to be exact—when I found myself standing in the back of a lecture hall in southern California the better to both watch and hear the best-selling author and religious iconoclast whose appearance I had come to cover. He began innocuously enough and managed to stay there for about two minutes. After that, he, and we with him, were off and running for a whole hour on "Christ Consciousness" as a road not only around particularity, but straight into the universalism of salvation for all regardless. Mercy over justice, no questions asked or even raised. Suddenly I had come up sharp and hard against my own beliefs in terms of conduct decisions instead of thought experiments.

It took me about ten minutes to regroup interiorly and persuade myself that Phyllis Tickle the observer could not only analyze cleanly but repeat accurately and even ponder later with impunity what Phyllis Tickle the believing Christian did not accept as even faintly acceptable. It took me months . . . or so it seemed, though I doubt that now . . . to become at home in my own soul with the discovery that I could permit—even indulge—such a dichotomizing of self. The truth of the matter, as I also came to realize later, is that I could not have done any of those things had there not been a prior process. That is, by the spring of 1993 I had already begun, without realizing it, to separate the believer in me out from the observer by the simple expedient of trying, very intentionally, to figure out what in the world it was I was watching.

I have no idea at all now—and doubt that I ever did, actually—at what point in time I finally arrived at a definition of religion that was refined enough to be of any use in my own thinking. So likewise, I have little real memory of what that defining metaphor looked like when I first began to employ it. It too has suffered the adjustments and tweaking as well as the nicking and bruising that give character to any well-used tool. I do know, though, how I define religion now. Or, to say the least, I know quite clearly the stance or platform from which I now observe it.

Religion is the rope of meaning. Extended, that metaphor can even be translated to something like "Religion is what connects the ship to the shore or anchors the swaying boat to its dock." I am not so compulsive in my use of images, but each to his or her own. The point is that regardless of how far one pushes the simile itself, every human society that we know anything about has eventually evolved a system of meaning to govern, secure, and justify its own experiences. The need to not live without rules and connection to something larger is apparently innate and intractable in us. Religion is the salve to that need; and the assuaging of that need is religion.

Just as an aside, but also as deeply pertinent, I must add here that even my most credibly atheistic friends and colleagues are daily in pursuit of right standards of conduct, relationships of care and compassion beyond themselves, and the driving need, as they usually put it, "to make a difference." That, I would submit, is religion; and the fact that it is nontheistic in its context no more prevents it from being their religion than the same concepts prevent Buddhism from being the religion of the Dalai Lama. The former system is idiosyncratic, at least to some extent, and the latter organized, again to some extent; but that is a logistical, not a substantive difference.

If religion is the rope of meaning in human life, then like any other rope or cable, it must have its component parts. That is to say that, like any cable, this one is composed of strands that are braided together for strength, wrapped in a mesh sleeve to deter their fraying, and then protected against the elements by a tough outer casing. The three interwoven and securing strands are spirituality, corporeality, and morality. The mesh sleeve is the common imagination; and the tough outer skin is story.

So long as the story holds, the mesh sleeve of shared imagination will hold its weave. If and when the encasing story is pierced or pulled back, the sleeve is exposed and begins to pock, baring the strands within to examination . . . even to the insult of being pulled up a bit out of their braid and into the open air, where we may look at them more closely, finger them, inspect them. Inevitably, the human society doing the fingering returns the strand it is considering back to the braid, usually even stuffing it into place with considerable attention, lest the cable itself have been weakened. Usually as well, if the story casing has not been put back in place, human hands will reach through the pocked mesh and pick up another strand in order to finger it awhile. In some periods of history, all three parts of the braid have been subject to major examination. At other times, only one or two. Our recent past and near future are a matter of all three under major examination.

One of the more disconcerting things for me over the mid- to late 1990s was the ease with which folk used the word "spirituality." They employed it with the abandon of those who honestly know what they are talking about. I am not, I hope, being precious when I say that I have never quite known what the word means, and therefore found myself using it less and less easily with the passing of the years. For me, it is close to a catchall bin of a word into which we dump all the nonvisible or subjective experiences we don't know quite what else to do with. The process is a lot like using the word "virus" in medicine to cover every set of symptoms not immediately diagnosable by protocol or laboratory procedures.

All of this does not mean that I do not use the word or — would it were so! — that I have a better, more precise one. It simply means that I could quite easily campaign for funding some kind of research group that recognized a bin when they saw one and were adept enough to dump it out and sort its contents into more clearly labeled, smaller bins. My strong suspicion is that such will not soon happen, though my other suspicion is that something very close to it happened with the Celts . . . or that is what I think my friend Tom Cahill would say.

Catchall word or not, however, "spirituality" is what we currently have, and "spirituality" is what we are stuck with for naming the first strand in the braid. As such, it does mean to include and denote all those pieces and parts of interior or nonlocative knowing that provide awareness of, as well as means of connection between, one sentient entity and another without the necessity of direct touch. Corporeality, as its name implies, is much easier to handle simply because it is, by definition, the handleable, seeable parts and accoutrements of religion: its buildings and altars, its sacred texts and rituals, creeds, priestly system, budgets, and programs . . . all the things that make visible the assertion of meaning. Morality is the third strand in the sustaining braid and shares fibers with the other two. Morality is the ethics of meaning, the governance of conduct as it is defined through human application of perceived divine or natural law and modulated through the restrictions of human character and circumstance.

The common imagination is that dear, if somewhat tractable, lacework of comfort that lets us all agree, to varying degrees, about who we are as a species or culture or group or individuals.

It tells us how the world works. Whether or not the explanations with which it secures us are accurate or not is not germane to its uses. What matters is that we all more or less agree on the world-view that it offers. And that system works very, very well, right up to the time when someone or something makes a tear in the story, for it is the story that must be right, must be accurate, must speak truth with a capital *T.* Everything—the integrity of the whole rope—depends on the story. In 1993, one did not have to go to California to know that the story was in trouble, but it did most certainly help clarify the issues; for California was the epi-center of story bashing at the time.

Chapter 17

• • •

Santa Rosa, California, is two hours by bus (with a couple of taxicabs thrown in for good measure) north of the San Francisco airport. As bus trips go, this one is pleasureable enough for me to recommend it as an adventure without need of a destination. Straight through miles of vineyards and into the heart of Sonoma County's wine country. The first time I made the trip, I thought I had died to this world and gone, if not to a theological heaven, at least to an aesthetically perfected one. Highway 101 exits to Highway 12, and Highway 12 turns off to Farmers Lane, and Farmers Lane at Fourth Street turns off to the Flamingo Hotel.

Santa Rosa, unless it has changed markedly—which I would find inconceivable—is an American town with a faint, almost ineffable European cachet and an ambience and architecture that appear to have been permanently arrested in the 1950s. Even the Flamingo Hotel is as solidly early–Holiday Inn in its attitude as it is midcentury in its decor. I have rarely been more comfortable in a place than there, nor have I ever been more aware of the inherent contradiction; for the stolid, functional Flamingo Hotel's greatest claim to fame undoubtedly is that twice a year it houses The Jesus Seminar.

The attack on story that exposes a culture's shared world-view or common imagination to pocking is, of course, really an attack upon the vehicle of meaning for that culture. In Euro-American culture, and most particularly in American culture, the sustaining story is biblically based and biblically carried. Both by demographics and by history, Christian story, Jewish story, and, increasingly in the twenty-first century, Judeo-Christian story have been the protective casing through which have trundled, in relative safety, all the connective explanations of life . . . or they had at a lay, or popular, level, until The Jesus Seminar came along.

The Jesus Seminar is a part of the Westar Institute and was founded in 1985 by a disenchanted biblical scholar named Robert Funk. The thorn in Funk's disgruntled side in the 1980s was what he saw as an institutionally sanctioned biblical naïveté in America's citizenry: dangerous ignorance about its story, if you will. Indeed, more than "sanctioning," Funk seems to have seen the Church and the Academy as joined together in a kind of deliberate conspiracy of obfuscation as a means of protecting their own hegemony. That is, they seemed determined to keep what they knew about biblical studies and contemporary criti-cism safely locked away from public scrutiny lest the story that sustained their positions of privilege be subjected to disestablish-ment. Lord knows Funk was right about the public naïveté part. Apparently he was right about the conspiracy part, too, at least to some extent.

The Seminar is exactly what its name suggests: a meeting of the highly competent for the purpose of studying an area of shared interest. In this case, the highly competent are called "Fel-lows" of The Jesus Seminar and are, right down to the last man and woman among them, excruciatingly credentialed and beau-tifully educated academics and clerics. In aggregate, they repre-sent the faculties of some of the most respected seminaries and universities in North America. There are now almost two hundred such Fellows in this country and Canada who circulate papers in New Testament studies among themselves for peer review, publish their work through Westar's Polebridge Press as well as through major commercial houses, and gather twice a year at the Flamingo to consider the historicity of the Christian biblical canon and its contents.

The sad truth in all this is that among the two hundred–some participating scholars and theologians, there are one or two who have lost their academic posts specifically because of their membership in the seminar; and in addition to the two hundred–plus participating scholars, there are a dozen or so others who have had to withdraw from Westar or face losing their own professional appointments. Intellectual freedom has never found an easy ally in institutional religion, save only during those brief periods of time when a reforming force achieves supremacy and is constrained to honor (and later ossify) the revolutionary thinking that had stoked its success. The Jesus Seminar was never destined to break that rule.

To give history its due, the inerrant literalness and/or historicity of the Christian story (and of the Jewish story with it) had been under seize in academe years before The Jesus Seminar was even thought about and in far more places than the Flamingo Hotel. As early as 1778, a German thinker named Hermann Reimarus had spoken of the historical Jesus, by which he meant to posit the possibility that the Jesus of Galilee and the Christ of history might not be one and the same. By which, in fact, he meant to argue that the Christian Gospels, which contradict themselves frequently, are fraudulent, being no more and no less than the deliberately manipulated products of men who were fanatically concerned with establishing a new religion up out of Judaism.

It was a disconcerting line of thought. More than that, it could become a downright dangerous one, and Reimarus's age managed to stuff it back into the dark out of which it had come.

As a complex of questions, however, Reimarus's work did not go away permanently. Prominent and influential theologians like

David Friedrich Strauss and Christian Gottlob Wilke, Christian Hermann Weisse and Johannes Weiss continued to raise questions in the nineteenth century about the lack of cohesion amongst the Gospels; about the lack of parallelism within the stories of Matthew, Mark, and Luke; about the distinct differences in nature and character between the Jesus of St. John's Gospel and the Jesus of the other three gospelers. Then, in 1906, Albert Schweitzer began to ask those same questions, but, given who he was, in a far less suppressible way.

I know all of this because Marcus Borg, the Hundere Distinguished Professor of Religion and Culture at Oregon State University and a Jesus Scholar as well as a Fellow, first told me some of it and then set me off on the trail of much more of it. He did so, in fact, in a taxi we were sharing. We were riding away from the Flamingo and toward whatever restaurant we might luck into off-site. He, I imagine, was in hopes of a quiet lunch away from reporters (poor man). I, on the other hand, wanted to escape for a while from a Seminar session that had been so far beyond any biblical scholarship I could lay claim to as to be positively disorienting.

Marcus Borg and I have become friends over the years since that first cab ride. Though we rarely see each other for long, we often pass in and out of the same venues and, with Dom Crossan (John Dominic Crossan, another of the Jesus Scholars), we sit on a board or two together. I am always grateful for those times of renewed contact. For one thing, I can never forget the kindness—and passionate concern, actually—with which a visibly weary scholar in retreat delayed his own comfort to give me a quick and much needed education. For another, even had he never been kind to me, I would still know that in Marcus Borg there rests the best combination of the academy's virtues: an almost pastoral concern for the delivery of fact in the most effectual and constructive of ways, while being, at the same time, informed by constantly honed intelligence and by absolute integrity of scholarship.

This is not a paean to Marcus Borg. He certainly does not

need such from the likes of me, nor do I have anything to gain by gratuitously offering it. This is not a paean to anybody, as a matter of fact; rather, it is offered as a kind of proof text or defense against some of the very foolish and unworthy accusations that were leveled at the Seminar in the 1990s by people who should have known better. If the Seminar conducted itself in something close to a Mardi Gras atmosphere (it did), that fact in and of itself does not mean the scholarship involved was erroneous. It certainly is not license for impugning the purity of the Seminar's vision — much less the purity of intention and motive of its members — on a personal rather than an ideational level. From the beginning, it was inevitable that at some point the discrepancies in the Gospel narratives and the difference between the Jesus-man of Matthew, Mark, and Luke and the Logos/Mystic of John would have to be addressed. Only the truth about the how and why of those things could set Christianity free from what Schweitzer himself referred to as "the tyranny of dogma."

When all of that is said and done, however, the fact still remains that, twice a year, there is, or used to be, a Mardi Gras at the Flamingo Hotel that has nothing at all to do with the outré pink birds scattered around its grounds. The spectacle is inside, in a large, low, dusky ballroom where the Fellows sit around a sizable square of tables across whose center they face one another. Around two sides of the room, there are . . . or were in the first half of the 1990s . . . two or three rows of straight chairs where paying observers and the media may sit. When the media show up for academic meetings, especially ones on biblical scholarship, there has to be more going on than meets the eye. There has to be a gimmick, and there is.

The questions under discussion in the 1990s had to do primarily with one question: What did Jesus really say and do, as opposed to what his followers represented him as having said and done? That central question feathered out into dozens more, of course, none of them original to the last decade of the twentieth century or restricted to just that place: How many of the parables and the aphorisms attributed to him were ones taken from other traditions or sources and simply interjected into the Christian story for political or doctrinal reasons? How many of the tales told about the events of Jesus's life were likewise borrowed from other biographies and inserted for practical reasons? How many of the sayings were manipulated to become more compatible with prevailing Greek philosophy and operative classical norms? Those are—or at that time were—freighted questions.

They were so freighted, in fact, that as each Seminar moved verse by verse . . . sometimes phrase by phrase, most often word by word . . . through the canonical Gospels of Matthew, Mark, Luke, and John, even some of the scholars themselves were hesitant to have their individual stances about the historicity of any given section be attributed to them directly. Accordingly, they devised a voting system. After interminable months of passing scholarly papers amongst themselves and after hours in session in Santa Rosa, they would as a group determine when the time for decision making had come.

In front of each Fellow's chair was a small container of colored beads. A black bead meant that the words or the event under consideration had absolutely no claim to having happened to, or been said by, Jesus of Galilee. A red bead meant the opposite: absolute historicity. The pink bead meant, as one would suspect, that probably the thing under study either happened or was consistent with Jesus' teachings and story. The gray bead was a "could conceivably be, but so unlikely as to not be credibly defended." The beads were the Seminar's ballots. A box was passed, and each scholar put in the bead that matched his or her best scholarly judgment. The colors, assigned a numerical value of 3 for red down to 0 for black, were tallied and their sum divided by the number of beads cast. It was, at first blush, a carnival.

Serious—deadly serious—scholars were sitting around a table voting on the faith that had sustained all of Western civilization for centuries, and they were doing it by throwing colored balls into a passing bucket? Preposterous! Preposterous, except that it did something more than shield each of them from the very real threat of recrimination. It got people like me there to watch the process. As Robert Funk, who devised the system, knew so well, the only way to get the genie out of the bottle — the only way to combat and fatally wound institutionally enabled naïveté — was to jump straight from the academy to the public at large. The only way to break through the walls was to play the trump card of democratized information. And in the pre–"rampant Internet" days of the early 1990s, the only way to accomplish that feat was through the media.

Chapter 18

• • •

Poignant and disturbing as they were, neither the anguished questions of theologian-philosophers like Hermann Reimarus nor those of a famous missionary physician like Schweitzer would ever, in and of themselves, have led to the establishment of something as bold and iconoclastic as The Jesus Seminar. Rather, the Seminar, while admittedly a predictable next step in over two centuries of accumulating scholarship, was also, and much more immediately, a response to twentieth-century scholarship unavailable to those who had first posited the central questions with which the Fellows in the Flamingo wrestled.

Some of that scholarship was in the field of textual criticism and had to do with questions about a given text's freedom not only from the deliberate, but also from the accidental, corruption of its contents by human copyists and, later, by errant machines and typesetters. By the twentieth century, orality itself had come to be recognized as a separate form of literature with its own conventions and rules. Oral transmission, like its hard-copy cousins, was understood to be subject to caprices, in this case those of human speech and human hearing. Whereas storytelling had once been perceived as simply a part of human experience, it was, by the late twentieth century, more accurately seen as an entity created up out from human experience and, therefore, as an art form, also with unique and informing characteristics.

Likewise, twentieth-century scholarship had come to appreciate more completely that our human expectations of History itself had shifted over the centuries. What had been understood, in classical and biblical times, as a goddess-inspired, creative act directed at capturing the meaning of things and events had begun to morph during the eighteenth century into our current conceptualization of History as the business of disinterestedly and perceptively recording the content of sayings and events as they actually and verifiably had happened. Whether or not that more recent definition of History is overly optimistic, if not outright disingenuous, is not the point. The point is that the perception of History as accurate record of events instead of as interpretive distillate had been imposed backward over the centuries. This unquestioning assumption of factual accuracy in all details was especially operative in American culture, where it still furnishes much of the foundation for our textual naïveté. Once, however, scholars began to relieve the West's sacred texts of a burden they never were intended to bear, the messages those texts contained began to convey a vastly different kind of truth.

Even so, textural criticism, form criticism, historical criticism, deconstruction criticism might still have stayed safely stored in the academic cupboard for another few decades—especially in view of how very unsettling they can be—had it not been for modern archaeology, expanding funds for excavations, cheap and ubiquitous methods of communication, and—once again—a growing press corps eager and able to take new stories to market, jig-a-jig-jog. From the middle years of the nineteenth century on, the Holy Land, the Middle East, Egypt had all begun to give up their treasures. Physical history was coming up out of the sands and dry riverbeds and tels of the ancient world. Whole cities, like Sepphoris, were being unearthed and others, like Caesarea, unburied. Long lost ships were found, and previously unrecorded ones analyzed in exquisite detail. Old roadbeds rendered up the daily detritus of former millennia, and new construction sites became treasure troves of mosaics and faintly visible frescoes.

What the twentieth century discovered did not always jibe with what the twentieth century had been taught by the pulpit or the academy, much less with what we thought we had been taught. Which to believe? Beyond that, what we discovered sometimes also illuminated with exhilarating consequence what we really had been told but had not been able to envision or imagine, much less accept. How to convey such excitement? By the 1990s scholars like Herschel Shanks had begun to address those questions through the very public means of accessible magazines like his *Biblical Archaeology Review*, while other scholars, like Charles Pelligrino, had begun using popular books to talk about unearthed wonders. *National Geographic* was right behind them; and PBS, followed shortly thereafter by the Discovery Channel, was catching it all on tape for America's living rooms . . . the democratization of information. Or in this case, the exquisite democratization of theology.

Yet even democratized theology and so organized and well credentialed a media spectacle as The Jesus Seminar still might not have been able to serve as ratchet and pawl in pulling back the rope's protective casing had it not been for two mid-twentieth-century discoveries that forever changed the course of this culture's informing story/ies. The discovery and excavation of the library at Nag Hammadi in Egypt in 1945 and of the Qumran library in the Transjordan in 1947 were the true conveners, forty years after the fact, of the meetings in the Flamingo Hotel.

Qumran rendered up 157 biblical manuscripts, all of them the earliest editions of their originals to be recovered and all of them offering a whole panoply of new sources against which to measure the integrity of contemporary texts in Judaism and Christianity. The codices recovered at Nag Hammadi, while less bandied about in the general conversation originally, were by the

1990s arguably a far greater threat to the inviolateness of the Christian story. Of importance critically was the fact that the Nag Hammadi codices were written in Coptic, the language of early Christian North Africa. The study of them, just from a linguistic point of view, began almost from the first to inform and expand previous scholarly understanding of Coptic, its dialects, and its libraries. Of far greater impact over the long haul, however, was the fact, first, that Nag Hammadi was a Gnostic library and, second, that Nag Hammadi rendered us up our first, essentially complete copy of the often-referenced, never-before-seen-in-the-whole Gospel of Thomas.

Chapter 19

• • •

December 7, 1941—the original December 7—was a Sunday. I was seven going on eight that year, and we were on our way to evening services when we heard the first wailing call of "Extry! Extry! Read all about it!" My father jerked his head toward my mother, and I knew they both knew . . . and whatever it was they both knew was something I did not want to know. I was sure of that.

My father pulled the car toward the curb, made a U-turn back up to the corner above the church, and said, "Here, boy, give me one of those." By that time even I knew; for after "Read all about it," the paperboy had called out, "Japs bomb Pearl Harbor."

At some point that evening or the next . . . I cannot remember which, and it has always struck me as strange that so vivid a memory floats free of its date in my head . . . at some point that evening or the next, the phone in the study rang and Mother answered. "It's for you," she said to my father. "There's trouble downtown, and some of the boys are involved. They need you to come."

My father was principal of the local university's laboratory school and one of the college's administrators. While he was not often called out at night because of some difficulty between town and gown, such a thing was not entirely unheard of; but this time was different. I knew that the minute he said to Mother, "Get Phyllis ready. You may have to bring the car back home without me." Which is how I ended up once more in the backseat of the old Plymouth and headed for town.

This time we went straight toward Main Street; but two or three blocks before we got there, the streets were already congested by hastily parked cars and randomly abandoned bikes. "We'll leave ours here and walk," my father said and then, to my mother, "I'll carry her." So he did carry me, right up to the head of Market Street and to the part of the block where the broad back steps of Kress's five-and-dime cascaded down to the sidewalk. A progenitor of sorts of the later twentieth century's Kmarts, Kress's was what we also called a "ten-cent store" because of its economical pricing. It was my favorite place. Full of wonders and the intoxicating aromas of bulk candies in bins. Toys of every imaginable kind. Beautiful dolls, and the very best puzzles. And then there were the dishes.

We ate on Kress's dishes every day of our lives. Mother's Haviland was the "company china," but the Kress dishes were "our china"; though every time I said so, Mother would laugh and say, as if it were some great, good joke, "Turn it over and read, honey. It's from Japan, not China." Joke or not, however, those ten-cent-store plates and bowls were my elegance. Set neatly on our supper table, they were my security and my assurance of a coming gratification. They were china by my definition, even if not by geography.

And, of course, it was the sound of dishes breaking that I heard first. In fact, there was almost no noise at all except for that of the dishes. Unlike the crowds I was used to at university ball games, this one was orderly, methodical, and intensely at one in all its members. Some of the men were indeed students. Most of the crowd, though, was made up of mature adults, one or two of whom even I recognized. Someone had beaten open the back doors of Kress, and a bucket brigade of men now lined the steps. Cartons of china were being silently passed, hand to hand, out from the store and down to the street. There, standing more or less in a huge circle and with the headlights of parked cars for illumination, dozens and dozens of men and women were seizing dishes—my dishes—from the opened cartons and then hurling them with a kind of icy-cold fury at the asphalt-paved center of their circle. And most horrible in mind then, as in memory now, was the near silence that surrounded their breaking, that sterile calm uninterrupted by human noise, that automation by madness of those who worked to destroy in the frozen quiet.

Over the years since that night I have seen far more mobs and riots than I ever wanted to see. Most of them, of course, I saw at a remove by means of video footage and news photography. Some I saw firsthand, for we were living in Memphis when Martin Luther King, Jr., was assassinated there and when, night after night, sections of the city were torched. Each of those occasions, though, was pillage for the sake of revolution or reformation. They were mob actions lacking leadership, but accompanied by the roar of a thousand self-appointed commanders shouting their fury and their own exoneration. What happened in the street behind the five-and-dime was none of those things.

What happened behind Kress's was cultural and spiritual surgery that was as sterile and gruesome and cold as any intrusive violation of the body can be. I have never been able to cast it away, nor have I ever been able to surmount my dread of the abyss from which it comes. City blocks can be rebuilt, and mobs can even be justified, to some extent, as the products of mass psychology gone amok. Cultural or intellectual or spiritual surgery . . . call it by whichever name you will . . . is otherwise. It cannot so easily be undone or rebuilt, nor can the onus of its beginning be laid at the door of unreasoned passion. Cultural surgery is self-discipline made pathologic by the doctrine of otherness. It is the calculated decision of responsible individuals to excise physically from their own existence some thing of worth in order that there may be no obvious ambiguities at large among them.

Only twice in my life have I had to deal intimately and personally with the ghoulishness of cultural surgery. Once was in December 1941; and once was fifty-two years later, almost to the day, when the reports and news shots began to come in to my office from every region of the country. Pastors and congregations were standing in silent circles again, this time in the parking lots and backyards of churches. They were gathering there in the dark nights of that dark December in order to burn a new book.

Unthinkable, but true. Men and women in the year of Our Lord 1993, in this privileged and literate country, were coming together to ritually burn a book, as if thereby to undo it. The book was *The Five Gospels* by Robert Funk and the Fellows of The Jesus Seminar; and it contained, in the four-colored clarity of red, pink, gray, and black inks, a public and annotated record of what the Fellows believed to be the actual sayings of Jesus of Nazareth. It contained as well, and also in four-colored editing, the first popularly accessible copy of the recovered "fifth" gospel, the gnostic Gospel of Thomas.

I did not know in 1993, and I still do not know, which was the greater offense, the Seminar's codifying of the four canonical books or their inclusion as equally authentic of the newly recovered Thomas. To those performing surgery by fire, such was a moot question, and they declined every opportunity to answer it.

Chapter 20

• • •

I spent an excessive amount of time in the 1990s—and even, truth told, in the opening years of this century—trying to avoid what for me would be the fool's errand of defining Gnosticism in print or on tape. There is no way for someone like me safely to do so; for the task requires a depth of knowledge and a scholarly finesse I simply do not have. That is, every definition of Gnosticism is incomplete and/or is offensive to someone and/or is inapplicable to some school of thinking or other. And even when none of those misfortunes accrue, so far as I can tell, any definition caught in print still is obliged to contain at least one small, derailing error that has been exposed by new discoveries in the space of time between the author's writing it and the publisher's finally publishing it. I offer all this in self-protection, of course, for it would seem that my time of trial has come at last.

It is probably not only safer, but also more genuinely useful to characterize Gnosticism than it is to define it per se. The consensus (not to be confused with unanimous opinion) is that Gnosticism is Christian or Judeo-Christian in origin. That is, Gnosticism arose originally not so much as a religion, but as one statement or interpretation or take on the story being offered by Judaism, nascent Christianity, and/or the confluence of them. Ambiguous as the ancient world historically was about an appropriate role for women in rituals and faith, many branches of Gnostic thought came down heavily on the side of the feminine. By and large, they were also the ones who revered Mary Magdalene as consort of Jesus, mother of his child, and, as such, the Holy Grail who received his seed. For those groups, in particular, one of the earliest and more operative predispositions was toward a concomitant rejection of paternal deity as creation's sole source and authority.

Across all of Gnosticism's distinguishing lines, though, the central tenet of salvation is very uniform and quite clear. Salvation, in Gnosticism, depends on sacred and secret knowledge, or gnosis; and it is this comprehension . . . this epiphany . . . this grasping of the arcane . . . that finally will release the soul from the fleshy prison in which it is trapped. Jesus of Nazareth was "the Word," or the Logos, as Saint John calls him; and for Gnostics, that means the gnosis, the Knowledge. It is, Gnostics believe and even as Saint John's Gospel suggests . . . it is the secret Knowledge transmitted through Jesus that is the means of salvation. The Jesus who died on the cross died as a man. He also died completely and permanently, but not as a sacrifice or some kind of appeasement of divine justice. He died in order that the Christ, the Gnosis, might escape flesh in order to show humanity how to escape its. He died that he might rise to, and be vitally functional in, the world of Light or the spirit world or the more authentic level . . . You may call it by almost any name you wish, so long as your words assume a dualism between the world of the flesh and the world of the spirit.

Light is the sustaining metaphor in Gnosticism, again across all its schools and divisions. Light is both the evidence and the symbol of the gnosis itself. Humanity, and indeed temporal creation in all its forms, are the result of a mean-spirited, lesser force or creature known as Samael, or the Blind One, who was himself a fallen or rebellious angel. The assignation of "Blind" One has to do with the fact that Samael had no understanding of pre-history (meaning of the Lightworld above him) or of any essence higher than himself. Thus he did indeed create both our world and our bodies just as Genesis says; but he created them as cages for the human spirit and simply for his own purposes and amusement. Following this line of interpretation, the serpent in Eden . . . along with a number of other suspect biblical characters . . . becomes a bearer of truth—of gnosis—and an emanation of love from the world of Light; for it is gnosis that the serpent offered Eve and gnosis that she gained by believing him . . . again, just as the Torah says. Eden's gift to us in enabling us to understand like gods and discern between the good and the evil was indeed a gift to the Gnostic way of thinking, for it marks the beginning of humanity's journey toward full consciousness.

Gnostic cosmology imagines a world of one or sometimes more ineffable and originating creatures from whom comes all else. There are also ranks or tiers of angelic or angel-like assistants that exist as effectual agents in quantities undreamed of in canonical Judaism or Christianity. That contagious understanding of the heavenly ranks has sometimes been a theological circumstance of great blessing in and of itself. Certainly it has been to my industry. In the late 1980s and early '90s, an appreciable part of the first, dramatic jumps in religion book sales was due to angels. Those were the years when at least two angel books were constantly on every best-seller list in the nation and when, as I like to joke now, every self-respecting refrigerator in America had at least two angel magnets stuck to its doors. And though this too may sound like little more than a quip, there is still some truth in my saying that I flew into *PW* in 1992 not on NorthWest Airlines, but on the wings of angels.

Independent of our popular confusion of angels, Gnosticism is still quite real and very much current among us. Even if, in the axial era, it did not commence as an organized religion, it rather quickly became one. It either developed or borrowed and adapted its own rituals; it engaged in baptisms, sacred meals, and burial rites; it even produced its own ecstatic practices. Today, for an increasingly informed laity, the best-known manifestation of Gnosticism as a formal religion is probably Manichaeism, a dualistic, Gnostic branch of Christianity that flourished in the third and fourth centuries across the Mediterranean world and as far east as India. (It still exists today, as a matter of fact, under the name of Mandaeanism in a few isolated communities of the Near East.) Manichaeism's popular fame rests primarily not upon its accomplishments, however, but upon one of its failures. Its limited notoriety today rests on the fact that Saint Augustine was a Manichaean Christian for over a decade before his conversion to Roman Christianity in 386 C.E. Thereafter, the good man spent much of his time fighting Manichaean Gnosticism as a fatal heresy, an effort in which he enjoyed varying success, depending on whom one asks.

For the generalist in Western history, Gnosticism is probably best known as the faith of the Cathars and of the Albigensians, who alternately ruled and harried Roman Catholicism in southern France for much of the twelfth and thirteenth centuries and who finally helped drive the Church into the fearsome reaction we know as the Inquisition. The most familiar presentation of Gnosticism for older Americans, whether historically inclined or not, is the work of William Blake, whose Christian cosmology and creative work are strongly Gnostic in both their content . . . and let there be no mistake . . . their appeal. For far more Americans, especially middle-aged ones, the Gnosticism most visible today is found in what popular parlance began, in the Age of Aquarius, to call New Age beliefs or, by a confusing extension of an older label, New Thought.

By the mid-1990s, much of this country's functional credo was New Age in sympathies, if not in confession. That belief system was, and remains, inherently fluid, just as it remains vigorously resistant to being codified; but it is still morally and culturally operative and presumably will continue to be, so long as it remains emotionally soothing. That is, for many contemporary Americans of whatever faith, Jesus of Nazareth is most comfortably understood not as a self-sacrificing god, but as a brilliant teacher, guru, and holy man who lived and died within history. His greatest gift may indeed have been that of leaving us the so-called Christ consciousness (though despite my icono-clast's best efforts to the contrary, that particular term is still not widely employed for naming the phenomenon). Many of us are also persuaded that somewhere, somehow, there is some partic-ular practice or arcane method—or, more often than not, some book—that can teach the aching soul how to know and shape it-self. We likewise believe . . . or at least half of us do . . . in the place of the feminine in sacred affairs, maybe even in the mysti-cally superior potency of it. Beyond that and by whatever route, we believe that there are ancient, but retrievable, ways into the light and its perfect discernment. And for almost all of us, love of neighbor *is* love of god; that is, that instead of the two being in-tertwined, the former trumps the latter and ingests it.

Gnosticism. Gnosticism, whose strange beauty and com-pelling ways have, from the beginning, wrapped themselves like lovely tendrils around every branch of Christianity and which, lest we forget, has also found for itself a nurturing soil in the Kabbalah of Judaism and the lush intricacies of the Zohar. Gnosticism, whose coursings through Western history rose to flood tide in the 1990s.

So great was that tsunami that in 1994, *PW* ran a three-page feature on the phenomenon and the new and forthcoming books that fell within its broad sweep. The piece was written for us by Rich Scheinin of the *San Jose Mercury News*. One of the more sea-soned reporters of the religion scene in America today, Rich laughed when I called to ask if he would take the project on. "Sure, why not?" he said. "I'm definitely living right now sur-rounded by it on every side. I might as well get up to speed for the sake of the paper as well as *PW*."

And up to speed he did get. He has continued to observe Gnosticism and become something of an expert on the subject. Lord knows, there's certainly been no lack of material to write about, not only in traditional books but, by the end of the millen-nium, increasingly in movies, the burgeoning genre of the graphic novel, and the resurgence of popular interest in the Magdalene, to name but a few. Thus, while it's true that many older Americans may discover Gnosticism's most familiar presentation in Blake, many others, along with almost all their children and grandchildren, will find its most intriguing and sympathetic presentation in less heady and more egalitarian places. Certainly since 1999, *The Matrix*, and its sequels, both cinematic and literary, have provided us all the appropriate sound bites and proportionate whiffs of classic Gnosticism needed to keep our inquiring minds interested and our cynical defenses down. Even *The Matrix* and its spin-offs cannot hold a candle, however, to the cultural and popular impact of Dan Brown's *The DaVinci Code*, again in all its permutations, literary and cinematic. Scheinin was right: Gnosticism is California dreaming.

Chapter 21

• • •

The Gospel of John is commonly referred to, even in lay circles, as the most Gnostic of the four Gospels, primarily because it is. The Gospel of Thomas has no such qualifiers attached to it. It *is* Gnostic. It is also what is called a "sayings" Gospel. That is, it contains parables, aphorisms, and teachings attributed to Jesus, but almost no biographical material about him. What it does reveal are precepts and stories that assume a heavily dualistic world, that interject into divine practice the feminine, that employ "the Light" as metaphor for sacred source, that acknowledge angels, and so on.

From the very beginning, there had never been any lack of references to Thomas in the records of the Christian movement. There had instead been dozens of quotations and lifts from Thomas in the writings of the Church fathers and historians. The majority of those citations, admittedly, were offered up as evidence of heresy, not as reasons for acclaim. There just had never been before Nag Hammadi, however, a more or less complete text that we could hold in our hands and say, "Ah, here! Here it is!"

Thomas was not, of course, the only Gospel to not make it

into the Christian canon for one reason or another. There were at least a dozen and a half credible "Gospels" that suffered rejection at the hands of the emerging eccesial hierarchy; but The Gospel of Thomas was the most documented, most cited "lost" one, and for that reason even more fascinating. Thomas also had, and still has, the aura of the suppressed, the cachet of the dangerous outcast. Nothing arouses antiauthoritarian Americans to action more than the suspicion of deviousness in high places; and by its history as well as its content, Thomas plays to all that defining emotion. Yet, in our culture's defense, it is also true that no one ever bothers to suppress or drive out that which is innocuous. High places and those in them move only against the dangerous or the divergent or the subversive.

By the fourth century, Gnosticism, of which Thomas is one of the prime representatives and most basic scriptures, was becoming all of these things. The Gnostics claimed to remember and/or to have found recorded in Thomas and elsewhere the words of a Jesus who taught a dualistic world, the importance of the feminine, the principle of Light, and the centrality of the individual's search for purification and salvific knowledge. In sum, by the fourth century, Gnosticism, with Thomas as part of its authority, posited a very different Jesus from that of the emperor Constantine and the Rome he was trying to secure for himself.

Newly converted (whether spiritually or simply expediently, we will never know), Constantine looked out across a disintegrating empire and saw a possible thread of hope for uniting it once again into a cohesive whole under his rule. In the virulent and ubiquitous spread of Christianity across all his empire might lie the theological seeds of an effectual loyalty between east and west, if only the emperor could manage to align himself with that faith and only if the cause of empire could somehow be aligned with the cause of the Kingdom of God on earth. For that to happen, though, the Jesus of Gnosticism had to go, which deed apparently was not possible unless Thomas went first. The will of the emperor and of the Church Fathers who followed his theological construct was almost effected, too. Indeed, it would have been completely so had it not been for some aberrant, rebellious soul who was not so easily persuaded and who secreted his copy at Nag Hammadi against the dawning of a better day.

The Jesus Seminar, from its inception, had appointed itself the task of subjecting the recovered text of Thomas to critical and scholarly analysis. One should note here—especially since as a fact it gets a bit lost in the subsequent fray—that the bulk of the most heavily Gnostic sayings in Thomas were deemed by the Fellows to merit black beads, with only an occasional gray thrown in for balance. That is to say, the Fellows found the authenticity of Thomas's record to be as suspect in places as were the works of the other four gospelers, and to be every bit as hostage as its canonical counterparts to the purposes and prejudices of its pseudonymous author. There was, in other words, little in the Seminar's color-coded edition of Thomas that, in and of itself, should have disturbed the most conservative of Christians. That was not the problem.

Whether it was the caprice of circumstance or the work of some kind of predestining design, no one can say. Regardless of its causes, however, the truth of the matter is that work of The Jesus Seminar in its five-Gospel analysis of the sayings of Jesus of Nazareth came to its natural conclusion in an America that, by 1993, was already deep into angels and the sacred feminine and into a kind of whispered, but not yet widely employed, popular consensus that sacred texts were of more use as poetry than as fact. It was all these things that lit the fires of December.

Over the years of my work at *PW*, I have inevitably changed in many ways, most of them I hope good, some of them surprising even to me. Of these latter, the most surprising and the most gratefully received is a change in my response to nonmilitant fundamentalism and conservatism in my fellow Christians. Not being much given to gentleness and even less so to humility, I am routinely amazed even now by the candid and genuine reserve I feel about condemning them publicly, and the visceral abhorrence I feel for the slash-and-burn humor that is so often employed against them. We are coreligionists, and that is certainly intellectual reason enough to curb my tongue; but what I speak of is more than that.

PW and age, or the combination thereof, have brought me, like some pseudo-Heraclitus, to an appreciation of the need in all things human for the sustaining tension of opposites. Unanimity of opinion frightens me just as much as would the mask of death above my chamber door, and for the same reasons. Even beyond that, though, there is in my heart great affection for many a conservative Christian with whom I differ intensely and frequently. And even beyond all of those things, I experience in almost every such encounter a mutual empathy for the pain we all pass through in trying to discern our God. Being increasingly sure that I am not so much called to be "right" universally as I am to be "careful" in terms of the lens given me for seeing, I am loath to scorn or condemn, and more prone than earlier to contest and resist only by prayerful and prayer-found words and ideas. My first awareness of this shift in the work of my always facile and sometimes overly clever tongue happened during the course of the burning of *The Five Gospels,* when as a reporter and observer of the book industry I had to make my own peace with how I would view and treat what was happening.

What was happening . . . and part of any interpreting here of events then is the result of a decade's remove from the intensity and confusion of the moment . . . what was happening was, in my opinion, the first significant public howl of protest against the possibility of a historical Jesus. Reimarus and Schweitzer had at last come out of their closets, and there would be no putting them back in again. What was happening was writ large on my radar, in other words, primarily as an early-warning alert of things to come . . . as the first loosely organized, but nonetheless nationwide, move to destroy what might validate disruptive questions; as the first populist and physical engagement of something that threatened the story by threatening its literal, as opposed to its mystical and evolving, authenticity and uses.

What was happening as well was public evidence of something that would characterize the decades to come: conservative and fundamentalist Christians were joining with one another across congregational lines to fire their protests. The affinity of attitude and worldview was trumping the loyalties of denomination. Even as I watched, alternately horrified and mesmerized, I perceived in myself a kind of reverence or quietness in the face of the creative inevitability of what was happening. Julian of Norwich once famously had said that it will be well, and it will be well, and all will be well. I thought that December that she was right. I still think so.

The decade since 1993 has seen the flowering . . . or, at least, the progressing evolution . . . of the things that were foreshadowed by that eventful year. Gnosticism has increased its hold upon our common imagination, in no small part because of fine and popularizing scholars like Elaine Pagels, whose *Beyond Belief: The Secret Gospel of Thomas* is sitting astride the nation's best-sellers lists even as I am writing this. *The Matrix* became the best-selling movie in DVD time; and the 2003 release of its sequels evoked more cover stories in more major media outlets, so far as I can tell, than has any other movie in history. Certainly *The DaVinci Code* has received more cover stories in more media than any other book in history, short of the Bible itself. In 2003 my own magazine did its first-ever cover feature on the Vertigo graphic novels of Neil Gaiman, whose ongoing sagas of the Sandman and Lucifer Morningstar and the old gods have driven the genre of graphic novel way beyond pseudo-respectability and straight into fiscal and cultural significance.

The pursuit of truth through the acceptance of mystery is a discernible and much remarked trait of most religiously disposed Americans under thirty-five years of age. And for most of us across generational lines, the authority of texts must now be tested against opposing claims, contemporary knowledge, and our new understanding of the role of history. The canon, as our grandfathers and grandmothers received it, no longer holds, whether that canon be Christian, Jewish, or Islamic. Quietly, just under the shadow of 9/11, the Italian newspaper *La Stampa*, through which the Catholic Church moves much of its news out to the general public, announced in a small bit of copy that the

Vatican would convene a group of scholars to consider the Christian canon in the light of recent scholarship. The discreet little announcement went on to say that the scholars would be looking at whether some deletions and perhaps some additions were required, although, the paper said, it was anticipated that few changes would actually be effected. So far as I know, that succinct three or four paragraphs announced the first time since the fourth century that the Christian canon has been subjected to official and established scrutiny.

Less quiet by several hundred decibels was the release in November 2002 by the United Synagogue of Conservative Judaism of *Etz Hayim*, its new pew Torah and Commentary, which questions the historicity of Abraham as well as of Moses and the Exodus, which suggests non-Jewish origins for the Genesis story, which assumes the walls of Jericho to be more story than reportage, which in general asks its readers to think and discern as a means to faith. Some of the best and best-known minds in Judaism worked on the production of the *Etz Hayim* ... Rabbi Harold Kushner, Chaim Potok, David Lieber ... but that did not make its release any more palatable or less heretical for the thousands of American Jews who felt the story had been betrayed ... and themselves with it.

An ocean and half a continent away, the same peeling back of the protective casing had also begun in Islam. A German scholar, Christoph Luxenberg, had successfully published the first credible, text-critical study of the Koran. In their review of Luxenberg's *Die syroaramaeische Lesart des Koran; Ein Beitrag zur Entschlüsselung der Qur'ānsprache* critics Robert R. Phenix, Jr., and Cornelia B. Horn hailed Luxenberg as having brought "exegetical scholarship of the Qur'an to the 'critical turn' that biblical commentary took more than a century ago," and European Islam, at least, groaned. For all the Western-born sons and daughters of Abraham, there would be no escaping from the reformation that had been quietly at work among them for several decades before they even began to suspect its presence. The only way out was straight ahead.

Chapter 22

• • •

Marcus Borg and John Dominic Crossan, by common consent, have been pioneers in the work of popularizing twentieth-century biblical scholarship. The Jesus they found by means of their scholarship was not, of course, the only Jesus being talked about in the lay press or lay circles in the last quarter of the twentieth century. Traditionalist scholars like Luke Timothy Johnson or the Roman Catholic scholar Raymond E. Brown were amassing equally impressive credentials and data in support of the canonical Jesus. In the end, though, groundbreaking . . . not to mention sales-record-breaking . . . titles like Crossan's *The Historical Jesus: The Life of a Mediterranean Jewish Peasant* and Borg's *Meeting Jesus Again for the First Time: The Historical Jesus and the Heart of Contemporary Faith* won the day in what my friend Jon Sweeney calls "water-cooler god-talk." That is, they not only carried the message out and excited a broad readership for the work of Jesus studies in general, but they also made their authors familiar names for the first time in an arena outside the academy and far beyond the Flamingo Hotel. Borg and Crossan, however, were only two parts of an increasingly public triad. The other member was not, first and foremost, a scholar, at least not by profession; but, rather, a clergyman and, ultimately, an activist. The third man in the triad was the Right Reverend John Shelby Spong, Episcopal bishop of Newark.

I first met Jack Spong not in Santa Rosa, but in San Francisco. To be exact, I first met him by appointment at 3:00 P.M. one November day in 1993 in the restaurant bar off the lobby at the Mark Hopkins hotel in San Francisco. The odd thing about this fact is not the time of our meeting so much as it is that neither of us ever got around to ordering anything more than a cup of tea until after Christine, his wife, came in at almost seven to say she was ready for a drink and some dinner and were we crazy to still be sitting in the same place four hours later. We were. Jack Spong is that kind of man.

I do not know, and never will, what Jack Spong thought about that day before the fact. I am certain he still remembers it, and according to him at least, just as vividly and fondly as I do. In today's media-drenched culture, those in the public eye, especially those who wish to stay there for very long, must quickly learn to project themselves impressively while at the same time evoking the sympathy of their hearers and seducing their loyalty. Had she ever read that last sentence, my mother, whom I seem to be recalling more and more frequently these days, would rather acerbically have noted that, "It certainly takes one to know one." She would have been right in this, as in so many other of her observations. I too have had to learn to think in sound bites and to project, with energy, my self and my points of view while, hopefully, eliciting the goodwill of those whom I wish to persuade or to entertain, as the case may be. There is nothing inherently wrong with that learned conduct, so long as one is aware of it both in oneself and in those whom one is interviewing. No, the problem is not a moral one, but more an interpersonal one.

The media-savvy, whether they intend to or not, instantly present to the perfect strangers gathered before them as co-conspirators and friends within a common cause. The result is

that a more substantive bond between them as people is sometimes precluded entirely or, at best, is simply never allowed to
mature fully. It doesn't take long, once one is in the business of
being media, to perceive this principle at work and to become
chary of its dynamic. To say the least, at three on that autumn
day in 1993, I was fully cognizant of the phenomenology involved in interviews; yet by the time Christine Spong came for us
at seven, I was without defenses and already involved in a friendship that I have valued and nurtured ever since.

That all having been said . . . and, in part, it is offered in the
name of intellectual honesty and truth in reportage . . . all that
having been said, the man whose sincerity and wisdom and insightful analyses won my loyalty to him, if not to all of his ideas,
exceeded that day the demands of both common courtesy and
media etiquette. We had that drink with Christine, and they ex-
cused themselves to wash up in order that we could meet again
for a late supper in the dining room. By midnight, I had . . . we
had, Jack Spong and I had . . . the foundation for a respectful affection and a sustained admiration, one of the other, that has
lasted now for a decade.

That decade has been for him and for the issues he is passionate about as tumultuous as any novelist could ever have invented
for him. By the time of our first meeting, he had already published a half dozen or so books that, while they had at first been
influential within the scope of his own voice and episcopal influence, were now threatening to level everything in front of them
nationally. That, of course, was why his publisher, HarperSan-
Fransisco, had wanted us to meet in the first place.

By the time Jack and I actually sat down together in San
Francisco, his books were solidly present on the country's best-
seller lists in both religion and in general nonfiction. In a way
their titles alone suggest the scope of their author's mission: *Res-
cuing the Bible from Fundamentalism: A Bishop Rethinks the Meaning of
Scripture; Living in Sin? A Bishop Rethinks Human Sexuality; This Hebrew Lord: A Bishop's Search for the Authentic Jesus; Born of a Woman:
A Bishop Rethinks the Virgin Birth and the Role of Women in a Male-*

Dominated Church; and, scheduled to be released four months later, in March, *Resurrection: Myth or Reality,* which would prove to be the most contentious or notorious or applauded of them all, up to that time

One has only to look at that list to see not only the major themes and concerns that would command Jack Spong, but also a good half dozen of those that would command American religion throughout the 1990s and well into the next millennium. The growing alignment of Christianity with Judaism . . . let me pause for a "Reader, beware" here . . . What Spong saw and what is presently very operative in America's religious culture is not a coopting of one communion by the other or even the undeniable assimilation of many Jews by interfaith marriage. What Spong saw, teaches, and, I suspect, still actively desires is the putting into position of the informing sensibility of commonality. What is at issue is the expanding presence and practice of the complementarity of two of the three Abrahamic faiths.

Within only three or four years of my first meeting Spong, I was standing on the floor of the annual Christian Booksellers Association International—a sizable trade show, to say the least—when I heard a shofar blow, looked up, and saw just beyond me a heavily trafficked booth with not only shofars for sale but tefillin and Tanukhs as well. "Here's to you, Jack," I thought as I watched Protestant Christian retailer after Protestant Christian retailer place orders for both the appointments and the translated texts of Judaism.

Jack Spong was prescient, though, about more than the coming rapprochement between Judaism and Christianity and the roiling need in both of them for a repaired story. He was prescient as well about the centrality of sex and gender to the internecine wars that, in 1994, still lay largely ahead of us. Those who have followed his career, even in the most cursory way, know that Spong was an early advocate of complete rights, both civil and ecclesial, for homosexual, bisexual, and transgendered people. It is a battle he had fought at considerable personal discomfort and professional risk, but one he has fought with dignity, absolute surety, and great benefit not only to the cause he supports, but also to the thousands and thousands of human hearts who have found in him their one hope for acceptance into God's church on earth.

When we met in 1993, homosexuality was a matter of no moment to me personally, one way or the other. I imagine, in fact, that it would have been difficult to find anyone in professional religion at that time who was more indifferent, if not outright blasé, about the whole thing than I. In my own defense, I have to say that what seems now like a mammoth insensitivity can, to some extent, be explained by all my years of serving as the academic dean of a professional college of art. If I had ever been asked during those years to estimate the proportions, I would probably have said that at least half of the young artists whom I adored and/or admired the most were gay. At least a solid percentage of those colleagues with whom I ate lunch each day or with whom Sam and I attended openings or partied on our free evenings were gay or had close friends who were. Whether one was gay or not was not nearly so present in our conversation, then, as was the question of where we were going to go eat or which painting we found most promising and why. A life in the arts is very much a life with people as they are, each person's measure being taken in terms of his or her talent and of the discipline being applied to using it. A life in the arts, in a way, is also a life in an artificial demimonde. The pain of being different is obscured there by the fact that, demographically speaking anyway, one isn't.

Such cavalier nonengagement would be unimaginable to me now, as well as personally reprehensible, in large part because since 1997 Sam and I have worshipped in a community church that is primarily lesbigaytransexual and where the priest is himself part of a same-sex union of many years' standing. We did not seek Holy Trinity because it was a "gay church," but because Sam's accountant kept saying to us, "You *have* to hear this man preach!," which he alternated with "You *have* to see this worship service!" As a result of having found Holy Trinity, though, the two of us have had not only an intense, firsthand exposure to what Don Morgan was saying about sermons and worship, but also an intense, firsthand exposure to what "gay" means in the real world of daily commerce and affairs. Inevitably, we have become politicized, whether we wished to be or not; and inevitably I have thought many, many times of Jack and of how he mourned, so long before most of us even saw it, the human loss and unnecessary pain patent in organized religion's primitive treatment of sex and gender.

Going into our San Francisco meeting, though, and for three or four years thereafter, I deeply regretted that Jack had embroiled himself with two such volatile, but seemingly disparate areas as theological reformation and the Church's position on sexual and gender equality. For Jack, of course, the two were and are Siamese twins, two faces of the same chimera, the Scylla and Charybdis of the waters his beloved Church is swimming in. From my perspective then . . . and to some extent in retrospect now . . . the power of Jack's theological challenges was compromised by his attaching it to what was popularly seen in the 1990s as a moral and basically cultural issue. Likewise, from my perspective then . . . and to some extent now . . . the correctness and God-given humanity of his sexual- and gender-rights position were obscured by the flamboyance of his theological iconoclasm. We will never know how things might have played down had he been free to chose only one or the other of those two battles; but then, as a fellow journalist told me not long ago, then he would not have been Jack Spong.

However all that might be, it is still true that as the months and then years of the closing decade of the twentieth century rolled along into the schisms and near schisms of the twenty-first, the accuracy of Jack's early positioning, particularly of homosexuality as an authority issue rather than a moral one, was increasingly validated. Abortion and the decades of still-unresolved discord over its definitions and practices are moral issues. They belong in that strand of the rope as naturally and completely as do questions of fiscal malfeasance or domestic abuse or any other human action emanating out from the individual into the existence beyond himself or herself.

Homosexuality, however, is not an action; it is one in a long list of defining variables that, once mixed and assembled in differing configurations, make up a distinct human being. The divisive issue in homosexuality, then, is not one of morality. It is an issue of corporeality within the rope of established religion. It is an issue of the immutability of a religion's corpus of traditional tenets; it is a question of the locus of authority for the interpreting of a communion's received scripture.

In all three of the Abrahamic faiths, textual proscriptions of homosexuality are there. What is not there is any discussion of the distinction between the practice of unfettered, omnivorous sexuality and the pursuit of physical love with another who is of like constitution. What is also and understandably not there is any recognition of the now-documentable fact that some 10 or 15 percent of humanity are homo-, bi-, or transsexual.

For the peoples of the Book, the tension between those two antipodes of proscription and of a text that does not reach out explicitly to circumstances beyond its own time has been a constant from the very beginning. In postmodernism's battle over homosexuality, though, that tension has found one of its most torturous jousting fields. Whether any one of the combatants likes to admit it or not, either of the opposing positions of proscription or progressive revelation may be assumed with credibility . . . or, at least, with impressive scriptural footnoting and citations. And therein, as the poet says, lies the rub . . . or as another one might have said, the groaning before the bar of the anchor's cable.

Chapter 23

• • •

In the years since 1993, Jack Spong and I have never differed, good Anglicans that we are, on such matters as the sacred fraternity between Judaism and Christianity or the equality of gender rights or even on the need to "rescue" Holy Writ from militant fundamentalism in any of its presentations, be they Jewish, Christian, or Islamic. One has only to look at the tragedy of each day's telecasts to acknowledge that fundamentalism of that stripe presents as death in human affairs, regardless of which religion it is that spawns it. For reasons of obedience and faith, let alone freedom and mercy, militant fundamentalism must be opposed by anyone who understands life to be the divine breath within time and the agent of a mystery beyond human comprehension. Thus, it is neither the rescue of the Bible from those who would never scrutinize it, nor a staunch opposition to a conservatism that would always codify it, that accounts for the divergent views between us. Where we stand separate from each other, instead, has to do with the nature of the questions each of us sees as pertinent to this moment in history.

By 1993, trying to revisit . . . that is, to re-form . . . some of the doctrinal positions expressed as definitive in Christianity's creeds was hardly a new idea. In truth, it was not even much of a cause célèbre for many American clergy who, by then and by their own admission, had simply decided, as dozens of them have since told me, "to believe one thing and preach another, because the people who had opted to stay in my pews wouldn't have tolerated it otherwise." The miracle of Jack Spong . . . the anointing of him, if you will . . . was that he never once went down that path of compliance. Worn as he must have been at times during the years of his active episcopacy, never once has he been known to succumb to weariness of heart or tongue. Right or wrong, he has fought the good fight as God gave him to see it; and that is all anyone can ever ask of the servant pastor.

In Spong's case, it was not so much the intellectual rigor of his scholarship as the autobiographical passion he brought to the issue that made his ideas of a liberated theology seem so freshly engaged and vital. He spoke in 1993 . . . and has in all the years since . . . with a pastoral concern that is palable. His evangelical yearning was and remains toward what he calls "the Church Alumni Association." Unlike any expedient and/or often honestly compassionate concern for those who did decide to stay in their pews during the last decades of the twentieth century, his almost exclusive concern is for the believing who did not so choose. On the spring afternoon in San Francisco, he persuasively argued for four hours to a reporter whom he had never heard of before, the need for a "credible credo" of faith for those evicted and wandering believers. His urgency held that it was they, not the Bible, who must be rescued from fundamentalism, lest they become lost beyond all repair to themselves as well as to the Church.

What the bishop was responding to that afternoon was a fairly rare kind of crisis in the history of religion, or at best one that rarely occurs in such proportions. The problem, at a pulpit-and-pew level where bishops live and academic scholars usually do not, was that in 1994 dramatic changes in biblical scholarship were happening . . . had for several decades been happening . . .

concomitantly with dramatic changes in the secular circumstances that are religion's working context. As a result, there
were numerous rifts in our traditional understanding of ourselves and of who we are in what world. To state the matter in
my preferred metaphor, one would say that because the story
had been pulled back and the weather had been rough, there was
a serious pocking in progress of the rope's inner sleeve. Holes
were opening up in the stabilizing mesh of the common imagination, of the part of the rope that holds spirituality, morality, and
all the stuff of organized religion together in a balanced and
working relationship.

In 1996, I wrote a book entitled *God-Talk in America*, in which
I referred frequently to the closing decades of the second millennium in Euro-America as a time of "reformation," with a lowercase "*r*," or as a time of "re-formation," with a hyphen. I gave up
such verbal coyness within four or five years after that. We are
in . . . or perhaps have just passed through . . . a time of cultural
shifts that have caused, are causing, and/or have been accompanied by massive shifts in spirituality, morality, and the established creeds and practices of Euro-American culture. Those
shifts can be—indeed, should be—construed as analogous, in
both cause and result, to the circumstances that preceded and
eventuated in the original Reformation, capital *R* and without a
hyphen. In this, Jack Spong and I are of one mind and have been
from the beginning, though we are hardly unique in our thinking
about this one, either.

Any observer has only to lay the more remarkable changes of
the last century or so beside a list of the more remarkable
changes of the fifteenth and sixteenth centuries to discover the
bases of our argument . . . or perhaps, better said, the culprit
events behind it. The original Reformation was a religious and
creedal response to good half dozen major—not to mention innumerable minor—changes in Western civilization. New worlds
had been discovered, not only in a round earth fully inhabited by
exotically different human beings, but also in a greater cosmos
where the old center had not held, where now the earth rotated

instead of being rotated around. Heaven itself was relocated by a reality no longer layered but mobile within a machinery of physical principles. The truths of one's childhood, like the universe's center, did not hold.

Where had the Church failed to understand these things? Why had it taught error and aggressively suppressed truth? Did it, in fact, know its conceptualizations to be error? If the answer to that was yes, then betrayal most foul and breach of trust beyond repair! If the answer to it was no, then the Church is run by such fools as we ourselves are, and who would believe the likes of us about the matters of God? So forget them all! —or, at best, acquiesce for the sake of appearances. Let each man or woman become his or her own priest.

All of which is remarkably like the twentieth century's reaction to man's walking on the moon, or being shown that life-forms evolve and humanity probably did too, or having to acknowledge that the roots of consciousness are physiological and subject to the laws thereof. Where was the Church when fact again began to trump original revelation in the twentieth century? And who's to believe any of the original when so many parts of it are patently wrong? So flee to small groups to discuss godly discernment among the equally motivated! Flee to house churches to worship in community by the Spirit's direction!

A sometimes alternative, but usually complementary way to deal with one's skepticism about ecclesia is to demand one's right to see the texts and tradition on which such obvious error was built. That kind of freedom of access, of course, was empowered five hundred years ago by the invention of the printing press; and Gutenberg's marvelous machine is most often cited as the initiating cause of the Reformation and, most certainly, as the primary means of its enablement. Great as was the liberating and iconoclastic power of the printing press, though, it had the limitations of producing an expensive product that traveled more among the wealthy and the scholarly with libraries than among the hoi polloi. The Internet, on the other hand . . . Ah, the Internet, the radio, the television, the cinema, the magazine, the newspaper, the

paperback, the public library . . . now, *there* is access. *There* is true
loss of hegemony to the elite and privileged. *There* is information . . . and misinformation . . . that will not be contained. Who
is to believe what in such a world? Where is the Church when
what is needed is not so much answers as a vetting and ordering
of the questions? And how can vested interest ever be expected
to illuminate faith or temper its own absolutes?

Back to small groups and house churches. Or back to communities of fundamentalism where the imperative of such questions is denied and their danger to the soul proclaimed. Or, most
wearying of all, back to the restive pew of discontent . . . or perhaps just away, instead of back to anything. Oh, Jack, here's to
you once more. It's your nightmare come real.

A good church historian would be quick, right about now, to
note that the Reformation occurred within a period of history
that had been destabilized in many other, equally significant
ways. It occurred within a time frame when the basis of power
had shifted from blood and land to fiscal wealth, much as it has
shifted in our time from wealth per se to information and the
control of it; within a time frame when the fiefdom as a political
and social organizational model had given way to the emerging
nation-state model of modern time, not unlike the present shift
from the nation-states model that has sustained us to the global-
ization of postmodernism; within a time frame when clerical
abuse of clerical office was so rampant as no longer to be contained *intra cathedra,* a similarity that warrants no comment here,
unfortunately; within a time frame when an evolving sense of the
individual and of human life itself as independent of, and worthy
apart from, a social unit was beginning to change the common
imagination about who it was that actually went to his or her
prayers when the bells tolled. That disturbing vagueness was not
unlike the confusion about the nature of "self" and the moral definitions of "life" rampant among us now in our post-Enlightenment age.

A good church historian would probably even push my list of
disruptive cultural shifts to include things like a change in under-

standing about the appropriate recipient for one's loyalties. That is, there was a shift then from Church to country or nation-state, just as now there is a shift from country to humanity. The then-new precept of separating politically generated, temporal power from ecclesial power ultimately gave us our American sense of a necessary division between the two; yet now there is a distracting confusion about the two again, this time about how they must interface within the domain of a democratized, diverse, and secular morality. In fact, even a mediocre church historian could carry the list from here into tedium itself, but hopefully the point has been made: The circumstances of Reformation find their analogues in many of the circumstances of the twentieth century; and I work under the assumption that two or three centuries from now, history will see the results of both eras as being comparable.

It is in this that Jack Spong and I vigorously agree, or at least it would seem so. In May 1998 he published a book . . . again, with HarperSanFrancisco . . . entitled *Why Christianity Must Change or Die: A Bishop Speaks to Believers in Exile.* In my business, it is a truism that a publisher's press copy about a new book is usually somewhere between blatant hype and a sound-bites précis. In this case, however, Harper's copy pretty much covered the bases: Bishop Spong, it reads, "has never before drawn his audacious stands on Scripture, Jesus, sin, and morality together in a modern creed. Now, in *Why Christianity Must Change or Die,* Spong offers his unified and brilliant new vision of authentic Christian belief in our time."

A year later, in 1999 and with very conscious intentions toward coordinating his work with the changing of the millennium, Jack released another book, *Here I Stand: My Struggle for a Christianity of Integrity, Love, and Equality.* A work of searing candor, it uses autobiography for the first time as the principal architecture of a Spong book and delivers his theology in terms of the painful way of its evolving. By any gauge, it is his strongest, clearest, most emotionally engaing book, in large part because it is also, at last, his "position" book. The title of *Here I Stand* is taken from the words of Martin Luther at Wittenberg; and the volume itself, like events that transpired in front of the door of the castle church in Wittenberg, concludes with the posting of a list of theses. In this case, the theses are twelve, not ninety-five, in number, but Spong subtitles them as "A Call for a New Reformation." And it is in that subtitle, or at least in its implications, that we begin to diverge.

Chapter 24

• • •

Jack Spong's twelve theses, as he himself points out, are couched in negative, rather than positive form. To reduce them here with anything less than the precision that he lends them is unfair; yet I must try, begging his forgiveness and the reader's. In overview, the Spong dozen may be said to deny theism as a tenable conceptualization of God. Given that premise, Jesus can no longer be conceptualized as the incarnation of theistic deity. Eden and its resultant theology are pre-Darwinian and no longer sustainable. The Virgin birth is a detriment to correct understanding of Christ's divinity; and in a post-Newtonian world, any assumption of the supernatural in the New Testament miracles is untenable. The concept of the cross as a sacrifice for sins is "barbarian," and resurrection is not, and never was, physical. Assuming, as it does, a multitiered universe, the Ascension story as given can have no credibility in a post-Copernican space age. No received text can morally or ritually govern human conduct for all time. Prayer is no longer a conversation with theistic deity and/or a request for theistic deity to act within human time. Life after death is not a matter of reward and punishment; and all human beings must be respected without regard to the externals of race, gender, ethnicity, or sexual orientation.

Martin Luther's ninety-five theses, when one looks at them at a remove of five centuries, present more like bullets or numbered emphases in a PowerPoint presentation than as discrete items. From number one to number ninety-five, Luther argues against the selling of indulgences. His position feathers out, of course, to challenge the extant definitions of papal authority, the accepted conceptualization of the hereafter, and the obligation upon the individual Christian to pursue within his or her own self the disciplines of love, mercy, repentance, and faith; but basically the ninety-five all depend from the central thesis of opposition to the selling of indulgences. In Spong's much shorter list (and laying aside his final call to human equality in all venues), there is likewise one central battle being waged, that against theism. And as with Luther, so with Spong; all the rest branch out from there.

Originating in the seventeenth century, "theism" is a label that, at first, sought only to name a worldview that was other than atheism. Within a century or so, however, it was being used to name as well a mind-set that was other than deism. A requirement in Judaism and Islam, theism is foundational to most contemporary Christian theologies as well. It assumes a personal god who is transcendent and the source of the created universe, which he governs totally but without violation to human free will and/or human responsibility. The theistic god is the source, as well, of miracles and may speak through revelation and other supernatural phenomena. The point here, however, is not so much to focus on theology per se as it is to engage the subtitle "A Call for a New Reformation," which is prior to Jack's argument itself and used to position it.

Sociologists are an odd lot engaged in an odd trade. They proceed by instinct and then validate by numbers . . . or at least most of them do. I can say that with some authority, I hope, because a great deal of what I have done for the last dozen years is a form of sociology. It certainly has been dependent upon the theories and data of sociology, and I am grateful. One of the tricks that I am most grateful for, to be specific, is the sociologist's profiling of a population by its generations. Not all sociologists are enthusiastic proponents of the practice, and almost all of them warn about the danger of overapplying generational characteristics to particular subgroups or individuals within a given generation. Nonetheless, there is such a wealth of insightful perspective and such an economy of conversation in speaking generationally that I find myself pulled to its practices from time to time, this being one of the times.

Those, like me, who were born after 1925 and before 1945 are charmingly referred to as "the Builders," which means that as children of the Great Depression we believe, above all else, in the safety and efficacy of institutions. So we build them constantly — everything from the Federal Reserve banking system to Social Security and the TVA, with churches and service organizations and Medicare thrown in for good measure. Those of our children who came after 1945 and before 1963 are the famous (or infamous) "Boomers." Children of the Vietnam War, the drug culture, and sexual liberation, they essentially disestablished everything, and still want to. Such is, of course, the nature of generations: What the parents do, their children must reject.

Indulgent to a fault, loyal primarily to their own well-being, resistant to any authority that bore credentials other than those of immediate experience, the Boomers rolled like a bulldozer gone awry over institutional religion. In their utter rejection of the established forms of faith, they did not, however, lose faith; they simply pursued it in places other than the church or synagogue. Their mantra was "I'm spiritual, but not religious," and a now famous sociologist of religion, Professor Wade Clark Roof, assigned to them *in perpetuum* the label of "a generation of seekers" when, in 1993, he published a widely read and popular study of them by that name.

The Boomers gave birth to the equally famous Gen Xers, or those among us born from about 1963 to 1980 or '81. Whereas the Boomers had been, in sheer numbers, the largest generational segment in American history — over seventy-eight million strong—and could affect every part of the nation's life, they also stayed true to their own principles of self-interest and bred sparingly. As a result, their Gen X sons and daughters are no more than about 15 percent of the country's population today and exert a concomitantly diminished influence on the world at large, though, interestingly enough, not on religion.

By disposition and circumstance, ironic in a most healthy way, Xers are so totally disgusted by their parents' perceived self-absorptions as to become "Friends," both literally and on prime-time television. They have found community in one another and, from there, have achieved an almost unprecedented sense of humanity and activist compassion. In matters religious, they asked, and ask, primarily for authenticity; and it is the religiously inclined among them who began and continue to sustain America's quest to find authenticity, in both Judaism and Christianity, by returning to pre-Enlightenment mysticism and the rituals of pre-Reformation times.

I have a treasured fellow writer, fellow Episcopalian, and industry colleague, Debra Farrington, who, in talking about Generation X, said to me one day that as a result of them, "The best I can tell we are all hastening toward the third century." Nothing could be truer of the X generation. The potency of their "ancient future" conviction and direction might not have achieved its own steamroller effectiveness, however, had it not been for a segment of ourselves known, tongue in cheek, as "the Wedgies."

The generation after the Xers is alternately referred to as the Gen Ys or as the Millennials, in recognition of their generational dates of 1982 to the turn of the era. Once more their numbers are substantial because, once more, the Xers rejected parental ways and bred with enthusiasm. The Millennials, at eighty-two million strong, are more numerous than the Boomers, and they evidence every intention of informing American culture just as monolithically. The older ones of them also show a fascination close to outright absorption with religion . . . which gets us to the power of Wedgies.

"Wedgies" as a term really was, of course, a tongue-in-cheek creation, but one with its origins in serious business. It was invented by *Salon*, the smart and influential online magazine, in response to the absence of any, more appropriate, academic term. "Wedgies" names the phenomenon of overlap that occurs when the youngest of a maturing generation meet the oldest of a rising generation and form a kind of subgroup that mixes the generational sensibilities of both. Our present Wedgies—roughly those who at the turn of the era were from sixteen or seventeen years of age to those who were thirty-three or so—have shared, reinforced, and given demographic ballast to the religious sensibilities of the Xers. They have, thereby, substantially increased the effectual influence of those sensibilities, to say the least. In addition to the defining characteristics of Gen X that I have sketched above, though, there is one other of perhaps even greater import here, not only because it would be significant in and of itself, but also because it is evangelically shared by the Xers and their Wedgies. That is noncontrarianism.

Noncontrarianism early became a distinguishing hallmark of Gen X, primarily because theirs was the first generation in the American experience to evidence it. Simply put, noncontrarianists do not believe that two contradictory things necessarily contradict each other. Lest in theory that seem to be a piece of foolishness, one needs to apply it as a principle. Thus, an Xer or a Wedgie sees no abrasion between "Do unto others as you would have them do unto you" and "You have to look out for number one. God helps those who help themselves." Or taken out of general culture and put a bit more into theology, between "Unless you eat of my flesh and drink of my blood, you cannot see the Kingdom of God" and "I have many sheep who are not of this pasture" or "In my father's house are many mansions."

Noncontrarianism does not just willfully ignore the apparently mutually exclusive appearance of such opposites; noncontrarianism simply does not see it as pertinent to the discussion at hand or, if seeing, perceives the disconnect as indeed being more apparent than real and therefore not operative. And unless I am very, very wrong, the impact of that kind of seismic shift in perceptual thinking will alter Western theology more dramatically and effectually than has any other since, probably, the Reformation itself.

Just as an aside, I probably should note here as well that, because they have become sufficiently enfranchised now to be recognized as a major new force in religious thought, the Wedgies have received a much more dignified name of late. Like their Boomer grandparents before them, they too got theirs from a book. In 2002, Colleen Carroll, herself a Wedgie, as well as an actress and a youthful journalist with the *St. Louis Post-Dispatch*, published a masterful and very well received study of her generation under the title of *The New Faithful: Why Young Adults Are Embracing Christian Orthodoxy*. As a name, "New Faithful" seems to have stuck . . . and that really does get us back to Bishop Spong and his theses.

Chapter 25

• • •

My most treasured example of Wedgie/New Faithful non-contrarianism in the flesh happened sometime around the end of 1998 or the beginning of '99. I have no memory of the exact date, because the beauty of the event itself has obscured its details. I was speaking in Atlanta, though, to a group of both lay and ordained Christians where my audience included a healthy number of young adults, most under twenty-five by the look of them. (The increasing presence of that age bracket at religion lectures, by the way, is hardly unique to the groups I address, and is a measurable example of what students of contemporary religion are talking about when they speak of the rising generation's absorption with matters of faith.)

During the course of my address, I must have mentioned the doctrine of the Virgin Birth as an area of current theological and doctrinal contest. After the lecture was over and the general questions finished, a young man—probably no more than eighteen—came up to me, shaking his head. "I just don't get it," he said. "Of course I believe in the Virgin Birth. Why wouldn't I? The whole thing's so beautiful, it has to be true, whether it happened or not."

Bingo! I could have squeezed him breathless right there. Instead I hugged him, and have since immortalized him by constantly telling and retelling his story.

What my young man meant, obviously, was, first of all, just what he said. He did not understand why the actuality of the Virgin Birth (or of any of a dozen other such matters of received doctrine) had anything at all to do with his embracing them as his truth . . . his functional, operative, informing, and transforming truth. At first blush, it is not hard, even for a world-weary Boomer, to grant the young man's position a kind of casual or tolerant acceptance. After all, there is a strong whiff of John Keats's "Beauty is truth, truth beauty" aphorism implicit in how he couched his statement. To go there and stay for long is, however, fairly difficult, especially for Builders and Boomers who want their mysticism, whether poetic or not, to be confined to nonworking hours.

To jump to Keats's now-clichéd lines is also to obscure the breathtaking subtlety of what is being expressed. For Xers, Wedgies, and those who will be the New Faithful of the present and coming age, the received stories that became the doctrine of earlier times . . . those tales that have been codified and refined and treasured and handed down to us by our forebears in the faith . . . those dear images through which they reported what they saw . . . are like the tube of a fine telescope or the supportive ring around the lens of a spyglass. They hold the range of one's eye in place.

Or those doctrines, polished lustrous and smooth by human hands as well as by divine ones, are like the icons of a new orthodoxy. To look at them intensely and with reverent affection is obligation in the life of faith. It is also . . . and this is what my young man was expressing . . . it is also to recognize in them a means provided for daily transport into the divine—or as he put it, into that truth which is beauty because it is always and only truth.

And to question what, to the New Faithful, is a very clear and irrefutable line of spiritual logic is about as antique an exercise as expending serious thought on how many angels can dance on the head of a pin, and just about as useful . . . which is why I question whether or not the Spong theses really call for a new Reformation. Rather, I suspect, they summarize, albeit in an exquisitely accurate way, the inadequacies of the last one.

The questions underlying theism are questions that rose up out of the Enlightenment and that gave that particular bit of intellectual exploration its name in the first place. The Enlightenment has passed into history, however, leaving behind the enormous gifts that came out of reason and its employment, but also leaving behind in its trail of glory a much healthier sense among us of reason's limitations and appropriate uses. A new time is upon us. For lack of a name for it just now, we speak of this time of shift as post-Enlightenment or postmodernism or post-Cartesian or a number of other "post"s. The very plethora of the hyphens speaks to our lack of clarity about what exactly is happening to us. A label will come in due time, of course; and it will no more be tongue-in-cheek than it will be immediate. A century or so from now our children's children will name our times with a concision forgetful of all our pain in getting here; but like all good labels, it will make the benefits of what we have lived through more accessible to them and more economical in application.

All of which is to say that Jack Spong, whom I have been privileged to admire and enjoy all these years, seems to me as one of a facing pair of noble bookends. The other is Martin Luther himself. As if they were holding hands to embrace the five hundred years between them, the two stand in my imagining as the beginning and the closing of a mighty era in Christianity. The processes set in motion by the questions of the former have solved myriad conundrums and resolved many postulates in religion and in secular life. As processes, they also worked, as does all human advancement, on principles that were beneficial at the time, but some of which proved worthless . . . even sometimes false . . . in a later time. Bishop Spong, in my imaging of him, offers Martin Luther an organized posting of the questions that did not make it across the divide, a statement of questions that are more historically worthy than useful within a new paradigm. And lest someone think that I speak here only of Christianity and presume to generalize out from there, I must add, in a somewhat edited form, my other most-treasured and also autobiographical proof text.

One of the great gifts of the latter part of the 1990s for me was the opportunity to meet with and sometimes speak as a participant in two or three Jewish think tanks and organizations. Certainly I have been, and continue to be, blessed and increased by those events. Perhaps of the greatest personal benefit, however, has been the number of times I have had to do a Christian mea culpa about my own lack of textural understanding or of just plain wisdom, both mystical and religious. This is not about one of those latter moments, however. Rather it is about the most poignant, to date anyway, of my encounters at a formal level with Judaism.

I participated sometime in late 1998 or early '99 . . . again, I cannot say exactly because my two stories are dependent, one upon the other. At some point, anyway, I participated at a gathering of primarily Orthodox Jewish clergy and religionists. During the course of our discussion, I spoke of noncontrarianism as the X factor in the emerging era and its effect particularly on religion. Instead of elaborating, I simply told my then brand-new story of the young man and his finding any question about the Virgin Birth to be a nonquestion, if not an impertinence. There was, I think, but cannot recall for certain, a bit of discussion, and we went on with things.

Weeks later—it was in the spring, I remember, because I was on Park Avenue just at the lunch hour futilely trying to flag down a cab—weeks later, I saw a young man coming purposefully toward me down Park Avenue, his yarmulke bobby-pinned down tightly against the tug of a stout spring breeze. When I looked more closely, I realized that he was one of the younger rabbis—thirty-one or thirty-two at the most—who had been part of the meeting I had participated in weeks before. We greeted each other, and then he said, "I stopped you because I need to thank you for something that I didn't really want to try to write you about." I nodded to indicate I understood, though for the life of me I could never have guessed what he was about to say.

"You know that Virgin Birth thing you did?" I nodded again.

"That's changed my life." Then he realized the humor of what he had said, and we both laughed. "No," he said, "I don't mean that way. I mean that my father and I have had so many arguments over the last four or five years that we had just about got to the point of not talking anymore about the stuff that matters a lot to both of us."

I knew his father by reputation as a prominent rabbi in a neighboring borough. I assumed, therefore, that what father and son both cared about was the matters of faith, but I still could not imagine where the conversation was going. Then he said to me . . . and I saw tears suddenly well just for a moment before he regained his composure . . . "What it was, you see, was that whenever I was home, he always wanted us to talk about Sinai and the Exodus and the tablets and that kind of thing. And when I would try, he'd get furious because I didn't want to talk about whether or not they happened. The truth was that I could hardly bear to sit there and have him do it. So I'd just get up and leave as soon as I could, and then he'd get his feelings hurt all over again. It was dreadful.

"But two nights after your Virgin Birth thing . . . I mean, I'd been thinking about it and it made such sense to me. It was the Christian take on what I'd tried to say to him about our stories and never could word it right or get through to him . . . two nights later I decided to try doing it your way. I called my mother and said I was coming to supper, if that was okay, and I went. Afterward, before he could start on theology, I said, 'I went to a meeting the other day, and there was this Christian there with a really interesting story.'

"I told him the story of what you had said about us Xers and historicity, but just as a story. After I finished, he was real quiet; and when he looked up, he was crying just a little bit. 'That's what you feel about our stories, isn't it?'

" 'Yes, sir,' I said. 'And it's why I can't bear to do it your way. I don't even want you to do it your way.'

"He's a wise man, my father, and a good rabbi. He just laid his hand over mine there at the dinner table, shook his head a little, and said, 'Judaism's is a large house. It welcomes both of us, you perhaps more than me, and that makes me know that I have been a good father as well as a good rabbi.' "

There was nothing to say after that, nothing that would not have dishonored the quiet and the sweetness around us. Because he was Orthodox and I a woman, we could not even embrace. Instead, I smiled, and he smiled back. "God bless always," he said and was gone on down the street, his yarmulke still fighting the bobby pins every step of the way.

O'Hare, My Home

Chapter 26

• • •

If, as seems true in memory now, half my working life during the mid-1990s was spent in California, then it is also fair to say that the other half was spent in Chicago. California was unfailingly kind to me in the intense, early days of my career as a road warrior; but so too, and equally, were Chicago and its environs. Pray God, that strange mix of cordiality and sangfroid which infects both those cultures will never leave them . . . or us. For whatever else it does, the spirit that informs Chicago and California breeds a distinct kind of intellectual generosity not only in their citizens but also in the institutions and events that each attract. In this latter category, particularly, Chicago excels. That is to say that while the Parliament of the World's Religions had been a foretaste for me of Chicago's ease with big things and big ideas, it has proved to be only one impressive line item in a long, long list of impressive spectacles and experiences.

In the book industry, there are two major events each year around which everything else takes its pacing and measure. Not unlike Easter and Christmas in the Christian calendar, Book-Expo America and the Frankfurt *Buchmesse* are the touch points of each year. Promotion is planned toward them, the release dates for new books are set in terms of them, private Day-Timers are blocked out four and five years in advance around them.

Frankfurt's international book fair makes my heart sing just to think of it, much less prepare to go to it. Occupying ten huge buildings and the whole of what has to be the world's largest fairgrounds, the *Buchmesse* is populated, from opening to closing a week later, with the costumes, languages, and professional passions of book lovers and bookmakers from every nook and cranny of the globe. If the Parliament is a carnival, Frankfurt is the world gone deliciously mad.

Publishing executives huddle for hours over deals amongst themselves, buying the rights to republish another country's literature into their own. Authors are as ubiquitous as the beer that flows from every tap; and book lovers . . . just plain readers, God bless them . . . wander dazed as satiated gluttons through building after building. There are sad moments at Frankfurt as well . . . sober ones, perhaps, is the better word. Each year during the mid-1990s when we both were always there every year, I would meet a dear friend at 4:30 P.M in an outdoor pub on Friday afternoon right in the middle of the fairgrounds. The Frankfurt fair happens in October, just as the weather is turning into winter in Germany and the days are growing markedly shorter. Especially in that beautiful city of shadows and half-lights, sundown in October comes early, so we went early to our beer, Stuart Matlins and I.

Stuart is the head of Jewish Lights, one of this country's predominant publishers of Judaica and ecumenical titles for both Jewish and general readerships. He lives in Vermont, we still see each other several times a year, and on the eve of Rosh Hashanah he always calls to wish me a happy new year; but we made it a habit in those years to drink together only on the Friday afternoons of the Frankfurt *Buchmesse*. As soon as we were done, Stuart went to his Shabbat and the lighting of the candles, and I, sobered but consoled, to my quarters. We had drunk, you see, to the memory of those who died there and to the wonder that in that place and in our time, Stuart, a Jew, could raise a glass with me, a Gentile woman, while we said a prayer together for all that had been lost to make it so.

But if Frankfurt's fair is my industry's winter carnival, BEA—BookExpo America—is its spring fling, and the fling happens (with occasional exceptions to appease the coastal dwellers among us) in Chicago. Also with very little variation, it happens over Memorial Day weekend, when Chicago, that city of high wind and lake-blessed sunshine, is turning from warm into . . . well, into Chicago. I have rarely been hotter or more bottled up in sweaty crowds in my life than on some BEA weekends in Chicago; but that seems to be a discomfort which we all either forget or forgive each year.

Less spectacular than Frankfurt's *Buchmesse,* Chicago's BEA is still a sweet cacophony of languages and intense negotiations. There, readers are not allowed into the exhibit halls, but America's retailers are . . . big-time, they are. With backpacks and shopping bags full to the bursting from giveaways and catalogs and prepublication hype, they buy and order and then barter the size of the former against better shipping rates and the power of the latter against publisher promotional dollars for in-store author appearances. The intensity would be overwhelming if it weren't Chicago and spring and—after all—the industry's favorite orgy. It's hard to be painfully intense under those circumstances, and most of us settle for being happily intense instead.

During much of the last century, religion books were hardly more than a minuscule part of the activity and presence at BEA. That is to say, the received wisdom was that religion stuffs went to religion readers and got there through religion retailers. General merchants usually maintained a small, almost always single-case section . . . traditionally in what the industry still refers to as the "ill-lighted, back left corner" of each store . . . of "Religious" titles. The scope of the titles gathered under that signage was almost to a store diffuse, poorly shelved, dusty, and intellectual rather than confessional, proselytizing, or pastoral in content. There were exceptions to this pattern, of course. There always are. During the midcentury years, Catherine Marshall, for example, became a great commercial success with her Christy novels and C. S. Lewis was a steady, profitable presence in general bookstores, as were Norman Vincent Peale with his books on confident living and Thomas Merton with his autobiographical *The Seven Storey Mountain*. They and authors like them were not as a rule shelved under "Religious," however, but under "Fiction" or "Philosophy" or that best of all catchall dodges, "General Nonfiction."

Occasionally, during those years, a fluke would happen and demand the general retail market's attention; but it was the mid-1960s and Harvey Cox's *The Secular* City before the flukes even began to look as if they might be seaworthy. It was, in some ways, a more telling event, though, when in 1972 *PW* reported that *The Living Bible*, a populist translation of Holy Writ, was the fastest-selling book in the U.S. market. It was also noteworthy . . . and briefly the world took note . . . when in 1975, Billy Graham's *Angels* was the best-selling book of the year, again according to *PW* tabulations. But such were the exceptions that confirmed the rule until the mid- to late 1980s, when serious, popular, religious inquiry, like a lion roused from its slumber, began to overwhelm those who had been so careless of its reputation.

By the time I went to my umpteenth BEA in 1993, but in my new role as *PW*'s religion editor, the world was singing religion's song . . . which, of course, was the enabling music behind my being there in the first place. But I remember that Memorial Day weekend in Chicago as one of the sweetest . . . such an unfortunate word, this one . . . sweetest "victories" of my publishing life. Instead of brazenly calling it a victory, however, I reported to Sam that BEA 1993 was a triumphal entry replayed and on a much more secular scale.

Had anyone told me, before that weekend, that I had spent years feeling defensive about religion's lack of place at America's intellectual and polite tables, I would have scorned my accuser with contempt rather than engagement. Why would I care one way or the other? Religion was central to my own life, but it hardly had to be so for everyone else's, did it? What kind of belief is it that demands respect for itself instead of in and of itself? Oh, how poorly and imperfectly we know ourselves.

Aisle after aisle of exhibitors' displays lined the halls of McCormick Convention Center in 1993, and booth after booth showed religion titles written, edited, and produced for the general reading public. Angels were everywhere, flying from book jackets and exhibit stanchions with absolute assurance. The saints were just beginning their comeback that year, and they could be seen everywhere as they came marching into the national imagination; and the New Age publishers not only occupied a huge area on the floor, but they appeared to have the most active block on the floor.

In a moment of sheer headiness, when I turned down the aisle and saw the traffic in front of me, I half-ran back to our own booth and grabbed Fred Ciporen by the hand. "Come," I said. "Don't ask, just come."

He did, and then stayed with me for an hour as we moved from stall to stall listening to general retailers and publishers talk "spirituality," "body, mind, and spirit," "self-help," "twelve-step programs," "meditation," "prayer beads," and "home altars."

"I'll be damned" was what he said to me after about ten minutes and long before we had even begun to make our way into all the exhibits. "Probably," I said back to him, "but isn't it wonderful ... just breathtakingly wonderful!" I remember that he looked at me as if I were half crazed; and I remember thinking I probably was. To say the least, I had never felt so high before.

Chapter 27

• • •

Those of us in the religion book business enjoy something close to an embarrassment of riches when it comes to trade shows. Frankfurt and BEA serve as trade and networking venues primarily for commercial or, given the lack of a better term, for secular books and book dealers. And while religion since the 1980s has been a constantly growing part of the secular retail market's profit margin and therefore of its inventory, there are stores and distributors, publishing houses and literary agents who do nothing except religion. As a powerful segment of the larger book market, these religion-only professionals function as a world unto themselves as well as one planet within a larger universe. Most religion distributors and publishers double-track, however, maintaining a strong presence in both camps. Most booksellers do not. There the divide is much cleaner. One is either a religion store (albeit, sometimes with some few general trade titles in stock) or one is a general-trade book retailer (albeit, and increasingly, with a decent religion section that now has subcategories and the signage to support it).

If one is in the former group and a retailer of Christian

books, one goes to either the Christian Booksellers Association's (CBA) trade shows or to the Religious Booksellers Trade Exhibit (RBTE). Both terms are regrettable misnomers, having that very kind of proprietary arrogance which drives people outside of religion to despair of there ever being any generosity amongst the godly, one toward another.

The Christian Booksellers Association was formed—where else?—in Chicago in 1950 and held its first trade show there in the old LaSalle Hotel. The misnomer it suffers under is that its "Christian" has no qualifying adjectives. A union now of about twenty-two hundred stores and/or chains, CBA is actually a trade association for retailers of evangelical, Protestant Christian materials. Even under that more specific wording, there is still a good deal of room for theological variety. CBA stores . . . which to this day still tout themselves as "Christian" stores to the implied exclusion of all others . . . run the gamut from the most restrictive inventory of fundamentalist Protestantism to the most ecumenical inventory. By and large, however, the gamut is still within books of political commentary, agenda-driven fiction, lifestyle aids, biblical exegesis, and pastoral or spiritual concerns that offer more answers than questions.

CBA, whose member stores now rack up annual sales somewhere in excess of $4 billion, have two sizable trade shows. One, CBA International, meets in July, though it now changes locations each year. The midwinter CBA-EXPO also roams about. And *PW* is there every time the doors of either one of them open. In fact, one of the subtle but informing stories of the 1990s and early 2000s has been the transformation of the CBA shows, especially the International, into exactly that: an annual, expanding coming together across great distances and at great expense of Reformation-formed, modernist book professionals. I never leave one of those shows without a reassuring sense of the counterbalance they offer to folks like me who enjoy the questions. I also never leave without that good sense of having just had a week of reunion with relatives I'm totally different from except in spiritual DNA and family stories. It is the shorthand of the conversations, the readiness of shared referencing, the bones of contention that are rubbed smooth by centuries of manipulating. It is all those things that make us love our kin even as we remark to ourselves, usually in congratulatory form, on our differentness from them. Ah, religion! May God bless it. Someone most surely needs to, anyway, for none of us seems either willing or able.

The RBTE—Religious Booksellers Trade Exhibit—is, on the other hand, "my" trade show. Not only because it traffics in the questions, but also because it and I have grown up together; its tenure as a show is only one year older than my own as a religion editor. More personally significant than that, however, is the fact that RBTE's has been the doorway through which some of my most treasured friends have stepped into my life, and I into theirs.

RBTE meets each year in St. Charles, Illinois, a suburb, naturally, of Chicago. If the Flamingo Hotel lends a certain 1950s droll earthiness to The Jesus Seminar, the Pheasant Run Resort and Convention Center in St. Charles lends RBTE a definite 1960 and '70s cachet of jaded weariness and decadent modernism. I love it. So far as I know, every single bookseller, sales rep, agent, publisher, or media person (including me) who comes into RBTE each year refers to our quarters as Pleasant Ruin, but with the greatest affection. The one time there was talk of a change of venue, there was a near mutiny within the ranks. Those long, dark halls, the glassed-in solarium with its incredibly loud, fake waterfall, the faux Bourbon Street of shops and restaurants, the exhibit hall that, like Goldilocks's third try at a porridge bowl, is neither too large nor too small . . . who could bear to leave these for some unknown horror that might work better and have less character? No, thank you very much, we'll stay right where we are.

RBTE was started in 1991, when I was, in my own benighted way, still thinking of myself as a retired publisher and full-time writer. As a result, I not only missed its inaugural, but I was totally innocent of its creation. By 1993, though, Daisy and I were both there with bells on. RBTE meets on the Monday through Thursday before Memorial Day so that on Thursday evening or Friday morning, the publishers, sales reps, agents, and media who walk both sides of the secular/religion divide can move easily by taxi from it to BEA in downtown Chicago. It is a handy arrangement both logistically and psychologically; and I have often wondered if my extreme joy at BEA that year was not at least primed by those immediately prior four days of my first encounter with RBTE.

RBTE, like CBA, is defined in terms of the retail buyers who attend and by the bias or segment of the religion market they serve. "Religious" therefore, really is intended, in RBTE's case, to function more as a distinction-making than as a describing adjective. That is, we can safely assume that both groups regard themselves as religious in the more ordinary sense of that word. In truth, the reason for the lack of precision in the self-definitions of both groups is that the distinctions being named lack a certain preciseness themselves. Most assuredly, the articulating of them lacks any semblance of political correctness, much less of mutual courtesy across the ecumenical lines.

The lines are as old as the Reformation and modernism. Some, looking at the history of the early church, would undoubtedly grant them an even longer heritage. For practical purposes, though, the differences are those between sensibilities and/or what Peter Berger in the last century called "structures of plausibility." RBTE serves Roman Catholic booksellers and Episcopalian booksellers with a goodly number of Lutheran and Methodist buyers and publishers thrown in for good measure, the whole lot of them being lightly salted with some Presbyterian and Orthodox materials for good measure. There is even an interfaith presence, primarily from publishers of Judaica but, increasingly, also from some Islamic and Buddhist houses.

It may be a cliché to say that RBTE deals primarily in books and stores and publishers who are more concerned with raising the questions than with declaring the answers; but clichés live for good reason. They are as useful as a shirt pocket for containing a slippery truth in an accessible place. But the distinguishing sensibilities involved here are more than intellectual. That is, most RBTE attendees indeed would argue with conviction, as I myself do, that the soul's maturing is better served by the constant juxtaposing of the received tradition against the perceived experiences of living than it is by a constant dependence upon received, but unexamined tradition. We would also, though, argue just as passionately that no one ever got to spiritual maturity (assuming, of course, that anybody ever does) solely on the basis of scripture — theirs, mine, ours, or anybody else's. Ritual too is necessary, for it exercises the body in holiness and incorporates it in its rightful place as part of the soul's eternal and indivisible substance. Polity is important, for in it rests the mechanisms of accountability and the readiest safeguard against the long, sloping slide into idiosyncratic theology. And mystery. Above all else, mystery — the not knowing that is at the center of all beauty — allows the ineffable spirit to, for a few moments, be known as transport and constituent part.

Beliefs, or just plain sensibilities, of such a constantly restless kind require not only a lot of books, but also a lot of variety within the range of books offered. No one profitably interprets experience in isolation. Rather, experience, once perceived and isolated in the consciousness, wants to be studied in terms of other, related human experience. How is it that a Buddhist meditates? What is creativity, and where does it come from? When the Desert Fathers withdrew into asceticism, they produced spiritual writing that speaks powerfully. What does that mean about how we should govern our own lives within postmodernity? What is the darkness in each of us and whose are the chattering voices? Prayer works, but what will we lose or have to change if we admit that it works; and why does it work for other faiths as well as ours? Where does one place dreams in terms of their origin and/or their meaning and uses? Where is the goddess in the received tradition, and how can any of us understand her presence so felt in life, but so absent in the tradition? . . . or is it? The questions go endlessly on, producing as they go a seemingly endless and richly textured flow of books, each one usually exciting further questions. It was to this group of newly empowered guides for America's religious pilgrims and spiritual seekers, then, that at the 1994 RBTE I was to give what was probably the most consequential speech of my life.

Chapter 28

• • •

By 1994 and the pre–Memorial Day week of RBTE, I had almost two years of trade-magazine experience under my belt. If I were ever going to understand my job—my ordination as Daisy had granted it to me—by then I did. Certainly I understood that Daisy was right about one thing: We dared not fail.

We might not save the world or be able, finally, to stave off religious triumphalism and inhumane aggression against another god's people; but we could do our part toward that end. We could take the vehicle of a powerful magazine and dare to say, "All ideas are heard here, impartially reported here, and respected here in terms of their product, not their origin." In 1992, that had been a trying posture to assume, and we had borne our fair share of condemnation and complaint during our first year or so of pursuing it. Some of the evangelical Protestant publishers were not happy that we put their book reviews in the same section as those of the New Age houses. Some of the Roman Catholic houses wanted to be separated in coverage from the Protestant ones. Some of the Roman houses even wanted to be separated from each other, as far as that goes. But by 1994, most of that sniping at one another and at us had died away into yesterday's news, and it was generally understood in the industry that religion at *PW* was religion, sans adjectives and sans qualifiers.

That happy and hard-won state of affairs did not mean, however, that I had quit being a Christian in favor of being a religionist. Instead, I tried to organize my thinking into two compartments, one marked *PW* and the other marked "P.T." I exerted every personal discipline I could muster toward being sure that the wall between the two of them was impenetrable. Obviously, that kind of intention is doomed from the beginning to be less than completely perfect in its mechanisms, but I think we came as close as any trade journal could. I know that I, as editor, came closer than I had at first ever dreamed I could. But when we were at RBTE, I could let all those barriers down and just enjoy. We were, by and large, Christians together; and more to the point, we were drawn from the same gene pool of peculiarities and penchants within that tradition. Editing my tongue before I used it was not a constant exercise during those four blessed days each year, and religious candor among ourselves was the order of the day for every single one of them. Beyond the sweet refreshment of being among one's own, RBTE by 1994 was also offering me a kind of professional exhilaration. The active presence of a postmodern neotraditionalism that some of us had claimed to see coming was now being evidenced by the surge of books and the variety of books it was evoking. Before 1991 there had been no national trade show across Reformation and/or denominational lines for Christians like me, nor had there been any professional organization for those who ran the cathedral stores or liturgical bookshops where I shopped. There had not, because the market was not there to justify it. But the last quarter of the twentieth century was indeed informed by a growing restlessness with the obsolescence of the Reformation's arguments and by a concomitant yearning, across denominational lines, toward the ancient in Christian practice as a way of finding its future. RBTE's very existence was a celebration of that most welcome change. It was, then, in a mood of personal candor, mixed with professional exhilaration, and tempered with an amazement that I of all people should be living and working in this of all times, that I stood up to keynote RBTE 1994's banquet.

I do a great deal of public speaking, primarily because my job requires it; but also because, like all recovering academics, I for many years earned my living by talking more or less publicly, though back then I called it lecturing, not speaking. Whether lecture or talk, however, I do enough of it to know that public speaking, if one does it long enough, becomes an art form of sorts and subject to all the caprices and triumphs thereof. When I am doing it badly, I distract myself with my own running commentary on what I'm doing wrong, where I'm not connecting, why the material is so intractable and unyielding in my hands. I am, when I am performing badly, very much present to myself, in other words, though in the most unpleasant of ways.

Most of the time, of course, when I am speaking, I am just speaking, and conscious to myself in much the same way that I am conscious to myself when I am driving: pleasantly aware, certainly alert, but confident of arriving somewhere before too long. Then there are those other times. Then there are those few times when, as I say to Sam, I'm not even listening . . . those few heady, delicious times when the audience is joy in my hands and the words come from some other than the me I know, and when, after the fact, I have only isolated moments of memory about being behind the podium or of what I have just said. I fully know only that whatever they were, the words and their delivery were as they should have been — complete, in balance, and born free to live awhile in God's good world. RBTE, in 1994, was one of those rare times.

Because I really do not have the presence of recall and because I have never asked to hear the audiotape of that night, I do not know what I said. I know only that going into that experience, all I had been able to hear in my head for days were the words of some of the grander and more poignant of King David's psalms: "Lift up your heads, O ye gates; and be ye lifted up, ye everlasting doors; and the King of glory shall come in. Who is this King of glory? The Lord, strong and mighty, he is the King of glory," from the Twenty-fourth Psalm.

Or that eternal favorite of the church, "the old 137th." "By the waters of Babylon we sat us down and wept, when we remembered you, O Zion. We hung our harps on the willow trees in that land, for those who led us away captive asked of us a song. And how can we sing the Lord's song in an alien land? If I forget you, O Jerusalem, let my right hand forget her cunning; and let my tongue cleave to the roof of my mouth, if I do not set Jerusalem above my highest joy."

They are the triumph songs of religious ecstasy and constancy. They speak to the persuaded heart as do few other words. How can we sing your song, O Lord, in a strange land? But let my hand lose her skills and my words their force if ever I forget the home of my beginning. There the gates shall be lifted up and there the king shall go, both in and out, as he wills. There we shall forever behold him and be ourselves wrapped in the consolation of his glory.

It comes no sweeter than that, no richer, no grander. And every religion bookseller and every religion publisher knows just as surely as I ever will that those are the gates and that the journey toward which we are moving, toward which we publish, toward which we retail, toward which we pray with our crowded shelves and our weary bodies. This, I think, must have been what I said.

The response was, as it is when the words are right, one first of quiet, some hasty wiping of tears, applause, and then the slow undulation from the back tables to the front ones of an audience rising to its feet. That always feels good. How could it not? It is affirmation of what I already know. More powerfully, though, it is a means of our rejoicing together—audience and speaker— over the goodness that has just been given us. At RBTE in 1994, however, it was the less immediate responses to the address that still stand as the amazement. They are probably also the reason that I positively do not want to listen to the tape of that evening lest the words contained there in some way fall short of the wonders that have been born of them.

Chapter 29

● ● ●

The morning after my address was a cordial one. On the exhibit floor, publishers waved from their various booths, giving me the victory sign or a broad hollo or both. "You aced that one!" sounds good to me anytime and anywhere. Booksellers were equally kind; but the people I most smile over, even ten years later, are the Episcopalian retailers who had worked for so many years in the hope that a time of equal market presence would someday come for them.

Nancy Marshall, who owns The Episcopal Bookstore in Seattle, and Jane Baird, who manages The Cathedral Book Store at St. Philip's in Atlanta, were in the early stages that year of the struggle to forge their confreres into a viable professional organization. They would succeed, of course; and by the turn of the millennium, the Episcopal Booksellers Association would have become what it is today, one of the most influential and respected groups in the religion industry. But in 1994 and in the birth throes of their effort, the two of them were bundles of an anticipation that could not confess itself. What they knew was within their reach and was good was also still so fragile that they dared not claim it yet. Being with them was like an exercise in being afraid to breathe. When Nancy came up to me that morning and, tears in her eyes, gave me a squeeze and the simple words of "Thank you," she gave me the greatest affirmation and one for which I shall ever be grateful, primarily because I knew the singularly anxious hope from which it came.

But the hours of morning-after glory could only last so long before work came slamming in to overtake me. I was there to cover a show, to talk about what trends merchants were seeing among their customer requests, about which publisher was considering opening which line of inquiry or new direction, about what was selling and where in the country it was hot and where it was not, about what the common wisdom saw as the why behind any of the above, about who was riding high and who, as a result, was not . . . About all the things that a trade journal has to report on for the general good and, sometimes, just for the general amusement.

By lunchtime, I was tired. Not exhausted, of course, just sort of bone weary in my head. I did not want to ask any more questions, and I certainly did not want to receive any more answers, at least not until I had had a break from the process involved in both. At probably no more than three minutes before the buzzer closing the show floor for the lunch break was due to sound, a blond dynamo (what else can I say?), a blond dynamo with a Yankee accent as thick as my southern one came charging around the corner of the aisle I was leaving, grabbed me by my forearm, and said . . .

. . . she really did. She said, and I quote, "I want you to come see my books. I know you don't know me, but the Holy Spirit just told me that I needed to come get you to look at my books."

In case there is any confusion here, or any lack of stereotyping either, let me say immediately that Episcopalians do not, as a rule, go around talking much about the Holy Spirit, especially not to strangers whose bona fides are unknown and most especially not in full throttle in public space. We regard it as poor taste, for one thing—as a lot like saying, "I had a really great lay last night" in the middle of a crowded elevator. We believe in the Holy Spirit and its efficacy just as surely as we believe in sex and its, but we don't mention them except among ourselves. Beyond bad taste and its implied violation of private space, public talk of the Holy Spirit in terms of having had some direct communication with or from it is almost always a signal among Christians that there is a charismatic or Pentecostal suddenly come among us. Among Episcopalians especially, it is interpreted as a signal that "one of *those*" has somehow drifted in.

I say this not to disparage, but to confess; for every one of those reactions and prejudices jumped up, front and center in my head, the minute Carol Showalter touched me and said those words. The next thing I should say, though, is that I went with her. That, ultimately, was and is the pivot point of the whole story and of my life since.

The Book of Acts records a number of pivot-point stories not unlike mine with Carol; and one of them I find to be particularly applicable here. The one I have is mind is the story about Saint Peter when he was on a missionary trip and staying at the house of one Simon, the tanner, in Joppa. It was noontime, and Peter, who was hungry, had gone up to the roof of Simon's house for the noon prayers. While he was in prayer on the roof, the story says, Peter had a vision of a sheet being lowered in front of him; and in the sheet were all the animals and birds and reptiles that Jews are forbidden by the law to eat. As he stared at the sheet of proscribed creatures, Peter heard a voice that said to him, "Peter, get up. Kill and eat." Good and observant Jew that he was, Peter answered the voice by saying, "No, Lord, you know I have never eaten any unclean thing in my life." The voice then said, "What God has made clean, you must not call unclean."

The sheet, we read, was withdrawn, but then twice more it was lowered with the same words of "Get up. Kill and eat," Peter's same answer of "No, Lord, you know I have never eaten any unclean thing," and the voice's same response of "What I have made clean, do not call unclean." Then, at last, Peter understood what he was being told. The faith he was teaching and living, the faith of Jesus of Nazareth, whose disciple he had been, was not to be given to Jews only. It was to be carried as well to the unclean, to the Gentiles, and this by law-observing Jews like him.

I believe that particular story is an almost word-for-word account of something that, in this case, historically happened. It has all the ring of the kind of authenticity that the writer in me reverences. Beyond that, it has its proof in the faith of millions and millions of non-Jews just like me who have been enabled into Christianity as a result of it. I believe that the voice spoke and that it was the voice of God directing by immediate communication the course of human affairs. I believe all that, and I had said so many, many times before Carol Showalter ever got hold of me. In 1994, it was the times when I knew the voice or presence of God had directly instructed me, however, that I was constitutionally and communally unable to talk about and/or comfortably hear about in other people's experience. I still have trouble with the former, but Carol and company have long since cured me of the latter.

What she has never cured me of, though, is the association in my head between her seizing me and Saint Peter's lowered-sheet experience. The parallel is certainly not perfect in all its parts, but what that sheet taught Peter, Carol has forced me to live out and acknowledge:

The voice speaks.

Separating it from other voices is the work of a lifetime of prayer.

When all else is said and done, obedience is the true confession of the voice's having spoken and having been heard.

Candor to others as well as to oneself about experiencing the divine is the root and mark of humility.

I don't have much.

I am trying.

That noonday, however, I had not even begun to work my way through a hundredth part of all that. All I knew was that I was following a middle-aged, beamingly confident, slightly over-weight blonde down an aisle I did not want to walk through to see a line of books I did not at that moment care about even in theory; and I was doing it two minutes before lunch because she had said she'd been told by God to fetch me. Weary as I was at that moment, the implausibility of the whole thing was still not lost on me. I remember in fact . . . and Carol would be proud of my saying so . . . I remember having a sense of being carried be-hind her, rather like an iron filing behind a magnet, as if it were beyond my own power to not follow.

Her books, when we got to Paraclete Press's stall, were clearly right on the edge of becoming something significant. Al-ready they showed the design and production sophistication that characterizes a successful line of books. Beyond that, judging by their titles and a hasty run down of their back-cover commen-taries, they represented a fairly clear sense of who their publisher was and what was the voice of the house from which they came. A few more seasons of editorial maturation, and they would be ready to be serious players in the religion-book trade. That was obvious.

The buzzer had gone off just as we had gotten to the Para-clete booth. The floor manager had already issued his customary three warnings over the P.A.; and the lights were dimming down toward off when Carol abruptly took the book I was holding right out of my hand. "No," she said firmly and with a shake of her head. "No, this isn't right. Will you come to us? Will you come to Cape Cod and look there?"

She said it as if . . . and this probably was what had indeed happened . . . as if she had just heard the voice again. I said, "Yes, certainly I will come." I have no idea why I agreed. I told myself later it was because I was hungry and wanted out of there at any cost. I also told myself later that there was no way *PW* was going to buy me a ticket to Cape Cod to visit one small and just emerging publisher. Nor, I told myself, did I think anybody, in-cluding me, was going to look kindly on my being given a junket to Cape Cod by any publisher. "Forget it," I said to myself. "This will be the end of it. You'll never hear another word."

By October of that year, I was on a fifteen-seat puddle hopper flying from La Guardia to Orleans, Massachusetts. The thing had a wound-up rubber band for a motor and millions of square acres of Atlantic Ocean beneath it for a crash pad; but twenty-seven harrowing minutes later, I stumbled down the angled ladder the pilot called steps and into the waiting arms of Carol Showalter and her husband, Bill. I was on my way to the Community of Jesus to spend three days looking at books and talking about manuscripts . . . or that was the stated agenda. Actually, I ended up spending three days falling in and out of astonishment with an unsettling regularity.

I had said to Daisy before I had accepted Paraclete's invitation, "Are you sure this is all right?"

"They're not paying you, are they?" she'd said.

"No."

"So, go," she'd said, "and have a good time. Visiting publishers is part of the job, and anybody who's based that far off the beaten track can be expected to have to provide transportation."

Wise woman, in all her ways. And I did have a good time, as Daisy by now knows very, very well.

Chapter 30

· · ·

The terms applied to any change, be it social, political, religious, or cultural, are often fractious and unwieldy. "Post-Reformation" as a way of naming our time certainly is; but one of the more visible characteristics of post-Reformation religion has an even more ungainly name, that of "postdenominationalism." Anyone who can say it discovers fairly soon thereafter, though, that in this case the bark is worse than the bite.

Postdenominationalism means, on its largest scale, the shy moving back into dialogue of the Roman Catholic Church, not only with Orthodox communions, but also with many of the larger Protestant ones. When, as happened in 2003, the Presiding Bishop of the Evangelical Lutheran Church in America can sit down in conversation at the Vatican with His Holiness the Pope for the purposes of discussing their joint declaration about the theological balance between faith, works, and grace in the plan of salvation, something more than ecumenism per se has happened.

At only a slightly less global level, when the Episcopal Church in America, which requires apostolic succession in the laying on of hands at ordination, and the Evangelical Lutheran Church in America, which scorns both that process and the theology behind it . . . when *they* two can enact a statement of "Common Mission" that provides, among other things, that the congregations of either may be completely pastored by the clergy of the other . . . when that happens, as it did in 2002 after several years of prayerful consultation, then something much more substantial than ecclesial good manners is afoot. At a quieter level, when the Protestant denominations of, for instance, Wales or Scotland begin to talk about sharing a common office space, a common administrative staff, and certain pastoral functions across all the old lines, some form of accommodation is definitely under way.

Part of twenty-first-century accommodation is, without doubt, a judicious pooling of resources in a time when declining censuses and shrinking coffers demand extraordinary measures; but to be too cynical or too fiscal in one's interpretation is to miss an underlying reality: The lines of division, once defended to the point of physical death or, more often, to the extreme of a believer's economic ruin, are not so taut of definition as once they were; and the energy those lines once commanded is now directed toward something larger than the separations they still rhetorically represent.

To interpret such current changes too pragmatically would also be to miss the smaller truths that, when the dust of the next fifty years dies down, will be the ones that turn out to have mattered the most. For example, in this country, by the turn of the millennium, two out of every five Christians who attended services regularly were actively attending them each week in two or more different churches or parishes or communions. If one can believe the sociologists who describe such patterns, there is no loss in this of self-identity, only a broadening of loyalties. That is to say, the Christians who belong in two camps will say something rather like "I'm a Baptist, but I like the midweek Bible classes at the Presbyterian Church." Or "I'm Presbyterian, but I love the Taizé services every Saturday night at the Episcopal

Church." The pattern, in other words, is the assertion first of denominational identity followed by the buts of activity and secondary attraction.

Even less remarked in America's secular chatter about its religious self is the steady growth of configurations like the Emergent Church movement or the all-inclusive church movement, the community-church movement or the ecumenical-community movement. Here, the telling shift is truly one of loyalty. "I was reared a Roman Catholic and I still go to Mass sometimes, but I belong to Sojourners" . . . or to Vine Street Community Church or to First Church of Collegeville or to whatever. The formula is still the one of "I am . . . but I belong . . ."

The Community of Jesus in Orleans falls in the ecumenical-community category. C of J is, in fact, almost a textbook-perfect case study in the evolution of that movement. When last I asked, the Community had members drawn from over a dozen different denominations, both Catholic and Protestant, all of whom apply the "I am . . . but I belong . . ." formula, although at its next, highest level. That is, at C of J, if one inquires, the answering formula unfailingly is "I was . . . , but now I am here," *here* being a faith family, but with a place-name, not a theological one.

Like many other, though certainly not all, of America's ecumenical communities, C of J is vowed and residential. Seventy or more sisters live under vows of celibacy as well as obedience and constancy in a convent that sits just across the quadrangle from the Community's church. A Ravenna-like basilica that is massive and almost painfully exhilarating to behold, the Church of the Transfiguration replicates, in all its appointments and details, the early churches of Christian history. Within its doors, the services are headily liturgical, the paraments colorful, and the clergy and Community members traditionally vested.

Just beyond the quadrangle and to the side of the sisters' convent is a smaller house where a dozen extern sisters live apart from the larger group, most of them holding jobs outside the compound itself. At a much farther remove from Transfiguration and the quadrangle that is the compound's centering point, thirty-some brothers live, also under vows of celibacy, in the Friary. Scattered about all this, in an area the size of six city blocks squared, are the Community offices, its support buildings, and the homes of the two hundred–plus members of the Community who live under the vows of obedience and constancy but not of chastity. Some of them are single, of course, but most are married and rearing children.

All of them, regardless of ecclesial station—brothers, sisters, clergy, and lay—live under the rule of Saint Benedict with all the liturgical nuances implicit in that statement. They observe the canonical hours and celebrate the Mass together each morning before the workday begins. Fully vested in monastic robes, they meet in choir, as need arises, to discern the course of the Community. They meet in choir as well to elect their prioress, to whom, once elected, they extend their obedience. They exercise hospitality with one another and to any others who choose to spend a day or a month or a year with them. They counsel one another actively and regularly in matters of spiritual growth and religious maturation.

In the thirty-odd years since its founding, the Community members have honed one another into the most radiantly confessional Christian family I have ever borne witness to. Much of that radiance comes from the fact that the pain of living one's faith is greater in community, because faith is more open to critical scrutiny there. The ego's protective barriers of silence or of withdrawal in distress are burned away, almost always with all the psychological agony that the verb implies. But the result is stunning. Like a mighty oak tree full spread and stately in the midst of a greening meadow, over three hundred people stand together as roots and branches to one another; and they know, these three hundred–plus people, that mountains can move, that the Spirit can come visibly and audibly upon us, and that submitting to one another is the generation of love. They have lived all these things and more.

The Community of Jesus has become my community, and Sam's as well. Though we function as no more than small satellites to that world, our prayers and our affections move with it each day; and our trips to the community are frequent. With regard to this last bit of business, I must say that things have been helped along considerably by my discovery, in early 1995, that going to Orleans from anywhere is a much less wrenching experience if one flies into Logan airport in Boston and simply catches the Plymouth and Brockton bus out to where Orleans waits, sweetly nestled in the inside crook of Cape Cod's elbow.

Chapter 31

• • •

Professional focus, if by that one means undivided attention to the job at hand, was just simply not destined to be part of my postspeech RBTE. Nineteen ninety-four was one of those rare years when America's commercial booksellers appease their West Coast colleagues by holding BEA in Los Angeles. For firms exhibiting at both shows, the realities of that appeasement are a strain on resources, not to mention a logistical tour de force.

The most common resolution to it is for exhibitors, whenever possible, to mount two entirely separate displays, one at Pheasant Run and the other in the Los Angeles Convention Center, with top sales and marketing people manning the show that is of greater importance to each particular house and leaving the details of the lesser show in the hands of more junior staff. The connective tissue in all of this, especially for midsized publishers, is that the head of house of those exhibiting at both shows usually has to leave RBTE a day early in order to make it to the West Coast in time for pre-BEA meetings and events. It works; but as a rule it also adds considerably to the stress or urgency levels emanating from those CEOs who are neither totally in one place nor the other.

Michael Leach is not a stress or urgency person, at least not in the usual sense of those words. He avoids it by staying on overdrive all the time, albeit in the most relaxed and more or less light-handed way imaginable. He is now executive director of Orbis Books, a Roman Catholic house and a central player within the religion market. From the beginning of his career, though, Leach has always been a force to be reckoned with, which is why in 1994 he was director of another influential, though commercially owned house, Crossroad Publishing. And the minute one says "commercially owned" about a religion publisher within Christianity, one implies attendance at both RBTE and BEA.

Case in point: In 1994, all Michael Leach had to worry about, presumably, was making downtown Los Angeles on RBTE Thursday in time for the usual drinks and supper meeting. Most people would have taxied into Chicago early Thursday morning and flown out of O'Hare before lunch. Not Leach. At lunch, suitcase and briefcase in hand, he was trotting through the lobby of Pheasant Run saying his good-byes. Only the Central-versus-Pacific time difference makes such fragile scheduling even faintly possible anyway, but Mike plays things like that near to the edge, primarily, I have decided, for the exhilaration of never quite knowing whether he will make it or not, while at the same time being entirely confident he will . . . which, by the way, he always does. It was not a whit out of character, then, that just as he was going through the lobby door to his cab, he waved at me and said, "I have to talk to you in L.A." Since at that point, I hardly knew Mike except by sight, I was caught by the intensity with which he addressed me.

"All right," I said.

"I mean it," he said, and was gone.

Three days later in another aisle, this time in the Los Angeles Convention Center, I quite literally bumped into him because I was deep in conversation with a colleague and not watching at all where I was going.

"I saw you and was trying to catch you," he said, after we had both recovered and run through our gamut of apologies. "You and I need to talk about what I saw the other night in that talk you gave." Not that it wasn't a superb talk . . . it was, he hastened to say . . . but about what had to happen next. Could we make an appointment, say for Monday in one of the rooms upstairs overlooking the exhibition hall? Say about one-thirty? Fine, I said, but why. He looked at me as if I were faintly retarded or, at the very least, inattentive. "Why, about what you're going to do with all of this."

By 1994, Mike Leach had published them all, from Henri Nouwen to Basil Pennington and back again. But he published in spirituality, not the sociology of religion as it is commercially applied, which by any stretch of a euphemism was still and nonetheless what I did and knew. Why he wanted us to meet was, therefore, more a puzzle than a compliment. Even sitting in his chosen meeting room two days later, looking at the lights and antlike people below us, I could not fathom what he had in mind.

There were two or three other people with us; and this was clearly an editorial meeting. Michael dealt with one of his better-known and more popular authors, talking about where the manuscript in process should go and what should follow it. From time to time, he turned to me and said, "What do you think? Will that idea fly?" or "Is that pretty much where you see the market right now? How about in eighteen months? Will it still be there for something like this?"

It was all publishing talk, the same conversation that I sometimes have as frequently as two or three times a week with editors and publishers. But what he wanted from me had to be more than this, for what we were doing in front of his authors could have been more economically done just between the two of us over an early drink. He dealt with another author or two, making each one feel personally attended to and passionately believed in. Mike's kind of affection and commitment was both genuine in its delivery and, as I was to learn, the very heartbeat of the Leach charm. He *did* believe, and his authors *were* central to his attention as people as well as writers.

As we all stood up to go, he said to me, "Hold it, just a minute, will you, Phyl? We need to talk."

Phyl? Excuse me, but nobody had ever called me by that deplorable abbreviation . . . nobody, that is, except Mike Leach, who has never stopped using it. And truth told, after all these years, I would probably bean him if he tried to stop. I most certainly, though, would bean anybody else who tried to preempt him in that habit.

By whatever name, however, the man wanted to talk, and talk we did for over an hour. What he wanted was indeed the result of something he had heard; but the other part of the Leach success story is that he often "hears" what none of the rest of us hears . . . or at least he had in this case. What Michael had heard in my overview of religion's newfound place in the center of America's book publishing industry was not sociology or statistics or even random enthusiasms. What he heard was "the rediscovery of the sacred" in America. What he wanted was a short book, informally told ("accessible, as if you were just talking"), and designed primarily for the industry itself and those interested professional religionists immediately outside it. The book would convey the scope of that rediscovery, but it would also project some of its future implications. He would like to have the manuscript in house in three or four months, if possible, so Crossroad could publish it as quickly as possible.

The other and third part of the Leach penchant for success is that he does seem always and entirely believable. Like catching a departing airplane by its tail feathers, one believes that if Mike Leach says it can be done, then it obviously can be done. I was hardly a naïf about writing books by that stage in my life. I had done it often enough to know it was a gut-rending process not ever to be entered into lightly, at least not by me. But somehow, and for whatever reason, what Michael said to me made sense. There was a story to be told, a description to be written and shared, about what was happening in America, a story about a landscape that was changing.

Crossroad published the result of our conversation, just as

Michael had said it would, in 1995 and more or less under his conceptualizing title. *Re-Discovering the Sacred: Spirituality in America* was true to the Leach metaphor physically as well. It has, emblazoned on its jacket front like a cartouche, a suburb of American sprawl caught in aerial view and in all its cookie-cutter sameness. What neither of us could have possibly guessed in 1994, though, was that *Re-Discovering* would jump beyond its initially intended audience and, in doing so, would raise more questions than it had answered, primarily ones about prior circumstances, ones like "Why has all this happened?" and "By what route did we get here?" Within a few weeks of *Re-Discovering*'s publication, Mike and I were once more huddled in conversation, though this time in the less dramatic setting of his cramped offices in Manhattan.

The "why it all happened" and the "by what route did we get here" questions and their answers became *God-Talk in America*, which Crossroad published in 1996 and which has remained in print ever since. The significance of *God-Talk* for me, however, was neither its success nor that of *Re-Discovering*. Nobody of right mind would believe an author who claimed that sales and growing readership did not matter to his or her ego, much less to his or her ambitions as a writer. I certainly would not believe me, if I were to say such a thing about my own experience with *God-Talk* and *Re-Discovering*. I do believe me, however, when I say that there was a consequence so much greater for me than all those other good things as almost to override and obscure them.

It had never occurred to me, before Mike Leach showed it to me, that what watching religion through the lens of book publishing exposed for me was of any worth or interest to those involved, not in publishing, but in religion per se. Without him, I would never once have appreciated the fact that cartography drawn for commercial reasons is still a useful mapping for other travelers. The response, first to *Re-Discovering*, and then to *God-Talk*, was by and large a deeply personal one from people who found in the books' removed perspective and market-referencing analysis a distance in which to understand and, apparently, accept the courses of their own religious biography. In listening to them, I began to understand that I too had gone, and was going, through the exact same process, albeit not with any self-awareness. Much of my joy in my work at *PW*, I realized, was a joy in a new kind of self-understanding. My faith had got where my faith was by the grace of God, certainly, but also by the help of circumstances which, divine in origin or not, I could isolate and appreciate. My work was an exercise in personal freedom, and I had never perceived it as such until Mike Leach threw me, like Daniel in the lions' den, smack into the middle of myself and what I was.

Chapter 32

• • •

I have never in my life wanted to be a preacher, and to this day I run from the word "homily" as if it were a fatal and highly contagious illness. There is in the preaching life the need to assume the weight of ordination and the authority of the priesthood. I would break under that burden and under the stance of right interpretation that assuming it implies. But I am a teacher. I love to discover . . . it makes my heart race and causes everything else to blur out around me. Yet once discovered, a new thing goes only half known and half enjoyed unless it can be shared, be told out to others, be rejoiced over in congress with the like-minded. What Mike Leach opened up for me was the door to a truth about myself just beyond that one.

There is in Judaism the tradition of both teaching rabbis and pulpit rabbis at the congregational level; there should be in Christianity. Pray God I shall live long enough to see the day. Meanwhile, what I have known since 1996 is that I am a teacher within the Church. Self-ordained perhaps, in a time where there is no ordination except Daisy's for my kind, but employed of God nonetheless. For an old woman, it was, and has remained, a startling discovery, and I have been like one at play in the Elysian Fields ever since.

I spend far more of my life now among church and interfaith groups than in publishing meetings per se. The paradox is that talking to people of faith in the places where they live and worship and wrestle with what they really believe means listening to people; and, believe me, having essentially unlimited access to a genre's readers and to their concerns is as great a benison in the book business as it is rare. Publishers and editors try to visit bookstores routinely enough to maintain some kind of working contact with the realities at the retail level of the industry; but those spot checks are about as near professionally as most of them get to the realities of literate, believing John Q. and Mary America.

The unexpected consequence of my more general and ever more public role as a presence in church and interfaith conferences has been to turn me into a kind of conduit. Through those experiences, flowing in one direction out to general religion audiences, is knowledge-based information about where pop culture is, has been over the last few years, is going in the near future, and about what difference that is shortly going to make in naves, synagogues, and auditoriums. Flowing in the other direction, back toward my industry, is exposure-gleaned information about what are the perceived needs in America's religious life; about where, in matters of spiritual, pastoral, and theological query, the energy is beginning to approach critical mass; about what, at pew and reader level, is the experienced articulation among god-talk, electronic pop culture, and the book; about where, for those attempting to live a life of belief, the old faithese of former times is beginning to break down completely; and — perhaps most important — about what a new rhetoric is going to have to sound like and how.

Being a conduit, even metaphorically, is more utilitarian than glamorous; and it certainly is nearer to plumbing than to the academic due process I had once been trained to. It is also immensely satisfying. Everything that flows through on its way somewhere else and without regard to the direction of its flow

leaves a bit of itself . . . its excitements, its insights, its understanding of present limitations and struggles. Above all else, it
leaves its steady, strumming vibrations of an awareness beyond
itself. It is of these things that I have become a student. They are
my reference library, my laboratory, and my instructors. But
they are also only one half, albeit the larger half, of what I have
been talking about publicly over the last five or six years. That
additional turn in the path was the third and last life-shifting result of RBTE 1994 and the speech I refuse to listen to in replay.

During the banquet that preceded the evening's address, I
was seated at a table near the front of the hall and conveniently
near the podium. Seated next to me was Tom Cahill, whom I
knew at that time only by job description: He was head of religion at Doubleday, a division of the world's largest publishing
conglomerate . . . which is a nice way of saying he was serious
business, especially in my business; and I was not naive about
why he had been seated next to me. This was going to be a working banquet, I thought to myself, before it became a keynote
address.

In 1994, Tom Cahill was still about five years away from being famous in his own right. *How the Irish Saved Civilization* was already rolling around in his head, though, as were *The Gift of the
Jews* and a myriad of other magnificent essays and books. I just
had not known any of that before the fact. As a result, while I sat
down to supper with a shrewd and highly successful publisher, I
got up from it acutely aware of the intellect, religious depth, and
absolute personal charm of my dinner companion.

During that hour, Tom spoke little of himself but a great deal
about the world of ideas in which he lived, into which he
presently published, and the outreaches of which he hoped soon
to explore as a writer. There was in him the generosity of the true
artist and the humor of the true believer, the eyes twinkling even
when the words were deadly serious. I remember regretting to
myself that my one time with Tom Cahill was taking place in a
preaddress circumstance with all of the minor distractions inherent in that situation.

After I had finished speaking, I went back toward our table, and Tom held my chair for me, as one would expect. As he pushed it in, he said, almost under his breath, "I have some people I want you to meet." That was it, nothing more, until the following Friday night at BEA, when the phone in my hotel room in Los Angeles rang, and it was Tom Cahill.

He was, he said, as he assumed I must already know, Archbishop Desmond Tutu's American publisher; and the Archbishop, Mrs. Tutu, and his press secretary John Allen were coming into town the next day, Saturday, in order that Tutu might address the convention on Monday evening as part of a promotional tour for his forthcoming book, *The Rainbow People of God*. Because of the press of crowds around him when he appeared in public, however, and especially on an extended tour like this one, the Archbishop preferred, when he was on the road on the Sabbath, to celebrate the Mass in his hotel room with his family, staff, and a few fellow Christians. Would I be able to join them on Sunday morning at ten in Tutu's hotel room?

Once again, memory fails me as to what I thought at just that moment . . . whether I was more starstruck by the Archbishop or ego-stroked by the invitation or dumbfounded by Tom Cahill, I cannot even begin to measure. I suspect I was stunned by a healthy hunk of all three; but I did manage to say yes.

"Good. I'll call you Sunday morning with the floor number where I want you to get off. I'll meet you at the elevator, and we will go together to the Archbishop's suite."

And that was that.

Chapter 33

• • •

The Friday evening of Tom Cahill's call was May 27, 1994. The Saturday of the Archbishop's arrival in Los Angeles, May 28, 1994, was exactly a month to the day after South Africa had completed its first free elections and Nelson Mandela had won the presidency of his homeland. The Sunday of our proposed time together was May 29.

In 1994, Trinity Sunday in the Christian calendar fell on May 29. As the Sabbath immediately after the Day of Pentecost (when Christians celebrate the descent of the Spirit upon the infant church), Trinity Sunday is a major feast day of the faith. The Sabbath it marks is the first to occur after all three parts of the triune God — Father, Son, and Holy Spirit — have revealed themselves overtly within human time: The Trinity is now complete in human experience as well as in Itself. No Christian goes lightly into Trinity Sunday. No one of any faith could have gone lightly into this one.

There were ten of us that Sunday morning: the Archbishop; Mrs. Tutu; John Allen, who had contributed several sections of commentary to *Rainbow*; Tom Cahill and his daughter, who was a college sophomore that year and at BEA with her father on a kind of father-daughter lark; an assistant editor at Doubleday; Tutu's agent and her husband; Patricia Klein; and me.

Patricia, an evangelical Christian, fellow Episcopalian, and friend of long standing, was finishing her tenure that year as the buyer of religion product for a large national chain of bookstores and was on her way to beginning editorial work for Tom. Tom had told me when he'd called on Friday evening that Patricia would be coming too. When he called on Sunday morning, he suggested that the two of us walk over together. "It's the Hyatt," he said. "The two of you come to the sixth floor, and I'll get on the elevator and take you on from there."

What I remember most about our walk to the Hyatt was how little we said. Pat is not a chatterer, but she is an able conversationalist who is given to deadly accuracy in nailing whatever is at the center of a situation or an issue. Her quietness, it seemed to me, was her way of nailing this one. It was Trinity, it was a month and a day after Mandela, it was a thing beyond the foolishness of words. Tom met us, as promised, and took us to another floor and then down the hall to the Archbishop's suite.

We were all there as observant Christians. There was no question about that, and it was the first thing that struck me as the three of us walked into the shadowy, more or less generic room that served as the suite's public area. In fact, to enter that badly lighted, long-nosed room with its pseudo-personal furniture and its glass-topped everything was, as nothing in life before or since has ever been for me, like entering the imagined catacombs of Christian history. Admittedly, there had been a suggestive cachet of surreptitiousness about the arrangements for our coming, an almost pleasant furtiveness about how we had been directed to assemble in such a way as to protect the Archbishop from harm or intrusion. Yet when Tom knocked on that door and we were admitted, there was more than the exhilaration of some sweet secrecy already operative in the room.

People whom I did not know and who apparently had not previously known each other were talking among themselves, making introductions and small talk as people upon meeting will. But a part of their individual attentions had already moved to the purpose of our coming. It was obvious in the stillness of their hands, in how they kept them in their laps or at their sides. It showed in the way their eyes drifted sometimes away from the faces of others and toward our surroundings, seeing nothing. It showed most in the soft, uninquiring conversations.

When we arrived, the Archbishop, wearing a black-and-aqua nylon jogging suit and white Nikes, was already seated in front of the double windows at the far end of the room in one of the place's two high-backed chairs. To his left was an octagonal lamp table and beyond that, the other and matching high-backed chair, still empty. To his right was another table — the low, square kind that hotels put in corners to fill up the incongruities between overstuffed low sofas and overstuffed high-backed chairs.

As if to thwart the Hyatt's decorative intentions, John Allen, in khakis and a white shirt whose sleeves he had long since rolled up over his elbows, had judiciously placed a straight-backed desk chair in front of the corner table. He was sitting there now or, rather, he was perched upon the edge of it now, his arms and legs all crossed upon themselves and his angular attention clearly focused on someone or something he was expecting.

To Allen's right and sitting on the sofa itself was Mrs. Tutu, as relaxed and nested in as Allen seemed restive and perched. A coffee table that, guessing by the depressions in the rug, had originally stood in front of the sofa had been pulled up toward the Archbishop as a makeshift altar and was within easy reach for both him and Allen. Three or four copies of the Scriptures were already on the table along with three or four copies of what I discovered later was the South African edition of The Book of Common Prayer. Around all of this were a desk chair or two and other, folding ones that had been brought in for the occasion.

"Please," the Archbishop said, addressing Patricia and me in that singularly lilting speech of the native South African when he speaks English. "Please be seated with us. We are waiting just now for the bread to come up from room service."

Had the Archbishop of the Anglican Church of South Africa danced naked in front of me I would not have been more taken aback; nor could I have been more efficiently and quickly thrust into the attitudes of his reverence. To be waiting for a bellman to bring up bread from the kitchen was so matter-of-fact, so unpretentiously reasonable, as to be the act only of a humble man. The Bread of Christ from the kitchens of Hyatt. I could never have done such a thing—which, I understood immediately, was a limitation in some dark way akin to the self-inflation that had allowed me to be flattered by all of this in the first place.

While we waited, the Archbishop made bits of small talk, but most of the time he deferred to Mrs. Tutu, who chatted with the room in general about her flight, the elections, her predictions for the Mandela presidency, and the state of her children. The knock came within no more than five minutes, and a young face peered around the door, proffering a small plate with two naked slices of light bread uncovered and drying on it.

"You want this, sir?" the boy said, his amazement that he had been sent upstairs on so unorthodox a mission was as obvious as his confusion about why there were ten seemingly sober people waiting for him to accomplish it. To the day of my death, I will be willing to wager good money that that young man had no idea to whom he was delivering two slices of untoasted sandwich bread or why, but I would wager the same money that he has not yet forgotten the fact that he did it.

"Thank you, I'll take it," said Allen, across the room before anybody else to take the plate and pay the tip. Making his way more deliberately back through the obstructing chairs, Allen pulled the coffee table a bit nearer to Archbishop Tutu, set the plate down on it, and resumed his own seat. He reached under the lamp table, took out his briefcase from beneath it, and from the briefcase took out a small, airline-sized bottle of Glen Ellen wine that he had obviously bought on his flight in. He set the bottle beside the bread and replaced his briefcase under the table. All the necessary parts of the Christian Mass were in place.

"Good," said Tutu. "Now we shall begin." And he started assigning roles. To Allen the job of leading the Prayers of the People, to me the reading of the Old Testament lessons, to Tom's daughter the reading of the Epistle. Next he spoke the prayers of consecration over the elements in a voice so low I could not distinguish the words, but in which I thought I could hear the occasional clicking sounds of his native tongue.

"Blessed be God: Father, Son, and Holy Ghost," he said, lifting his head and addressing us in English; and we responded in kind, "And blessed be his kingdom, now and forever. Amen." The opening prayers were said, the Gloria recited, the Kyrie spoken; and long before even that much was done, I, like everyone else in that room, had already slipped effortlessly into the habits of a lifetime, walking once more without self-awareness or any awareness at all along the familiar road into the center.

The Old Testament lesson and the Epistle were read and then, as celebrant, the Archbishop read the Gospel, rendering it mellifluous and rhythmic with the rise and fall of his almost-familiar English. The readings finished, he turned to us and said, "It is Trinity Sunday, the first in the freedom of my people, and I am pleased to observe it here with you. Today we celebrate the three parties of God, the community of God as the Father, of God as the Son, and of God as the Holy Spirit."

It was the voice carrying me now, the modulations, the simplicity, the pastoral intimacy of it: "Father, Son, and Holy Spirit, God is a society and we are created in his image. The idea of a single human being is therefore a contradiction." And he began, in the soft persuasive litany of his melodic speech, to weave the spell of our common sonship. As he spoke, I slipped further and further into an understanding that was so clear to him as to become transparent through him. What I employed as a religious principle and moral convention, he was.

Then the homily was over as unceremoniously as it had begun, with his turning simply to the words of the Nicene Creed: "I believe in one God . . ." We repeated with him the time-hallowed tenets of our faith and then waited as Allen took up the Prayers of the People.

If I had experienced the spirit of the priest in Tutu, I had at least been prepared before the fact to some greater or lesser extent by his position and his episcopacy. I had had no prior warning about John Allen. Instead, it was the priesthood of all believers that rolled out of him, filling that room and those of us gathered there in it with all the urgency and poignancy of primal belief. He prayed as one talks to the landlord, he prayed as one talks to his daddy, he prayed as one talks to the suffering, he prayed as one talks to a lover, he prayed as I had never heard prayer before; and Mrs. Tutu prayed with him, filling his pauses and breaks and silences with petitions of her own for her country, her family, her husband, her faith and constancy, her friends. And punctuating them both was the voice of the Archbishop, sometimes in English, sometimes clearly now in his native tongue. The three of them rose and swelled and peaked and receded and rose again like an ocean calm before its own strength, and there was no doubt among them, no hesitancy, no modesty. They were as one body somewhere where we could still see them and almost go, praying with expectancy and absolute surety. These three were no chimneys for the fire of God. They were the fire in consultation together with God Himself to shape the world; and they were being burned by the fire. They were, in fact, luminous with it.

What happened after that—the celebration of the Mass itself, the final blessing and dismissal, the more secular good-byes—they all happened and in their proper sequence. Patricia and I left, as we had come, together; and though we have made mention of the morning several times since, we have discovered each time that there is nothing to say *about* what we experienced there, only that it was and is and will always be God-with-us.

Chapter 34

• • •

"Post-Cartesian" is another of those stifling terms that one would like to, in turn, stifle. The sad truth is that it, like so many of its kind, has not even a near rival for accuracy in naming one of the major characteristics of our times.

René Descartes was the early-seventeenth-century French philosopher and mathematician who gave the West, among other things, its favorite aphorism: *Cogito, ergo sum.* I think, therefore I am. We have built almost four hundred years of Western culture and human self-understanding on Descartes' premise. One can hardly say, then, that it was a mistake. Clearly it was a great key for our forebears in unlocking the anterooms of individuality as an operative construct in human affairs. One cannot even say that Descartes's "I think and therefore am" was an error per se. But we do have to admit that it was more an enabling concept than an eternal verity, which insight is why the late twentieth and opening twenty-first centuries can only be called post-Cartesian.

The Cartesian declaration of thinking as the property that defines the human being as a human being had been under assault in academic laboratories and learned papers for several decades before it got into trouble popularly. That is, before it hit the abortion street wars: Is it human before it can think or is it human because it may potentially think or is it human if we know from tests that it can never think . . . and the less raucous but equally sticky conversation about euthanasia, which, by the way, often hinges on the exact same set of questions. The death blow for the Cartesian definition of our defining hallmark at a popular level, though, was not a moral argument but the far more concrete one of artificial intelligence. Once Deep Blue had defeated Garry Kasparov at chess in 1997, "post-Cartesian" described every luncheon counter and coffee klatsch in Middle America just as surely as it described the most ivy-covered of lecture halls.

All of which led, and leads, to a very arresting . . . in fact, downright unsettling . . . question. If thinking is not what makes us human, then what does? Who are we?

And the truth of the thing is that we cannot go on until we answer that one. Oh, we may make fancier machines and fight wars that are more mechanized or conquer our ignorance about physical laws and space. We may learn to feed more folks more efficiently, and we will undoubtedly figure out how to make the wealthy wealthier. But we cannot proceed morally—and, therefore, religiously—until we can slip some new formula into the slot where Descartes's solution was for so many years. Humanity undefined is humanity not really present conceptually or rhetorically. There is a suspension in the conversation until someone tells us how we can know that we are and how we can understand the "are-ness" of our "are-ing." And into that suspension of conversation comes the voice of Desmond Tutu.

It is called—this aphorism he is speaking—*ubuntu,* after the African theology from which it comes. I did not know that in 1994. I was, in fact, totally innocent of it even as I listened in a Hyatt hotel suite, mesmerized and persuaded, to a homily that was rife with ubuntu thought. The aphorism is "I am, because you are." Its implications are enormous:

I know myself only insofar as and only as long as you are there to reflect my self. Without you, I am not. With you, I am.

Quantum physics. Without the observer, the observed is not because it is indeterminate. Once observed, it is determinate and therefore is as it has been observed.

There can be no horror much greater than that which is contained in those words, and no grandeur that exceeds them. If they are not Tutu's gift . . . and he says they are not . . . then they are Africa's gift through him to the present and emerging era of humankind. They are the sharing of this title. Pray God we use them wisely.

Chapter 35

• • •

Tom Cahill, Irish rascal that he is, was far from through with his gifting of me, even after Archbishop Tutu. Before BEA was done on Monday afternoon, he had written for me on a half sheet of paper the name Eric Major, followed by a couple of phone numbers, a fax number, and an address. "You are to meet him in Frankfurt," Tom said, "regardless of whatever else you do. I shall send along a letter of introduction, but you will have to arrange your own appointment. Just be sure you do it."

As early June began to give way to mid-June, I did indeed turn my attention to Eric Major, only to find making an appointment to meet him in Frankfurt almost disconcertingly easy. Frankfurt appointments are not lightly come by; but apparently Tom had done his thing . . . and/or the Cahill name had done its. Major is a Brit . . . Lordy, Lordy, is he ever a Brit! The quintessential one, in fact, in everything from demeanor to appearance to speech and bent of humor. In 1994, he was head of Hodder Religion in the United Kingdom, meaning he oversaw one of Britain's largest religion-publishing programs. Yet when we met, he was as relaxed as if he had no concerns beyond our immediate conversation.

The two of us chatted (to use his term) for over half an hour, and I left our time together with no more idea than I had had to start with about why, in Tom's scheme of things, we had needed to meet. I also left enormously glad that we had. Patently knowledgeable about religion publishing in Europe as well as in Britain and her former territories, Eric could have talked publishing to my benefit for the whole of our conversation. He did not, however, seem interested in going in that direction except incidentally. He talked rather in terms of himself, his family, his friendship with Tom, why he was doing what he was doing and what he hoped still to accomplish. It was not until some two or three days later that I realized he had used each of those easy revelations as a means of getting me to furnish the same information about myself, my life, and my purposes. I was as charmed by the discovery of how cleverly I had been manipulated as I had been by the man himself.

Eric Major and I will remain friends for, presumably, the rest of our lives; and today he is probably the man in publishing of whatever kind or genre whom I most admire and most completely trust. The increased intimacy in that statement comes from the fact that in 1996 Tom Cahill was at last able to break free of his duties and become the writer he yearned to be. His last act as publisher of Doubleday's religion program was to persuade Eric Major to leave England in 1997 and take over the Doubleday program in this country. And it was as head of Doubleday's religion that Eric Major, by 1998, would become my principal publisher. If there has ever been a more affectionate and cordial relationship between author and publisher, I don't know of it. Nor, for that matter, can I think of many people to whom I am more indebted than I am to Tom Cahill.

There is, however, one other gift gained from Chicago's plethora of them that I can never come and go through O'Hare without rejoicing over. This one I got, at least in its opening permutations, in 1993 and not at BEA but at yet another show, this time a publishers' tabletop show.

In general, one should avoid the syndrome named "tabletop shows." They work. Goodness knows they work; but what they offer in efficiency they, as a rule, lack in elegance . . . or, actually, in just plain comfort. The tabletop approach involves renting a banquet hall somewhere cheap (relatively, that is) and having a small and select number of publishers spread out their books and their literature about forthcoming books on bare tables while invited and ticketed retailers go up and down the three or four aisles, order blanks in hand, actually doing business instead of just merely networking. Everybody loves the tabletops . . . everybody, that is, except those of us who have to cover them, and I do that as infrequently as possible, believe me.

In 1993, however, I was a bit more enthusiastic and less sardonic about such things. The show was, naturally, in Chicago; and its being in Chicago was part of why I had elected to attend this show instead of any one of several others that fall. I could kill two birds with one airplane trip by going to Chicago.

The day of the show was cold and rainy outdoors; but outdoors was positively an illuminated delight compared to the gray-carpeted and faintly dank cavern that was the basement floor of the modestly priced hotel where the show was being held. I had had to more or less feel my way down the hall from my elevator to a sunken foyer or vestibule of sorts where at least a few ceiling lights were on. Presumably, drab though it was, this lowered level was the meeting-and-greeting space for the adjoining ballroom when social rather than commercial affairs were afoot. Since I dislike stand-up cocktail parties with an unrighteous vengeance anyway, I remember assessing the whole drear thing as a particularly torturous and unappealing example of the places where such things usually occur. Then I looked up from my funk and saw the woman who was my other reason for coming to Chicago and with whom I had an appointment, though at first sighting I honestly was not sure it was she.

Her name was Lynn Garrett and she lives in the Chicago suburb of Evanston. A dancer by previous profession and still, to this day, possessed of a dancer's body and a dancer's grace of movement, she looked almost nothing like what I had expected. She was sitting, apparently in complete comfort, on one of the gray-carpeted steps and reading in light that was too dim even to be called milky. The hair, though, was the inspired thing. Shoulder-length and blond, it kinked and waved, albeit in orderly fashion, all over her head. I looked, decided "too elegant . . . couldn't be," and had started into the ballroom–cum–tabletop showroom when I heard her say, "Phyllis? Phyllis Tickle?" We must have talked for over an hour on those steps before it occurred to either of us that there was work to be done and, after work, more comfortable physical circumstances in which to get to know each other better.

By the winter of 1993, I had developed a chronic and well-founded anxiety about the thinness of my writing stable. If there was one overarching need in the program just then, it was the need for more writers who were both journalists and trained in religion. That combination of journalistic skills and religion expertise is rare now; it was as rare as hen's teeth in 1993. How we stumbled onto Garrett, I no longer remember. Probably she wrote me with a résumé. It doesn't matter. What matters is that she was a trained journalist who had been a working journalist when she'd decided to go to seminary and earn an advanced degree in religion studies. Pure gold could not have looked any better to me on that cheerless day than she did.

And she could write . . . oh, my, could she ever write! Within less than a year of our meeting, Lynn did her first full feature for *PW,* covering the previously more or less arcane world of religion book clubs. And neither of us has looked back since, except that our roles have changed. She is now the editor and I, part of her staff. When the time came for me to step back a bit, I looked at Daisy and Daisy looked at me, and we both said, "Lynn!" as if in one voice.

For this and all thy blessings, Chicago, we do most surely thank you.

The Farm In Lucy

Chapter 36

· · ·

Thoreau once famously said that he had traveled widely in Concord. As observations go, that one for years seemed to me to be uncomfortably close to preciousness. It was The Farm In Lucy that changed my haughtiness into respect. Somewhere about the time that we were preparing to celebrate the first anniversary of our moving to Lucy, it began to dawn on me that I too had been traveling widely in Concord for several months.

Those early years of farming were too physically grueling to be romanticized, certainly by me, anyway. But from the first, they and the experiences caught within them began to teach and change and temper us. In cities, man is the measure of all things. From the scale of its architecture to the placement of its impediments and its delights, the city accommodates itself to the size of humanity and the stature of human needs. In the country, our kind is the measure of nothing.

Not one thing in the country is to human scale, not one thing is tailored to human need. All things necessary are provided, but not furnished; they must be asked for. And all the things being asked of are larger than the ones doing the asking. "I will lift up my eyes unto the hills" is not "I will lift up my eyes unto the sky-scrapers" for good reason. Skyscrapers fill me and everybody else I know with exhilaration. To this day, I still sometimes stand on Fifth Avenue and gawk like a bumpkin at them. They make my joy soar with the grandeur of what we are and what our sort can do. How great we are is a religious experience. It is just simply not the same part of religious experience as How great You are. Having learned the first part of that lesson fairly well in my years as a city dweller, I have for almost thirty years now been learning the latter part in Lucy.

Beyond the rather dramatic and sustained change in physical habits and values that moving from urban to rural experience forces upon one, there is an almost contradictory corollary, one that lies at the heart of Thoreau's observation. When intellectuals, especially writers, move to the country to sustain themselves there, they have often made a statement without recognizing it. Or at least in my case, it went unrecognized for a long time. What head people frequently are saying is that ideas in the tight spaces of the city can all too easily become elaborations upon one another . . . an impenetrable curtain of words . . . an embroidering of the already domesticated. What thinkers and ponderers are looking for in rural living is often an escape from such redundant accomplishments and from the fallacy of thinking one is in control. What they seek—what I now know I sought—is to work again within an immediacy between need and source. The foreshortening of the space between impotent self and infinite power does not increase human vulnerability; it simply strips our fragility of the emperor's wardrobe it tends to wear in town; and vulnerability, for writers, is fecund stuff, pregnant with awe and desperation and release. And if foreshortening of the physical is good for one's spiritual and aesthetic self, some distancing from the heat of analysis and argument is tonic and health to the intellectual self. In this, paradoxically, it is the ability to control the flow of incoming argument and a certain removal from immediacy that are beneficial. To speak in cliché, I can see the forest as well as the trees much better from here than when I am standing in the middle of them. And seeing is not all that happens.

The haiku poet Basho centuries ago wrote, "I looked into the eye of the newt and saw Fujiyama behind me." I think that is the greatest love song any poet ever wrote to his own place in the world. I think as well that it is a kind of motif of consolation. The poet may not travel to Fujiyama, but he may, through his own particularity, experience the awe of seeing the holy mountain's great contour and he may know the richness of holding it forever as talisman in his mind.

The Farm In Lucy has been my newt, and American religion, my Fujiyama for over a dozen years now; but it was not until the mid-1990s that I actually began to learn how to watch for the contours. It was not until then, in other words, that I fell in love not just with my job, but with the subjects that were and are its content.

Chapter 37

• • •

As religion continued to swell in market share and to perform consistently as the book industry's fastest-growing
segment of adult trade publishing, there was a conversation or
two about moving the religion department . . . meaning me . . .
into the New York office. The idea was short-lived, fortunately,
primarily because none of us could see that I would actually be
there often enough for any advantage to accrue.

Unlike other parts of American book publishing, religion is
not concentrated in the Northeast. Quite the contrary. It has several foci scattered across the country: Nashville, Grand Rapids,
Chicago, Downers Grove and Wheaton (both just outside
Chicago, by the way), Colorado Springs, and San Francisco, in
addition to Boston and Manhattan. Likewise, religion's professional organizations, shows, and meetings are intentionally peri-
patetic. What I needed, in other words, was a good airport, an
office that I could leave for a week or two at a time without fear
of something's having been moved or borrowed or simply reshuf-
fled, and a sturdy laptop.

We bought the laptop. That was easy, even if traveling with
its bulk sometimes was not. Memphis has a superb airport,

thanks to its being a NorthWest/KLM hub and, perhaps more significant, to the fact that FedEx's national hub is there. FedEx in particular seems to take it as an unkindness when anything about its hub does not work properly at all times. As a result, those of us served by Memphis International enjoy an ease of access to everywhere that it would otherwise be totally unreasonable of us to expect. That left only the matter of an office.

Since it was obvious that I was always going to work from Lucy, it was equally obvious that some adjustments would have to be made; and the only way to make them was to reconfigure the erstwhile double garage yet once again. This time, it was the former-shipping-room half that I moved into. With the remains of the kitchen stoop and garage steps right at the end of my desk, with our outside refrigerator bumbling along in the corner, with twenty-two-foot ceilings that no longer had garage-door tracks but did have an infinite variety of spiders, with the shipping table shoved against the supply cabinet, and with our coonhound keeping watch over it all, I moved in. I moved in with the serious petition of "Please, Lord, don't let anyone ever ask to see where *PW*'s religion division is, or we'll be dead in the water."

Jerry-rigged as it was, the thing worked. We wired in a data line and a portable line and a fax line. As my workload accelerated and Sam started to order the second land line, I drew my own line. There was only so much voice mail and so many incoming calls I could handle. But the ability to control the flow of print materials . . . the mail, the UPS, the FedEx, the Airborne, the other express deliveries . . . was not so easily exercised. Sam finally built an outside bin for deliveries and pickups. It did nothing to diminish the glut of books, galleys, and manuscripts, but it did make the coonhound's life easier. She could bark twice at each delivery and, having done her duty, go back to dozing as soon as the bin's lid slammed shut again. Even the size and configuration of the space itself were not a problem. There is something about ridiculously high ceilings that makes for a sense of airiness even in the midst of cramped quarters. The only real problem was me and how I think.

The first time Daisy ever walked into the Lucy office she was more or less associated with, she stopped dead in the doorway and said, "My God, Tickle!"—which pretty much covered the situation. I tried to tell her . . . had tried a hundred times before to tell her, in fact . . . that I think with my hands. I have to handle what I am thinking about. As a trait, it makes one lousy in abstract math, but fairly good in tree counting and positively gifted at organizing by categories. It was this latter that Daisy had walked into, ill-prepared despite my forewarnings.

By 1994, the major thematic shifts that were beginning to course like rivers at flood tide through American religion were finding their most accessible and discernible expression in religion books. The only way I knew to monitor those currents and gauge their potential impact as well as their probable origins and future directions was to sort books and press releases and galleys by ideas or general constructs. For me to accomplish this, Sam, on almost a monthly basis, had bolted more and more standards to the garage walls, setting shelf braces and boards as close to one another as he could, while I and my stacks slowly metastasized all over them. The old cabinet tops became presort holding pens for books and galleys that might or might not be keepers; and the floor became a warren of stools and upended trash cans turned into makeshift stacking tables.

It would have been a totally unacceptable mess, except that it was funny. It was even funny while Daisy was standing in the middle of it all shaking her head and declaring that no mental processes could possibly be furthered by this much physicality. But looking back now, I wonder if anything more elegant or even more conventional would not have thwarted what had to be done during those mid-decade years. Religion was so new a surge in book publishing and the changes in it so radical and fluid that perhaps only physical piles and actual stacking could have caught and mapped them. However that may be, the truth of the thing was that a walk along the twenty-two-inch-wide path that led through the stacks and encumbrances from the driveway door to our kitchen door was a walk through history in the making.

Chapter 38

• • •

When America began to realize, in the late 1960s, that it was well equipped with institutional religion and religious institutions but was pretty much bereft of any spiritual activity at all, it set about, in good American fashion, to solve the problem of its newly perceived emptiness. Because almost all of that first searching and seeking was done apart from established institutions and faiths—they were, after all, the culprits in all of this—a great deal of it became a kind of Yankee adventure in an individualism that invented its own guides and took no prisoners.

There was nothing inherently wrong with that process, I suspect, although I also realize that many clerics would probably disagree with me; for it was in the New Age that most of the mainline, established congregations began to shrink. Whether right or wrong, inspired or perverted, this country's search for spiritual discipline and a palpable contact with the divine more wandered than tracked as it made its way through pseudo-Buddhism, aromatherapy, yoga, angels, mantras, and ten dozen other bits of shamanistic sleight of hand. Much of the initial swell in religion publishing was due to the fact that each wanderer in these woods seemed compelled to share his or her adventures and discoveries, idiosyncratic and individualistic or not.

But by the mid-1990s some of that naive and largely unvetted rush to publish the account and methods of each subjective experience without regard to its spiritual legitimacy had begun to wane. Seekers were beginning to mature, and so too was their understanding of the New Age and the substantialness of its intentions. As maturation increased, so also did the credibility of much of what the early pioneers had discovered and then refined. As if totally unaware of the irony involved in such a shift, New Age, in effect, went mainstream. It was no longer the fringe that sought health of soul, a holistic life experience, and a life in the spirit. It was Middle America who had now discovered that there was more and that they wanted it.

In 1992, a tiny little publishing house, Gold Leaf Press, joined with a woman named Betty Eadie to release *Embraced by the Light,* Eadie's account of her own near-death experience. It should have made no difference in the larger world . . . the press was too small, the subject was too suspect, its only distributor was too regional . . . except. Except that in April 1993 I got a call from the religion buyer at Ingram Book Company, the country's largest book distributor and in no way, shape, or form regional. Did I know, he asked, anything about a Betty Eadie or a book entitled *Embraced by the Light?* I didn't. Then, he suggested, maybe we should begin to find out, because it was getting a lot of buzz in the Far West and now he was getting orders for it.

I have thought of that conversation so many times since; and whenever I am tempted to think I'm good at my job, I remind myself that I have some monumental oversights to balance the lucky guesses. Ms. Eadie was one of the former. By September 1994, *Embraced* had broken onto the *New York Times* best-seller list, where it stayed for over a year; and the following June, Bantam Books paid $6 million for paperback reprint rights, at that time the largest sum ever paid for such rights. Within a matter of months, thereafter, near-death-experience literature was everywhere. America was ready to believe in resurrection and contact with the divine in a whole new and unmediated way.

In the fall of 1994, just as Eadie was breaking onto the *Times*
lists, James Redfield published *The Celestine Prophecy: An Adventure* and once again the nation was rocked by massive sales of a
book laying claim to direct interaction between the spirit of the
creature and its creator. Redfield would go on to do pocket
guides and additional titles about the insights that were his experience. Every one of those spin-off volumes also hit the best-
seller lists, almost as quickly, in fact, as they came into my office
door in Lucy.

There is a rule of thumb which says that, in general, a piece
of religion writing becomes canonical or scriptural when it can
be shown to have evoked commentaries and ancillary reference
guides independent of its author. Within two or three years, *The
Celestine Prophecy* had begun to do just that. Reading groups of
adherents sprang up faster almost than one could track Redfield's appearances or report his sales. Unlike the near-death-
experience titles, which generated few if any groups of disciples,
Redfield's work had struck a different or additional note, one
that would be increasingly important for years. He offered a
morality that, while basically Judeo-Christian in tenets, was
fresh in its rhetoric and spiritual and holistic in its approach.
There was no shame or threat of damnation to beat the sinner
into compliance. Rather, there was light and joy and peace of
soul and harmony within humanity to be gained by embracing
the insights of the prophecies. It was a powerful message. It was
also a powerful exposé of where established religion had failed
for decades to make its point . . . where it had failed to mind all
three strands in the rope of meaning. For too long, spirituality
had been neglected and morality rendered formulaic by culturally and socially invested institutions. Both strands were now
turning into dangerously disruptive and unmanageable agencies
in the shaping of the country's new religious sensibility.

Within a matter of fifteen months or so of *Celestine*'s publication, Neale Donald Walsch published *Conversations with God: An
Uncommon Dialogue*. He too produced several more spin-off volumes, all of which sold in literally record-breaking proportions.
Life in Lucy became life in a broadcast booth, reporting on a

game that had no rules. By 1994, Marianne Williamson had joined the circle of major players, securing her place as another beloved guru to thousands with her *Illuminata: Thoughts, Prayers, Rites of Passage*. Andrew Weil and Larry Dossey, both physicians, drew massive audiences when they spoke about their books on spiritual healing and about the inviolate connection between and amongst body, mind, and spirit. Every morning, in fact, it seemed to me that there was a new sage or counselor emerging to join the others already there. What was happening?

At a practical level, what was happening was quite clear and simple to America's booksellers. One retailer in Chicago put it most crisply when she shrugged her shoulders at me, jerked her head back toward what in 1995 was still the ill-lighted, back left corner of her shop, and said, "It's simple. What they used to take to their pastor's study, they now bring in here to me." Put another way, books had indeed become portable pastors; and as a job description, that one has held right up to the present moment.

What was happening at a religious or faith level, however, had already happened. There had been a rebellion in the troops, and the Dosseys and Weils and Walschs, whatever else they were and are, were and are most assuredly proof of that rebellion. Excitement was the order of the day . . . spiritual excitement, an unleashed inquisitiveness about other ways of being in the world, a romp through the costume bins of anthropology in search of rituals that were risqué or outré or both, a rush to feel. . . . Oh dear Lord, this above all, let us feel.

Chapter 39

• • •

![flower ornament] An urgency to feel, left unexplored, smacks too much of
residual existentialism, which ours may in part have been in
the 1990s. Unlike the almost paralytic angst of Europe's midcentury, America's fin de siècle was energetic in its pursuit of
surcease. It also was fairly bold in its exploration of contiguous
subsets of ideas. Before a new and light-suffused basis for moral
formation and spiritual travel could be entirely trustworthy,
though, one had to know more about the darkness, both present
and past. One had to know more from those who had traveled in
it, those who had taken up residence there, those who had simply studied the agents of governance there.

It made perfect sense, therefore, that books like Elaine
Pagels's *The Origin of Satan* and Andrew Delbanco's *The Death of
Satan: How Americans Have Lost the Sense of Evil* both made best-
seller lists when they were published in 1995. One was fairly ac-
ademic, and the other, more popularly accessible in its telling;
but between them, they managed to cast a broad net across
America's reading needy. Less than a year later, in March 1996,
Dennis Covington hit the lists with what, at first blush, would

seem to have been the most unlikely of strong sellers. The book was *Salvation on Sand Mountain: Snake Handling and Redemption in Southern Appalachia,* and first blushes have never been more wrong. *Salvation's* success, like that of its predecessors, made its own perfect sense, because it added a missing piece. It brought to the investigation the experiential evidence and testimony of those who live among us presently, but in an almost premodernist milieu.

What Pagels and Delbanco and Covington really did, of course, was no more than open a conversation that was to occupy American thought for years to come. They and those who followed them recognized . . . or perhaps just intuited . . . or perhaps just experienced themselves . . . the restless need to go in and see. How much of what terrifies a child about his grandfather's basement will still terrify the adult who revisits it? How much of that dirt-floored and dirt-walled excavation will be dry and cool and efficacious in the storing of food for the winter? How much filled with abandoned tools worthy of repair? How much a burial ground for things and lives better forgotten? How much a tunnel into other places where fear and the fearing have sought sanctuary? What, my children, what of the darkness?

For almost a century, those questions, certainly not new ones in humanity's experience of itself, had been relegated to the still-fresh discipline of psychology. But when the talk of spirituality became common parlance across class and geographic lines and our concern with it a questing one, the perceived area of investigation had to be broadened. For talk of spirituality—even for spirituality itself—to be valid, it must assume some locus beyond the human psyche. And if there is a locus, then there is a creator for it or a landlord of it or, at the very least, a principle of governance present within it. Jack Miles effectively initiated that piece of the investigation at a popular level in 1995 with his brashly titled *God: A Biography.* Not only did the book make essentially every list and book column in the country, but it went on to win the Pulitzer Prize in 1996. Those who had not been offended by the audacity of Miles's title were offended by the presumption implicit in it; and both groups were vociferously offended when the book won a Pulitzer not in history but in biography, the category it had so irreverently claimed for itself.

But offended or not, readers and seekers read; and far more than a provocative title was the reason behind their reading. Miles had opened up the next stage of our national conversation about the history and constitution of personae who, being other than us, still operate within our perceived geographies of body, mind, and spirit. In approaching God as a subject susceptible to biography — Miles insisted that his was a literary and not a theological inquiry — Miles also marked — or maybe just legitimized — the start of a new direction in Jesus studies as well. Popularly received books, after Miles's and including his own *Christ: A Crisis in the Life of God*, would increasingly often treat biographically the holy men, women, and occasionally ideas of the Torah and the Old Testament. Even the canons themselves became proper subjects of quasi-biographical investigation for those trying to rediscover sacred word as the divine living and alive within history.

There can be little doubt that the business of trying to know the other-than-human agencies alive in the realm of the spiritual can be pursued very effectively by means of biography; but that method of analysis and engagement is as applicable to our order of creatures as it is to the extrahuman one. At least that would seem to be the conventional wisdom among American readers. From 1993, when Kathleen Norris published *Dakota: A Spiritual Geography*, right up to the present moment, there has been a steady flow not only of spiritual biographies but also of what *Dakota* really is, spiritual autobiographies. Travelers together encouraging one another and warning one another, yes; but more important, travelers addressing one another with a subjective candor that could never have accrued even a half century ago.

If autobiography was a major tool of spiritual research in the 1990s, so too was science, and most especially physics and the cognitive sciences. In fact, as the shelves in Lucy grew in number at an alarmingly rate, it was obvious even to Sam, as the carpenter on the job, that I and/or religion had left our traditional turfs and were coming very close to occupying his as physician and scientist. The whole twentieth century had pivoted on science, of course. It had opened portentously with the anguished cries of "Error most foul" pouring from millions of anti-Darwinists, and matters had gone straight downhill from there for several decades.

The tension between an established body of religious thought and a burgeoning, exhilarating, irrefutable, and highly practical body of discoveries about ourselves and our physical universe was as intellectually ridiculous at the time as it is now in retrospect, primarily because, as Yogi Berra would say, it was déjà vu all over again. We clearly had forgotten Copernicus and lost all memory of Galileo. That having been said, it is still true that theology changes slowly for good reason. To change theology is to adjust the rope and change the berthing of the boat; and to move too quickly in that endeavor is to risk damaging the hull and the sailors as well as the cable tethering them.

By the mid-1990s, as my shelves were filling up with popular trade books about belief in a time of astro- and nuclear physics, I found myself buying—an act that really did fill Sam with consternation—buying popular books on physics in order that I might have some hope of understanding what was going on in religion. The people writing the science-and-religion titles I was handling and the people who were reading them had largely been born and educated in the latter half of the century. I, on the other hand, had not. When I took physics, Einstein was still very much alive, and his ideas largely still privileged. Beyond that, when I took physics, in the late 1940s, girls in the main didn't do that . . . at least ladylike ones did not. As a result, I was the only female in a class of thirteen; and as a result of that distracting disproportion, I have always regarded my understanding of even basic physics as a bit suspect.

But I did not have to have a huge command of physics, much less any of chaos mathematics—thank God—to understand in 1994 the message patent in what Frank Tipler was telling me and all the rest of us in *The Physics of Immortality*. A professor of mathematical physics at Tulane, he was talking Omega Point Theory and the, to him, clear mathematics behind the inevitability of end-time and resurrection. What he was declaring as well, beyond his equations and conclusions, was that one who had begun as an atheist had ended as a believer, convicted by the pursuit of pure science. What he was also asserting was that the best theology of our time was being done not in seminaries or departments of philosophy, but in physics laboratories. Tipler not only carried that message cogently, he also carried it in so populist a manner that *Omni* made him and his work the subject of a major feature in its sixteenth anniversary issue.

Certainly, Tipler's was and is only one voice in at least a hundred equally prominent and articulate ones I could cite from those days. He is significant, though, and I often cite him as proof text, primarily because his mathematics . . . that is, because a good 250 pages of *Immortality* . . . are so obtuse and intricate that there is no way anybody short of a professional mathematician could comprehend their argument, much less their elegance; yet . . . yet those pages sold. They sold and they reverberated, because the need was there. And the need was not, I submit, for the mathematics that Tipler's pages contain, but rather for the witness they bore: Those who would save their souls, serve their God, and know meaning in their own self-presence can find assurance here that what theology has a stranglehold on is not God, but dogma.

That sense of permission to move with relative impunity into whole bodies of new information about the universe and humanity's role within it has been hard-won, and only a fool would think that history will write of us that one or two scientists or one or two books effected it for the rest of us. History will say, however, that as surely as a growing accommodation between science and religion was a hallmark of the 1990s, so too was the work of men and women like Sir John Templeton or Father John Polkinghorne or Kitty Ferguson or Huston Smith central during those years to the emancipation of the spiritual seeker from the tyranny of the no longer credible. Templeton, a financier's financier, even went so far as to establish in the mid-1990s a publishing house, Templeton Foundation Press, for the express purpose of producing popular trade books about the holy interplay between science and religion. The well-pursed Templeton Prize for Progress in Religion is likewise Sir John's doing and is awarded each year to that person whose work has best exemplified or advanced the lived interface between fact and faith. But the physics of our universe, both small and great, was only one part of the battle waiting to be won.

Chapter 40

• • •

Because of the efforts of influential and credentialed believers and because of the corrective effect of a century of
democratized information, the integration of physics and astron-
omy and mathematics with the stories of religion was a work already well in progress when the new millennium came. As the
calendar rolled from the 1900s to the 2000s, though, it was fairly
easy to see, even from a farm in Lucy, Tennessee, that the work
of integrating religion and physics might just pale before the face
of what was to be required of us next. If the discoveries and theories of physics and its complementary disciplines had described
and determined the twentieth century, the cognitive sciences and
all the disciplines subsumed under that label were going to define
and determine the twenty-first. It is they that will give order and
quantitative description to the post-Cartesian questions we have
to solve, if we want ever to move on in our religious formation.

A historian someday will look at the exploration of consciousness in the twenty-first century and date its beginning, if
not from the ancients or Descartes or even David Hume in the
eighteenth century, then certainly from the mid-1970s. Broadly

speaking, he or she will be correct. For those of us working in the trenches where ideas impact popular thinking and therefore the naves, synagogues, and mosques of America, however, the whole thing really began in 1993 and went backward from there to pick up what had been said but not assimilated.

In early 1993, a man named Peter Kramer published a book called *Listening to Prozac: A Psychiatrist Explores Mood-Altering Drugs and the New Meaning of Self*. If someone were to ask me to name the hundred books that, in my dozen years of watching religion publishing, have most shaped our situation as we enter the twenty-first century, I would have to list *Prozac* as one of them, though it never one time came across my desk for review or any other kind of professional attention. None of us, including *Prozac*'s publisher, I suspect, knew at that time what an impact it would have on believing and religious America, though the subtitle admittedly should have given us a clue of sorts.

By August 1993, *Christianity Today*, the premier magazine for America's Evangelical Protestant Christians, found its readers so neck-deep in Kramer and *Prozac* that it did a cover feature on him and his book. The problem was . . . and here words fail even the professional writer in me . . . the problem was one of exquisite pain. To use the old crutch of "If I had a dollar bill for every time . . . ," the truth is that if I had a dollar bill for every tear that has been shed (a fair number of them in my presence or on my commandeered shoulder) about the drug Prozac, I could build a cathedral. It may sound foolish to those who do not intentionally engage God every day for guidance in the governance of every part of life, but to many devout Christians who do, Prozac and Kramer's book touting it were either God's greatest kindness since salvation or Satan's cruelest joke since Eden.

Depression is rampant in America, and the religious are no more immune than any other group. As a disease, depression changes who one is to one's self . . . to one's consciousness of one's self . . . and turns one's interior into a frozen hell burning, like Dante's, with hoarfrost, stalactites, and tormentors. Prozac, for many so afflicted, relieves that paralyzing pain and releases the sufferer back into normal, functioning life. If, however, one goes from even mild depression to release from it, one cannot avoid perceiving that he or she is, as we say colloquially, "a different person."

What do those words, so casually said, really mean? And who or what is the *real* "person" in this exercise of differentness? What is the relationship between conscious perception of one's self and one's actual self? Between one's conscious perception and one's soul? If I block what I feel by drugging it, am I in any way different from an alcoholic who does the same thing? Do I not thereby block the voice of God coming in to tell me something about my life and how I need to change it? Can God mean for me to hurt this way? But on the other hand, how can I know the voice of God except through my consciousness? What is consciousness, by the way? And who am I with or without it? Oh, mercy! Mercy! Lord, have mercy!

As the sales of *Listening to Prozac* increased and then increased again, so too did the ubiquity of the questions and the torment to which they gave voice. More pastors than I ever want to know about, much less engage in debate, apparently counseled that consciousness is God's territory and not to be messed with under any circumstances or by any means. The faithful must soldier on, they taught, and find in prayer and fortitude the instructive purposes and message of their pain. Many of those who wept with me had been so counseled, of course. But many—maybe more—of them who wept were men and women whose pain had driven them to seize the relief offered, but who, having also heard the pastors, now feared for their souls even as they continued to use Prozac or one of its pharmaceutical cousins.

To appreciate the reach of what I am saying here, one must understand that when I speak publicly, I speak almost always on the sociology of religion. By its very definition, that is not an intimate or emotional or personal subject and, as a result, not one that attracts the nonthinker or the uneducated. The people whom I have listened to and sometimes held after those lectures are not stupid people, nor are they unprivileged or intellectually lightweight. Quite the contrary; they are thoughtful, most of them empowered, informed, and deeply frightened . . . frightened, as was the early twentieth century, by the abyss between what science can do and what religion can consecrate. The difference now is that the abyss is interior rather than exterior, experiential rather than theoretical or mechanical.

When I say that after Kramer, America's popular intelligence began going backward to pick up the pieces, I mean that the cognitive-studies work—commercially published—of men like Daniel Dennett and Douglas Hofstadter and Sir Roger Penrose and the indefatigable Edward O. Wilson began to enter more broadly into the general conversation. In 1981, Hofstadter and Dennett had published *The Mind's I*, a kind of opening salvo that was more understood and incorporated after the fact than originally by its lay readers. In 1991, Dennett, the director of the Center for Cognitive Studies at Tufts, published *Consciousness Explained*, its thrust toward materialistic argument fairly obvious in its title. And then, in 1995, came *Darwin's Dangerous Idea*, which took on "evolution and the meanings of life."

E. O. Wilson had already published *On Human Nature* in 1978, and his *Consilience: The Unity of Knowledge* in 1998 was an even more popularly read and influential contribution to the role of evolution in who we are as conscious intelligences. When Antonio Damasio of the University of Illinois published his *Descartes' Error: Emotion, Reason, and the Human Brain* in 1995, he supplied the tools of informed speculation for bright but ordinary readers. As if that were not enough, in 1999 he published his controversial *The Feeling of What Happens: Body and Emotions in the Making of Consciousness* to an ever-increasing readership. Even the still fairly difficult science of men like Stuart Hameroff of the University of Arizona is finding, like Tipler's mathematics, sympathetic popular audiences not only through blogs, print articles, and books but also through movies like *What the #@%*# Do We Know?*, the 2004 independent film turned mainstream by a fascinated public. Certainly, the *Toward a Science of Consciousness* collections that Hameroff has edited are influential now and, one must assume, also predictive of the eventual power of his work to inform lay thought and self-understanding.

To list even a few of the more present popularizers and enablers in a public conversation as dynamic and roiling as the current one on the nature of consciousness, the self, and, by natural extension, the soul is dangerous, and I know that. Anybody trying it runs the very real risk of appearing foolish more for his or her omissions than for the inclusions made. The effort here is not so much to be exhaustive, however, as to establish the scope of the discussion, which, case in point, has become so substantive that Amazon.com now posts a "Listmania" of "Mind and Brain Books" for its customers' convenience.

More than circumscribing the scope of the discussion, though, the intent here is to establish the location of the discussion about what are the linchpin questions of god-talk in this new century. The questions about what exactly are our constituent parts . . . the drive for more defensible definitions for constructs like mind or soul or consciousness or spirit . . . the determination of the responsibilities and nature of the will or intentional processes in all of this . . . the projection onto the divine and the private engagement of it in view of such radically altered understanding of our subjective structure . . . these and their inevitable corollaries, while not always worded so specifically, are part of water-cooler conversation; and the books that fuel and inform them are part of reading America's dens and bedroom night tables. That is what makes the difference . . . that, and where the questions are *not* being discussed and the books provoking and guiding them are *not* being read. The silence in the halls of ecclesia is more deafening than the murmuring in our streets.

Chapter 41

• • •

The shifting piles of books and articles in the old garage during the mid-1990s, and the categories of ideas and practices they represented seem now, in memory, to have been a living environment that tolerated me only so long as I did not impose myself or my preconceptions upon it. I earnestly hope that, in this case at least, memory is correct. If, though, my reporting of the patterns I was tracking in those days was, in the main, not compromised by my own opinions or desires, the reason is less my sworn intention toward objectivity and more the result of circumstance.

"Circumstance," when used as a pack animal to convey the otherwise inexplicable or the untouchable, almost always makes me edgy, especially when I am the one using it. Like a mirror that won't lie, it shows me what I am hesitant . . . or just simply ill-prepared or untrained . . . to receive into my working metaphysics. Having been reared as a Presbyterian and therefore as a Calvinist (I bolted straight to the more pliant theology of the Episcopal Church at seventeen, two weeks after I left home for college) has done nothing to diminish my fear of "circumstance," the word, and of the muddy thinking it permits.

It was circumstance, a secularist would say, that brought Michael Leach and me together, but I doubt it; or at least I doubt the impersonal and accidental tone implicit in stating the matter that way. Not for one minute do I believe that Michael and I lacked direction in our meeting or in our subsequent work together. Unquestionably, either or both of us individually could have chosen not to go through any number of prior and requisite doors, thereby preventing our ever even having met. I am sure of that. Instead, something so seemly capricious as his and/or my having chosen Door A instead of Door B on multiple, earlier occasions led eventually to our being able to go through other doors together.

The intricate lacework of interlocking possibilities that comes from that kind of thinking defies human conceptualization . . . which does not mean that it even faintly troubles the divine one, however. So I have no trouble saying that by the machinations of multiple choices approaching the oxymoronic state of directed chaos, Mike Leach and I arrived at a working relationship, the end results of which were consecrated by the means and methods of their coming about.

I have no trouble with that theologically or humanly, because, so far as I can tell, *Re-Discovering the Sacred* and then, immediately after it, *God-Talk in America* hurt no one, rose up out of no one else's pain, and presumably even did some good by clarifying and informing as well as liberating. I know beyond any shadow of a doubt that those projects were good for both me and my stacks. That is, I know that writing books of reportage about religion in late-twentieth-century America kept me honest in a way that I could never have achieved sans their presence in my life and my garage during those critical years. If one is going to write, especially in book form, about something so freighted as religion and its constantly changing contours, one had better be damned sure that there is some support for his or her commentary. I learned early on that while I might be wrong about something and would be genuinely regretful as a result, I would be far more regretful, compromised, and downright embarrassed if I could not cite some sort of credible underpinnings for my error.

Knowing, as I wrote both *Re-Discovering* and *God-Talk*, that
what I was saying to the world beyond the farm was only as valid
as what the piles of books and clippings around me could testify
to meant that I approached those piles not as the guru or teacher,
but as the seeker and the taught. "Tell me," I would say to them
each morning before I began another day's writing; and they did.
I am grateful . . . more grateful than I can say, actually . . . and
therefore loath to lay so great a gift at the feet of Circumstance.
The other brake upon my own fancifulness or enthusiasms is not
so easy to lay elsewhere, however, for it involves hideous pain
and another's loss.

Chapter 42

• • •

In 1986, Douglas Paschall, professor of literature at the University of the South and, by common agreement, the dean of Tennessee letters, assembled an anthology of works by Tennessee writers entitled *HomeWords*. The publisher was the University of Tennessee Press, the sponsor was the Tennessee Arts Commission, and the occasion was a statewide celebration of Tennessee herself, called "Tennessee Homecoming—'86." It was, to put it colloquially, a very big deal, the "it" being both the year-long celebration and the book.

Long after the banners and bands were forgotten, though, the book lived on and continued to be read. Since such a thing had never been tried before, I think it is fair to say that most of us involved in Doug's project were a little surprised, as well as a lot pleased, by how much our fellow citizens, fellow southerners, and fellow literati nationally applauded the book and its unusual lens of statehood and political occasion for viewing and discerning an aesthetic.

Given the response to *HomeWords*, it seemed almost—this word, again—almost predestined that the Arts Commission and

University of Tennessee Press would want Doug to do another, perhaps more extensive, collection. Nineteen ninety-six was to be the bicentennial of Tennessee's statehood. It would also be the tenth anniversary of *HomeWords'* publication. Producing a new compendium as part of the bicentennial and the anniversary seemed an inspired idea that served well the purposes of all the parties involved. The decision to go forward was finalized in early 1993, but by 1994 Doug still had done little or nothing about it. A few letters of invitation had gone out, but many of those were not even being followed up on. No one could understand. All too soon, however, the reason was obvious. Douglas Paschall, beloved and honored and necessary leader, was ill. He died of pancreatic cancer that Christmas, the project still burning in his mind right up almost to the end.

Before Doug died and during one of his last "good days," Alice Swanson, director of the Literary Arts Program for the Tennessee Arts Commission, made an afternoon trip to see him. While she was there, Doug, with the narcotics pump working away in his side and his attention already dulled beyond much conversation by pain and drugs, gave her such files as he had managed to accumulate before illness overtook him. Alice took those two boxes back to her office in Nashville and then called me. "There's nothing," she said, "nothing here." And then she corrected herself. "Actually, there's just enough here so it's going to be harder than if there were just nothing."

Alice was, and is, a much loved and much appreciated colleague as well as a personal friend. I don't think there was ever any doubt in either of our minds that between us we were going to try to finish what Doug had begun, and on schedule. The only hope we had of accomplishing that, though, was for her to take on the lion's share of the administrative load through her office in Nashville and for me, in a sense, to reactivate St. Luke's for the few, harried months between us and the posted publication date of May 1996.

What had to be reactivated at my end of things was not the suprastructure of a publishing house; the University of Tennessee was supplying that. Rather, what was needed were all the old contacts, all the files of phone numbers and addresses and data of easy access, all the credibility of an established track record. What was needed as well was something I hadn't used in over seven years. What was needed was editorial instinct. The rush that only editors know when what is being read is playing with perfect pitch in your head or . . . most blessed of all for an anthology editor . . . when what is in your hands and head tells you its notes can also be a discrete and complementary motif within the greater symphony.

We made our deadline, Alice and I; and *Home Works: A Book of Tennessee Writers* was published, only three weeks late, in June 1996. We had them all—or most of them, anyway: Shelby Foote and Andrew Lytle, Nikki Giovanni and Coleman Barks, Stanley Booth, Abraham Verghese, Alan Lightman and Madison Smartt Bell, Steve Stern, Charles Wright, Cathie Pelletier and Sharyn McCrumb, John Egerton and Will Campbell. There were 108 of them in toto, and they covered the bases in genre and voice and age. Many of them had scattered to other parts of the continent; but all of them were still working and all of them still bore Tennessee in their blood and their aesthetic. It was glorious. It had also been instructive.

The opportunity to once more work and think professionally in terms of art and purity of voice instead of dogma and orthodoxy had certainly been balm to me personally. Like the emotional relief of being delivered from overmuch religious fervor by the sheer distraction of the constitutionally unfettered, *Home-Works* had also helped buy me the distance I needed to walk more judiciously up and down that twenty-two-inch wide path from garage door to kitchen steps. When I would veer toward dishonesty or just plain misinterpretation and weariness, if *Re-Discovering* or *God-Talk* did not pull me back, then art did . . . art that, with its avowed refusal to accept moral preconceptions, was just beginning in the mid-1990s to rejoin the general conversation about religion in subtly new ways.

As I had rolled my office chair back and forth from anthology work to *PW* copy that was constantly on deadline in those days to my breviary at the appointed canonical hours to *God-Talk*'s accumulating chapters, I had rolled my attention and my working affection in and out of at least a half dozen distinct jurisdictions within the vast and largely uncharted world of subjectivity. So does anyone who encounters art at a hands-on, working level. When subjectivity itself is the area of exploration, though, art can appear to be a tool, not a jurisdiction. It can fool the eye into seeing it as a secure and safely traveled bridge between the profane and the holy. The error is that there are no safe bridges into the holy. The question of the origin of art has existed within the community of artists and philosophers since the beginning of recorded history. By 1995 and '96, though, the question had wandered . . . or at least some undisciplined tendrils of it had wandered . . . out from the site of its original planting. All the traditional and well-worn dialectics about art and its sources had, by then, begun to morph into water-cooler conversations about the relationship between spirituality and creativity. By mid-decade, discussion groups and conferences on the subject were rampant. By century's end, such sessions had become almost canonized as holy investigations not of the originating question, but of how to exercise a craft as a means toward intercourse with the sacred. The problems inherent in that kind of dialogue are myriad and, for the writer in me, oppressive.

Pursuing any creative activity stills the attention and, assuming the desire of the pursuit is already turned toward engaging the divine, invites a heightened awareness of the intangible. There is no question about that. Such an employment, by default, though, is already directed toward a spiritual or religious end rather than toward an aesthetic one. There is considerable hazard, however, in confusing art with craft, not to mention in equating the aberrant madness involved in art with the creative intentionality of crafts or applied art. Even if that were not true, discussions about the relationship between creativity and spirituality can never be unrestricted discussions about the sources of art, simply because the wording of the question itself already prejudices toward its desired conclusions. All of which is by way of being a confession, I suppose. The truth is that, like too enthusiastic an analysis of "circumstance," too casual an analysis of human creativity makes me edgy because, as any proper Tennessean would tell you, "Thar be bars in them woods." And during the months of 1994 and the spring of 1995, Tennessee writers had kept me inoculated with liberal injections of Tennessee caution about both the bears and the woods.

Chapter 43

• • •

Few—if, indeed, any—major shifts in human affairs occur without harbingers. Assigning a date to such a thing and saying, "Aha! Here it is, and here is where it happened" is always a bit simplistic, yet simplicity also has its economies. One of the major shifts in religion in the closing years of the last century was a growing acceptance of entertainment as a proper means of doing theology. As a shift, this one has had several faces and many children. Like dating the breakthrough of cognitive science into popular awareness by the publication of *Listening to Prozac* and moving back from there, I (and a lot of other commentators, for that matter) find it useful, if not exactly precise, to date the shift toward entertainment from 1994 and the institution of *Touched by an Angel*.

Touched by An Angel is the chosen point of departure for a number of reasons, not the least of them being the show's intentionality within the purview of pop culture. By 1994, television had certainly had its successful religion-oriented moments. Joseph Campbell's PBS work with Bill Moyers on *The Power of Myth* had established the fact that America would embrace well-done and informative religion programming, a fact that Moyers's work continues to confirm. In addition, there had been, from time to time, individual episodes of popular, entertainment-oriented television that dealt with a religion theme or issue. None of these is the same, however, as having two ordained ministers—in this case, Della Reese and her producer—deliberately choose to engage the world of faith by means of fiction in an electronic medium geared to prime time.

The most immediately obvious difference was one of the sheer range of impact. Every Sunday evening "god-talk" was going on in America's living rooms . . . at one point, in almost a half of America's TV-watching living rooms . . . without regard to whether those living rooms were in Bel Air or the local trailer park. Reese had managed to cut across all the usual divisions of class and education and geography. She had, in effect, burrowed right down to the mother lode that is humanity's need to believe and then had begun to mine it for all it was worth to her as an ordained and pastoral believer.

Story is as old as religion, and some would say religion even has its origins in story. There is nothing new in that. And when it comes to matters of theology, one of story's great uses traditionally has been the very fact that it is susceptible to as many interpretations as it has hearers. There is nothing new in that either. What was new, however, was the vast reach of story when it is done electronically and the resultant "discovery," as it were, of mass-produced story as a vehicle for proselytizing and/or homogenizing. Now story, turned toward an end other than itself and dressed in the guise of entertainment, if it were well crafted, could enter a pluralistic culture and become a persuasive salesman for a predetermined perspective on God, angelic agencies, sin, human salvation, and any number of other such issues.

The implications of all this were enormous for television and those who produced their shows by means of it, whether that meant commercially as with *Angel* or even, a decade later, *Joan of Arcadia* or independently as with, for example, *Veggie Tales*. The music industry had, of course, been one of the heralds and agents of change here, "Christian" music and concerts having begun more than a decade earlier to employ secular means and popular sounds for religious purposes. But movies were to become the most dramatic example of all. Here too there had, of course, been prior warning.

The French film critic André Bazin once observed that "Cinema has always been interested in God." He was far more correct than even he knew, though he did not live to see that validation. By the closing years of the millennium, America's theaters were flooded with religion-oriented movies: *Seven, The Truman Show, American Beauty, Dogma, Magnolia* — the list goes on; but by 1999, the list comes to *The Matrix*, and *The Matrix* (along with its sequels) is pure god-talk. Film had, in essence, taken pride of place over nonfiction as a vehicle for initiating, informing, and furnishing a whole new bank of common reference points for god-talk in America. The implications of that were enormous for the book business as well as for the film industry.

As the general public became more and more accustomed to receiving religious, theological, and doctrinal formation through entertainment, the growth in religion fiction became almost pathological in rate. What had begun in the late 1970s as a few simple, straightforward tales of nonerotic romance ("The bosom heaves, but the bodice doesn't rip" was, and remains, the standard description among publishers and booksellers) and faith-oriented western paperbacks had grown by the late 1980s to a flow of innocuous paperbacks. If hardly substantial, that stream of books was still well defined enough to position itself in the market under the rubric of "Christian Fiction" as a way of signaling its Protestant bias and evangelical intention. By the mid-1990s, however, the stream was swelling into a river that was on its way to flood tide.

In 1995, a pair of writers — actually a writer, Jerry Jenkins, and a popular, evangelical, and heavily apocalyptic preacher named Tim LaHaye — published through an, at that time, relatively small, Protestant Christian house the first in a series of a projected twelve novels. Taking the series approach is standard operating procedure in Christian fiction, so initially there seemed little worthy of note in the birthing of yet another run of novels within that marketing approach. Beyond that, 1995, midway as it was of the last decade of a passing millennium, was already beginning to feel the titillation, as well as the half fears, of endtimes. The end was coming, the end if not of creation, then of something we all had known and come to understand as the second millennium of the common era. It was exhilarating and troubling and as near to Halloween spooky as most adults could ever remember a thing being in their maturity. Given that half-pleasurable, half-anxious attitude at large in the general culture, the fact that a preacher of end-times doctrine had decided to go public through fiction with his message of 666, the Beast, and Armageddon likewise made perfect sense. What made no sense, at least at first blush, was what happened after that.

The Jenkins-LaHaye title for their series was Left Behind or, as the novels are popularly called now, The Left Behinds. From the beginning, the individual books had projected tantalizing, theologically teasing titles like *Soul Survivor* and *Armageddon* and *Desecration*. And from the beginning they sold as no other series of books ever has before or since. Within less than a decade, seventy million units of the novels and their spin-offs had been sold into an American market that was . . . that was what?

In the 1990s, one of the things most happily overlooked in popular thinking about religion in America was the subtle but growing divergence between the observant Christian American and the Christianized American; the increasing difference, as the scholar Philip Jenkins would say over and over again, between Christianity and Christendom; the ever-greater distinction between the growth of Christianity and the growth of a cultural construct not necessarily requiring religious observance, but operating within the mythic context of the culture's dominant religion.

Thus, by 2003 approximately 83 percent of Americans could, with sincerity and without apology, tell demographers that they believed in the doctrine of the Virgin Birth of Jesus. Since only about 84 percent of Americans claimed Christianity as their active faith at that time and given that the Virgin Birth was one of the most, if not the most, divisive and hotly debated issues within postmodern Christianity, there would seem to have been a rather obvious disconnect between the two figures. Or there would have until one realized that over 40 percent of those who claimed allegiance to the doctrine of the Virgin Birth were unchurched. Indeed, some 17 percent of them were self-avowed atheists. Why then accept as an operative premise something that is alien to one's beliefs? Because the Virgin Birth is not alien.

The Virgin Birth empowers Christmas, this culture's major holiday; it enshrines the holy feminine toward which we all turn in distress; it images the best, emotionally, of moral purity, compassion, and divine tragedy. It is, in short, as unassailable and incontestable within the patterns of the culture as it is distressing and assailable among many of those who address it as integral to their doctrinal progress. It is, in short, a clear example of the needs of the cultural Christian as distinct from those of the observant Christian. So, too, is Apocalypse, that arresting belief that at some time this thing we call creation will end in a great holocaust of fire and falling stars and earthquakes and demons set loose from the chambers of Hell. So, too, is the memory, half nostalgic, of a spiritual fear that once upon a time corrected a man's course and held a woman's true.

The Left Behinds sold, in other words, but not always and/or only to Christians. By the closing years of the 1990s, merchant after merchant had begun to say something like "You know, I can't ask a customer his or her personal faith when they're standing in front of me at the cash register; but I know enough about enough of my customers to know that a bunch of them who're buying The Left Behinds aren't any more Christian than they are stupid."

"So, why?" I asked a time or two, until I began to perceive my question as itself being stupid.

"Because," the answer always was, "because they're a good, Stephen King kind of story that's a lot more likely to actually happen." And in 2002, for the first time since the keeping of such records began, a Christian novel was the best-selling book of the year across all genres and all lines. The Left Behinds were not, in any way, being left behind. A new era in American god-talk, in its vehicles of expression and its rhetoric of choice, had been born.

It would be inaccurate, however, to leave the matter here without noting that, as with *The Matrix* and the changes it both exemplified and empowered, so too with The Left Behinds. Other Christian writers, like Jan Karon with her Mitford series, for instance, began to amass huge popular readerships and sales by fashioning fiction that spoke equally to the cultural Christian and the observant one. Other books, like Anita Diamant's *The Red Tent*, for instance, did much the same thing through variations upon the same theme, in Diamant's case by speaking to both contemporary Judaism and its cultural analogue of American Judeo-Christianity.

There was more to the story than that, though. As the public's acceptance of religion as a suitable subject for entertainment fiction had grown, so too had the storytellers, whether screenwriters or print novelists, grown bolder in what they dared. Entertainment that occupied itself with the exploration of faith and belief shifted, bit by bit, ever more toward fantasy for its conventions. It was so much easier to treat the definitions of good and evil, and all the theories about the sources of both, and the unanswerable questions about the relationship between the two, not to mention our yearning for heroes in a time of confusion, or the loss of our clarity in a real world of conflicting values . . . so much easier and so much safer and, truth told, so much more effecting . . . to speak in fantasy.

Let Narnia be reconsidered. Let *The Lord of the Rings* speak of Frodo and teach us about our world by exposing us to that of Middle-earth. Let Harry Potter draw the lines clear once more, and let the manga depths of the graphic novel bring back to us the comfort of holy heroes. Let Philip Pullman instruct us in his dark materials and in the salvation that lies on the other side of the hellish destruction of what has been and can no longer be sustained. And through it all, like a lovely, soothing, violent melody, the threading constant of a kind of neo- or pseudo-medievalism.

The questions of the Enlightenment—the questions that had engendered and then enabled Western technology and intellectual prowess—were no longer the questions of the popular imagination. The questions now were about what could not be deconstructed, what could not be analyzed into its parts, what could not be at all, except through the mysteries of divinely held chaos and relational existence. The questions once more were about the thin places, about what one sometimes catches briefly out of the corner of one's eye. The questions were about God as magnificent and angels and devils as present and violence as a holy endeavor. And the last place we had engaged those questions with rigor and attention had been the Middle Ages. By the change of the millennium, we were well on our way back to that place where last we had lived all those things. We were going home again, home, even if briefly, to a sensibility that knows without conjuring or discipline that there is more than we can see and that it wants us.

Chapter 44

• • •

Like many another Appalachian native of my age group, I grew up on the often-repeated, often-heard adage of "God doth provide." Such a frequency of use arose, at least in part, from the Calvinism—my mother called it fatalism—pervasive in almost all of the South during those years. Part of its frequent employment was due, I am sure, to the experientially realized truth contained in the words themselves. The connection between today's unanticipated need and the uncanny mercy patent in yesterday's having provided the tools with which to meet it is usually clearer in mountain light than in urban haze.

Despite those geographic and cultural circumstances, however, among the adults of my childhood "God doth provide," as often as not, was neither a statement of resignation nor an observation upon natural providence. Rather, it was a confession of faith, simply and unself-consciously stated in the patois of that place and time. Like a stele in the courtyard of their hearts, there stood in most of those men and women the sure knowledge that God is. Everything else was merely that: everything else. What was in the physical life could never be more (or less) than the waxing and waning and waxing again of life's means, but the core itself was immutable and always. It was in that immutability that God provides for humanity and out of it that, for them, He must be reverenced.

I spent years of my younger life trying to dissect or deconstruct or, perhaps, just disrespect any bent of personality that could declare itself so formulaically and so frequently. Later, in early adulthood, "God doth provide" came to be for me not only cloyingly pious, but also embarassingly naive about how the larger world really parsed things beyond the unanimity of the mountains. Then, as I grew older, the principal adage of my beginnings became for me like Pollyanna-speak at its most dangerous and most insensitive levels. It smacked of a kind of exhibitionist exposure of one's own private space or else, and worse, a deliberate, evangelical intrusion into the private space of another. Only by living into late maturity have I come where I am now: full circle, humbler, and as aware as were my forebears that God provides, albeit in not always immediately apparent ways.

The Farm In Lucy, even as it morphed for me into more and more of a rural sanctuary from which to do the city's business, did not cease to be a farm. Or at least it did not cease to be subject to all the physical rewards and dangers that go with farms. Among the more obnoxious and odious, if rather minor, of the latter is the chronic infestation of one's fields, from March until late November, by ticks. Ticks, in fact, constitute another one of those "If I had a nickel for every time . . ." parts of my life. The children, when they were living here, routinely did a check on themselves and each other after every excursion out to the fields. I still do a check on Lucy, the coon dog, every day or two. And in the sill of the kitchen window there sits, and probably always will, a disgusting juice glass filled two-thirds of the way up with a hypertonic solution of salt and dozens of tick bodies pickled and floating in it. I rinse the bodies out every few days in the summer and add salt to the toxin of their extermination chamber, but I long since gave up on any other means for disposing of them. Grab a tick, pull surgically, carry same to the windowsill glass, watch with relish as it struggles for less than ten seconds, and then go back to work, because this particular show is over. If such seems ghoulish, you need to live my reality. The Farm In Lucy is not Walt Disney's world.

There is also now a certain amount of personal animus in my tick routine, a kind of long-standing pleasure in seeing my species outlast theirs at least one more time, even though I know my victory may be snatched from the jaws of their defeat at any moment, and indeed probably will be. Sometime in late May or early June 1994—neither Sam nor I can remember which—I got busy and forgot to do the tick-check routine until I was ready to take my morning shower. There, right where the waistband of my jeans had kept it safe, was a handsomely fat tick that had obviously been feasting all night on whatever I had had to offer. When they are full like that, but not quite glutted enough to fall off by themselves, ticks are truly a nuisance to remove. Squeeze one of the things the wrong way or too hard, and blood goes everywhere. Which explains why, if I cannot remember when, I nonetheless can most certainly remember how I got him off (ticks are always "he"), because I had to do a double contortion to see him in the bedroom mirror while removing him without rupture. After that, on to the windowsill and the tick's final, abbreviated bath. That was that.

Sometime later, the time being again unclear, I developed a rash of sorts all around the place where I had been bitten. Sam and I remember now with a sad mixture of incredulity and bemusement that I treated the rash with a dab or two of cortisone ointment. Nothing more. Tick-borne fevers in any of their multiple presentations and pathologies had not yet happened in our part of the world, or at least none had ever been reported. Never once did it occur to me or Sam, as it now does to every sportsman and farmer in western Tennessee, to worry about any consequence other than an annoying rash, much less to treat anything except the annoying rash. To give it its due, the redness went away and I, guilelessly, praised the cortisone ointment for its efficacy.

It was a Friday afternoon, mid-July and hot as only hell and western Tennessee can get. Almost three o'clock and time enough to get the mail before afternoon prayers. I was alone as usual at that time of day. The children were grown and gone, and nobody had ever heard of a doctor, much less a driven one like Sam Tickle, being at home in the middle of the afternoon on a working day. I trotted down to our mailbox happy as a clam at high tide, Friday being the most hopeful day of my week, as a rule. No phone to speak of on Saturday, and nine—ten if I was lucky—hours to play catch-up with my desk. I was lugging mail and more or less sorting it as I went when, suddenly, as dramatically as a sniper's bullet, it hit me.

Pain is never remembered, they say, and therefore never susceptible to being described. That seems to me a mercy now, for I would never, never wish to know again, even briefly, what that pain was. My head ripped apart and seemed to roll away from me, crashing onto the concrete driveway beneath me. I was almost as far up the driveway as my parked car, and I made it to the hood before I collapsed against it. Physicians' wives are not naive about the body and what can happen to it . . . wrong, sometimes, but not naive. I was wrong this time, because I could step out of my agony long enough to think, "Stroke!" and to say, "House." I do not remember making it back into my office, but I do remember that in the midst of the unbearable pain in my head, I could not breathe. Something was wrong with my heart, but whatever it was was secondary to my head. I remember as well that the Sam Tickle who never left the hospital before five or six o'clock on a working day suddenly came driving up the driveway, into the door I had managed to make it through, took one look at me, and said, "Something told me I should come home."

I don't know what he did. That part doctors' wives never quite get right anyway; but he did it . . . except for the head. I had a fever of 103 and I had a heart that was going all over the place with arrhythmia. In view of those two things, I suspect he ruled out stroke with the most cursory of neurological checks and then moved on, because I was much more likely to die of the heart than a headache at that point. He worked, the fever broke, the heart stabilized even if I didn't, and the headache pounded on. Saturday dawned hot and miserable, with my headache appeased a bit but still wretched. The fever rose and Sam beat it back down while my heart managed to behave normally. Sunday everything except the headache was better. Monday, Sam went to work, leaving behind cautionary instructions about being quiet, calling if I felt unwell, ignoring the headache, doing nothing, drinking the juice concoctions he had left for me, and so on. I made it all the way through lunch.

This time there was no stopping my heart, and I couldn't breathe. I somehow managed to punch in his beeper number, he saw our home number, and he was to me almost before I could understand what was happening. This time it was a wild ride into the emergency room. This time it was Dr. Tickle banging open doors, shouting orders, and pushing a gurney. I remember the roll of words from triage up the hall to wherever Sam was taking me of "My God, it's Dr. Tickle's wife," which is about all I remember, except the headache. I spent the next two days in cardiac care, wired to the wall by various things and at times weeping with a headache nobody thought it was safe just yet to treat. The fever was back and roaring, but its explanation was as illusive as swamp gas. Infection . . . obviously; from what . . . not so obvious.

Tuesday afternoon, Sam went over to the Department of Infectious Diseases at the university. He had always, even after going into full-time private practice, retained an adjunct teaching post at the university, but he had not yet met the new chairman of the Department of Infectious Diseases, a Yankee who had joined the faculty only a few weeks before. To this day, I do not know the man's name, but I do know I have never been happier to meet a Yankee. Sam asked if he would come look at me, the chairman agreed, and Wednesday morning he came. He came, that is, as far as the jamb of my CCU cubicle when, my chart open in his hand, he said to nobody and everybody, "It's tick fever, you fools. Give her tetracycline."

I got two capsules within ten minutes, and two more four hours later. Somewhere along the way and before I got two more, the headache went away . . . mercifully, mercifully away. By Thursday, Sam was grousing that we had acquired thousands of dollars of hospital bills only to come up with a disease that could be cured with capsules that cost thirteen cents each, retail. He was grousing because he was relieved and because both of us knew by then that there really was not going to be a cure. My heart would never be the same trustworthy thing it once had been.

We came home, and I rested about one full day before the itch to work again overwhelmed me. My desk was a disaster, as was the house and the farm and everything around them. How so few days can do such damage to orderliness and timeliness is beyond my comprehension. Not being stupid or willful, however, I paced myself, only to hit the ultimate irony that my heart's going into arrhythmia had no apparent relationship to anything within my conscious control. I went back into the emergency room once or twice over the next few months, but mainly I just grew anxious during them. I was not afraid of dying from this thing so much as I was paralyzed by my accumulating memories of the experience of drowning that always attended it. Dread, like an archdemon, entered my life, and I became absorbed with my own chest.

Never before in my life had I ever been so distracted by anxiety about my body. I found my preoccupation to not only be tedious as all get-out, but also destructive. I could give 98 percent of my attention to what I was doing, but always there was that other 2 percent that sat somewhere over in the corner watching me . . . watching and waiting for the frantic thrashing to overwhelm me. It was no good . . . no way to work . . . no way to be all that I had to be if Daisy's vision were to be fulfilled. So in December 1995, on the third anniversary of a job I loved, I wrote my letter of resignation. Sam persuaded me to hold it a little while to be sure. In January, I mailed it. I was sure.

Chapter 45

• • •

Daisy Maryles has the most distressing habit of consistently being Daisy, no ifs, ands, buts, or maybes. She is as sure as tomorrow morning's sunrise and as constant as Gibralter's rock. This time, however, she fooled me. Or she fooled me by being Daisy in a way I had never had occasion to see before.

I sent my letter, and nothing happened. Several days went by, and then a week, and then almost two weeks. We were to the end of January when the phone finally rang. "No." That was the message in sum, though it took her a few more words than that, commencing with, "Tickle, Tickle, Tickle, what do you think you're doing!," and going on from there.

In the three years of Daisy's and my being together, the work of covering religion for a trade magazine had expanded enormously. Work always expands under any set of circumstances; that is the nature of work. In this case, however, the work had expanded exponentially because the religion market was in wild career; and keeping up with it was way beyond the strength or acumen of any one person. Accordingly, some months earlier, we had added another staff member, Henry Carrigan, to oversee the whole book-review part of the department. A secular academic

241

with seminary training and a review bibliography of his own that would give anyone pause, Henry has now gone on to become, first, in 1999, the head of Trinity Press International and then, in 2003, the American publisher of T. & T. Clark Publishing, after the merger of those two houses. In January 1996, however, Henry was just what he has continued through all these years to be, a deeply respected colleague and a treasured friend.

"We have Henry," Daisy said, "and we can adjust the rest." It was almost immediately thereafter that we both said, "Lynn!" There were a few anxious days while Lynn pondered and we waited; but—another example of "God doth provide"—in good time she took the job.

"You can do whatever you can do or want to do," Daisy had said on that first phone call, "just as long as you don't quit." That was all well and good, but the "what" of "whatever" had to be defined. Robin Mays, ever the marketer as well as the sales manager, somewhere along the way, probably in late 1993, had sneakily created a thing called *PW's Religion Marketing Newsletter*. The sneaky part was not the fact that she ran the thing, complete from production to mailing, out of her office in Atlanta, but that the editorial content had to come out of mine, a fact that had not at first been clear to me in her initiating conversations about *RMN*. In fairness to Robin's memory, I must say three things, however:

First, the newsletter was conceptualized as a friendly or "family gossip" piece just for religion publishers, not for the whole industry. Because one of its main purposes was to keep each house aware of advertising opportunities, upcoming industry meetings, and upcoming *PW* religion features, much of the little publication's actual content was not editorial at all. It was lists and dates and facts that Robin herself assembled and fashioned into content. In reality, then, what editorial meant for Robin's newsletter was really a one- or two-page essay under the banner of "From the Editor's Desk" that I wrote and in which I could say almost anything I wanted to, including a very great deal that I could not say in the magazine itself.

The second thing is that the newsletter almost from the beginning was a popular success. Chatty is good sometimes, especially in a high-tension industry; and chatty apparently was a lot more than good in this one. The third thing is that I absolutely loved doing those editorial pieces. The essay has always been my preferred form of writing, and the opportunity to express opinion and theory instead of just fact was delicious to one with my turn of personality. Beyond that, the feedback was downright heady. It followed then that during all those months of my grinding out "From the Editor's Desk," Robin had not only failed to be even faintly contrite, but had actually began to gloat by saying things like "I told you it would work" and "I knew you'd love it." And I had growled back with some kind of rebuff about her being a consummate con, but not with any real conviction, as we both knew.

But what had begun sneakily was, by January 1996, to become the first part of my "what." Lynn would be the mother magazine's religion editor; Henry would continue as its religion book-review editor; and I would be editor-at-large for religion, meaning *RMN* and continuing coverage with Lynn and Henry and Daisy of the various trade shows, along with participation in staff work and speaking engagements. I was relieved at a level I find it hard even now to express. The magazine and its religion program were no longer held hostage to the caprices of my health. If I became ill, the work went on just as scheduled. Whatever I felt as Daisy began to make it all work out was, this time, a definite "God doth provide" kind of security.

But Daisy did not effect her solutions a day too soon. In March, I missed my first speaking engagement. That month, I was to address the annual meeting of the Protestant Church-owned Publishers Association in Monterey, California. PCPA was, and is, a small and almost painfully dedicated group of like-minded professionals who find their work defined by the exigencies of having to answer not only to their markets, but also to the tenets and oversight of their various denominational boards. Not an enviable position, but one most of them occupy with humor and mutual empathy. I had attended their meetings a time or two before, but being asked to keynote their annual gathering was a real compliment to *PW*'s program, and I had treasured the invitation as such. But I was not in Monterey at the appointed time that March. I was back in CCU.

Chapter 46

• • •

The Protestant Church-owned Publishers Association engagement, while it was the first scheduled address I had ever failed to show up for, blessedly was also only one of the two that I have ever had to cancel, at least so far. The reason for that is that March 1996 was serious enough to lead to serious accommodations.

Once more, it was the Emergency Room and Sam's barking orders and the wave of "It's Dr. Tickle's wife." But this time, after all the fireworks were over and my heart had stabilized, it was also the cardiologist sitting beside the ER table talking to Sam as much as, perhaps more than, to me. The diagnosis was the same one I had heard before: "Her heart's in great shape, especially for a woman her age, but the electrical system is blown to hell," which I thought pretty much covered the bases, colloquially speaking.

There was one drug, however, he said, that might work. It would take three days in CCU to monitor my heart as I began to adjust to the drug and, should I ever have to come off it, another three supervised days to withdraw me. If it worked—and he thought it was worth giving it a try—I would have to take a pill every twelve hours on the dot. There was no more than a fifteen- or twenty-minute window on either side of the hour, and if I was delayed for some reason, then I would have to skip that dosage and hope. Could I do that? Would my schedule and/or my disposition allow that? Sam and I said yes, and so the adventure that is my current existence began.

Every morning at 6:00 A.M. CST and without regard to where in the world I am, I take a tablet; and every evening at 6:00 P.M. CST, again without regard to where in the world I am, I take a tablet. Having lived this regimen for several years now, I am still convinced that only technology makes it possible. Almost the last thing the cardiologist said as he dismissed me for home after my three days of merging into the drug was actually said to Sam. "Get her one of those wristwatches that alarms," he said, and he wasn't kidding. Without that raucous beeping, I would never keep the appointed hours; and thus I have come to say, even of so secular a thing as a Casio, "God doth provide."

The other thing the cardiologist said as I was leaving the hospital was not quite so easily or humorously negotiated. My miracle drug had to have some help in order to do its work. I would have to be down and quiet for at least ten to twelve hours each night to give my heart time to rest. Thank God for Lynn. Thank God for Henry.

But for all my thanking God and my referencing of adages in telling this long tale, I am just now coming to the core of my understanding of my forebears' words. Over the years of accommodating my schedule to one I would never have chosen for myself, I have come to embrace this change in life patterns first with respect and, nowadays, with gratitude. This does not mean that I find it always pleasing to have no evening social life, or that I like having to be abed late on the morning before an evening address and then late on the morning after, thereby destroying two days for one night. It certainly does not mean that my regret for Sam has diminished any over the years. Actually, it has increased, especially since his retirement from active practice in 2000.

Sam is the most gregarious person I know; and one of his long-anticipated joys of retirement from medicine was going to be the freedom to accept any invitation without having to look at the duty schedule first and even to have a late-night drink with friends without fear of the phone call that would require a totally clear head if a patient were to live. None of that pleasant socializing can be for us as a couple now, at least not in evening hours. To his credit, he has gone forth alone and found friends with whom he's comfortable as one half of a half-absent duo; and he has learned to attend many evening events alone. But it's not the same, and we both know it . . . not what we had planned on and dreamed about . . . not what we had thought it would be. There is, though, the other side of the coin.

After March 1996 the decree came down from Sam, as if from Sinai, that there would be no more trips abroad without him, and as few cross-country ones as possible. I told him he was being absurd, and one of his daughters, who wishes to remain anonymous, said, "So what's with you, Daddy? She's supposed to tell people, 'The queen only travels with her physician?' " But even filial sarcasm did not dent his determination. Thank God, again. We went to Frankfurt and the *Buchmesse* together that year for the first time. He joined me in my love affair with Germany and with Wiesbaden in particular, and together we commenced our eternal betrothment to Amsterdam, that beautiful city of good beer and uncanny light. Now, when we speak of taking a personal vacation, Sam's first reaction is that he wants to spend a week in Amsterdam doing nothing but sitting at a sidewalk table, sampling Dutch beer, and watching people. Barring the freedom of a private vacation as opposed to a working trip, he wants to do whatever we have to do that will permit at least two days of such sitting and watching something somewhere on either end of the whatever.

We have, in fact, become quite expert at attaching two-day holidays to the front and back ends of work-related whatevers. As a result, we have laid down memories in our shared life that would otherwise never have happened . . . everything from stolen overnighters at the beach to thousand-mile road trips for the joy of the countryside, of meals in small-town cafés, and especially of the car time together. These are unexpected and generous provisions for which we both are thankful. But the provision that has mattered most is different even from such pleasures; the gift of illness has been my education in prayer.

Chapter 47

• • •

Prayer is the most opaque of humanity's spiritual practices, although I would never have said such a thing ten years ago. I would never even have known to say it, in fact. Ten years ago, I thought I pretty much had prayer figured out; but that was before long nights in bed gave me hours of freedom to go wandering around in that strange landscape of cul-de-sacs and transport, crystalline chapels and anguish, gray-soft instruction and gentle birthings.

The old ways of mid-twentieth-century American Protestant Christianity, the ones that effected on me what the Church now calls "Christian formation," taught its youngsters about spirituality no more frequently or adequately than it employed the term "Christian Formation." Neither spirituality nor religious formation had at that time yet been articulated as separate from "being a Christian," a pleasantly generalized term that was as unparsed as it was ubiquitous. "Christian Education" was the working term in those days and generally referred only to Sabbath Day instruction. It was understood as well that the purpose of such instruction was first and foremost to make sure that every member of each congregation within a denomination, especially every young, aspiring member, understood exactly how to be Christian as "Christian" was defined by the stated doctrines of that particular denomination and as evidenced evermore thereafter by each member's observable conduct. For those of us who grew up under those midcentury contingencies, most Christian Ed was the purview of a lay Sunday School Superintendent and his volunteer staff of earnest mothers.

I can honestly look back over all my own years of Church School and say that, almost to a man and woman, I would wager that the volunteer teachers and superintendents of my own experience truly wanted to do their duty by God and their children. If motivation alone were enough, in other words, there would have been nothing inherently wrong with the system that shaped me. But sincerity of purpose is rarely, if ever, enough; and there was, implicit in the system itself, such a disparity of teaching skills and, more tellingly, of religious sophistication and introspective candor that preprinted curriculums had to take precedence over any free-form tutelage in the life of faith. I will always think that an informing and inciting part of the deluge of demand for spirituality books, retreats, conferences, and practices that overtook American religion in the 1990s had its headwaters in the anemic and soul-shy Sunday Schools of the American midcentury.

Be that as it may, however, the point still remains that I, and all my churched contemporaries, were taught. Were we ever taught! The number of facts that can be used to corset interior experience never ceases to amaze me, even today; and nowhere is that more true than in dealing with the matter of prayer. The curricular way to engage it was—and frequently still is—by typology. Thus take the four finger knuckles of a child's closed fist and name the first A, the second C, the third T, and the last, little one S. The result is ACTS, because prayer acts. One is to understand that "acts" here really implies an efficacy we would normally use the word "works" to convey; but "works" won't do as a mnemonic here, for it spells only itself while ACTS spells out the four kinds of prayer: Adoration, Confession, Thanksgiving, and Supplication.

Each of these knuckles can—and did—occupy two or three Sundays of elaboration in a Church school year, along with numerous opportunities for every child to share some example of each type of prayer from his or her week just past. When one got beyond Elementary Sunday School into Junior High Sunday School, one even learned to begin ACTS on one's thumb knuckle, thereby allowing for one more letter and the resultant acronym of ACTSI, the I standing for intercessory. The theory was—and probably correctly so in those less media-informed days—that intercessory prayer, when studied as a routine practice, requires too much awareness of the world's pain to be good for small children to contemplate.

There was, predictably enough, much discussion also of where one was to pray, in what posture, and whether aloud or silently. There was, so far as I can remember, no discussion about the difference between corporate, or common, prayer and private prayer, nor any recognition that almost all people pray at one time or another, even those who do not believe in god as such. I do recall having to tally up how many times in a week I had prayed, an exercise not unlike putting red paste-on stars beside my name each Monday in grade school, a star for each book I had read since the previous Monday. Meditation had not yet been invented as a nonintellectual exercise, at least not in America; centering prayer had not yet been heard of; and liturgical prayer, sometimes heard being chanted by monks in swashbuckling movies with stars like Errol Flynn or Cornel Wilde, was foreign, antique, effete, and, for all of those reasons, definitely suspect. Besides, proper people were too busy for all that, because being Christian meant that one was to be gainfully and visibly employed throughout his or her working day.

By the 1960s a great many of Protestant America's religious "givens" had begun to suffer cultural onslaughts they could not survive. Certainly by the time I turned thirty, in 1963, my Protestantism had blessedly suffered and succumbed to a lot of them.

Sam and I had three children by then, always a maturing experience that brings a lot of things into play subjectively, especially those supplicating, thanking, and interceding parts of prayer. Beyond that, I was teaching in the English department at Rhodes College in Memphis, an institution well known for its dedication to unfettered thinking and honest intellectual exploration. Had I not already been so bent by maternity and disposition, the stimulus of that place alone and of my constantly inquiring, constantly learning colleagues would have brought me to seek a prayer life that could transcend the knuckles on my closed hand.

My solution, which I stumbled across within a year or two of my thirtieth birthday, was more accidental than well thought out or deliberate. Starving on a steady diet of the prayers I shot off as occasion evoked them, I had begun to cast about for more than the caprice of circumstance to give shape to my interior life. I suspect now that I was frankly looking for something—some book or manual or fiction—that would either instruct me in how to understand and domesticate my need or, barring that, show me by example how someone else had managed to assuage a similar one. Either way, I was in the far back recesses of an antiquarian bookstore when I discovered, in a pile of books that were quite literally moldering there, a breviary. It was, to be precise about the matter, the 1941 edition of *A Short Breviary for Religious and the Laity* by the monks of St. John's Abbey in Collegeville, Minnesota. I still have it. For that matter, I now have another just like it that I shamelessly begged from the St. John's archives several years ago as a replacement copy for the original, which I have worn almost beyond use.

I had never held a breviary before, had not a clue how to make all of its ribbons and colored rubrics work, and was too proud or ashamed or just young to ask. Instead, I bought the thing, snuck it home, and began to teach myself. In those days, one did not learn to drive a breviary any more easily than one learned to drive a car. In both cases, desire was certainly the first prerequisite, but after that the need for sheer information kicked in. Fortunately, a life spent in and around university campuses had taught me my way around a library, and my faculty position gave me free access to roam through all of Rhodes's very fine one without having to go through a librarian or the front desk for what I wanted. I read. I practiced. I learned to drive that breviary. By the time I turned sixty-three, in 1996, in fact, and was completing my first full year as contributing editor in religion at *PW,* I had spent over thirty years of my life driving it, and I had loved the doing of it. Had I been asked about such things back then, I suspect I probably would have even said that I had discovered, in the dual disciplines of praying the breviary and offering my own ACTSI, the sum total of all there was to employ or pursue in the world of prayer.

Poor fool, poor soul. Both were much in need of interruption.

Chapter 48

• • •

    "Praying a breviary" is not exactly the world's most common, much less most self-explanatory phrase, nor is the exercise it refers to uniformly named. Sometimes called "observing the liturgical hours," sometimes called "praying the daily offices," sometimes called "keeping the divine hours," sometimes called by any number of variations on those themes, using a breviary means stabilizing and disciplining one's prayer life around the rhythms of the working day and the thoughts of the Church universal rather than around one's own experience or even that of a particular time, place, or communion.

    One rises at 6:00 A.M. to pray the office of Prime, *primus* having been the Romans' word for "first" and 6:00 A.M. having been the first hour of the Roman commercial day. At 9:00 A.M., one lays aside whatever he or she is working on and prays the office of Terce, so called because it was the Latin word for "three" and 9:00 A.M. was the third hour of the Roman day. Twelve noon, being the sixth hour of that day, is called Sext, and the prayers appointed for that hour are observed. Three P.M., obviously the ninth hour of a day that began at six, is called Nones and is observed by the prayers appointed for it. After that, the easy and obvious naming-by-numbers system disappears, primarily because the early evening office fluctuates in timing with the setting of the sun, *vesperus* being the Latin for "evening" and giving the next, much more generally familiar office its name of Vespers.

Compline is the final office of the day for most laity like me and/or the uncloistereds. Said at bedtime, it recognizes the completion of the working day, praises God for its gifts and His mercy, and commits the soul to His care in sleep as in wakefulness. The cloistered and many lay religious observe one or both of the remaining divine hours. *Matins* is the Latin for "morning" and, therefore, the name for the midnight office, observed just as one day dies and another commences. *Lauds* is Latin for praise and by extension is the name for the loveliest office of them all, that of praise as the believer greets the cock crow with thanksgiving that so great and beautiful a consistency of order and pattern should have once again been given to us as creatures.

The hours, as is clear from their names, are set by the clock and established in so fixed a way that the observing of them is commonly referred to nowadays as "fixed-hour prayer." There are variations, of course, slight and cautiously established, but still sometimes there. A monastery may determine, for example, that Lauds and Prime can be observed as a combined office at an appointed hour or half hour somewhere between cock crow and 6:00 A.M.; or an abbess may conclude that the half hour of 2:30 P.M. better suits the patterns of the nuns' workday than does three o'clock; or in much the same way, a layman—a teacher, for instance, or a shop foreman—may have to observe Nones at 3:30 P.M. instead of three because of a school's closing time or the changing of a shift. Whatever those adjustments may be, always the pattern, once established, is adhered to by the praying community or the individual observant, and always the effort is directed toward retaining the hour or half hour whenever possible. The reason for this is simple.

Saint Paul speaks of a constant cascade of prayer before the throne of God; and from the very beginning, Christians have understood this to mean exactly what it says. When I, at 6:00 A.M. arise for Prime and medicine, I join all the other Benedictines and fixed-hour pray-ers in my time zone. For those few minutes and regardless of where we physically are as individuals within our time zone, we are together in the communion of our prayers. The words we speak to our God are the words that have been raised only an hour before in the time zone just to the east of us; and when we are done, they are the words that will be raised before Him by our fellow Christians in the time zone immediately to the west of us, until the globe itself has been circled by our prayers and each day brought to its ending so another may begin. It is the communion of the saints horizontally and across all space.

The words of the day's offices are as fixed in their own way as are the hours. Each office each day is different from the same office on any other day of the year, because the prayers and readings for each are drawn from the prayers and readings assigned to it on the basis of the liturgical, rather than the physical, year's calendar. If this were not so, the resurrection readings in a breviary or the ascension praises, for example, would rarely fall on the exact days of Easter or Ascension, since both of those events are dated from the physical cycles of the moon. By following the liturgical calendar and its assigned readings, however, breviaries around the world, and from whatever varying sources, all tap into the same words at the same, liturgically appropriate day. And the words themselves are the wonder of the thing . . .

The words of fixed-hour prayer are not, as is true with other forms of prayer, the words of the person praying, nor are they the work of his or her own creation. The words of fixed-hour prayer are the psalms and holy writings of the millennia. They are the monotheistic tradition flowing down through the centuries from Eden's time to ours. They are the birthright of the observant prayer practioner and the soul's surety of a wisdom finely honed and proved true. They are the songs of the fathers and mothers since the calling of Abraham; and by joining that chorus, each man or woman who prays slips joyfully into the long ribbon of life that is the vertical communion of the saints across the ages. Amen. Amen.

I speak from time to time to groups about fixed-hour prayer, though truthfully, as I grow older, I find myself more and more reluctant to "talk" publicly about prayer in any of its forms. As my experience of it has grown, so too has my sense that most of what is said formally, whether by me or by somebody else, is little more than chatter, the chirping of magpies in December or of children in their toddling. When I do speak about fixed-hour prayer, however, always at some point the same question is asked. Though the words may vary a bit from group to group, the substance does not:

"What will doing fixed-hour prayer do for me?"

The answer, likewise, is always the same: "Absolutely nothing." The question has violated the gift.

That having been said, there are inevitably results or consequences of living the Divine Hours. At the most superficial or mundane of levels stands the business of time itself; and time is the consequence that continues now, even after all these years of fixed-hour practice, to amaze me. I had been living under the regimen of praying my day every third hour on the hour for some four or five years before I began to perceive the economy of time that is built into such a routine. I am relatively sure that the reason for this is more psychological than holy or religious; but the truth of the thing is that those who spend an hour or so of each day's allotted twenty-four in praying the offices appear to have more time than do folk who do not keep the hours. Or certainly we perceive ourselves as having more time.

Perhaps, in my particular case, that sense of having more time means only that after all these years of having to reach a closure of sorts every three hours of my day, I have somehow learned to accomplish more within each of those time blocks. Or perhaps the explanation is just so physical a thing as saying that the intense diversion of an office allows the body, both brain and gut, to clarify and return, as a result, more efficient in its work. I have no idea about the mechanics. I only know that such is true.

But I also strongly suspect that determining to keep the offices as a way of increasing one's secular time is doomed from the outset to fail. Fixed-hour prayer will have its adherents on its own terms or not at all; but the terms are faith's most cordial ones.

The daily office is a chapelette, though of course there is no such word. It is a routinized interruption in the day, though of course it is not itself within time, and only one's passage into it is temporal. It is a way station along the side of the road where pilgrims stop and rest, though of course way stations are usually humble, wooden structures holding no more than a single icon; and the office is neither a matter of fabricated materials nor does it contain them.

No, instead, the Divine Hours have come to be for me as the first singing stillness in the place that is prayer. Their words always an invitation to explore; their very exercise, by long tradition, a set of maps and connections helpful for journeying in nongeography. Moreover, without the hours, I would never have traveled beyond my own fist or, at most, beyond my psalter and my Book of Common Prayer. I know that. Those tools and those alone would have been for me a sufficiency, and my lazy soul would have slept through its own adventures. But then there was this little tick who, almost a decade ago now, gave me other hours in which to walk about out beyond the cage of words. Who, indeed, could not be grateful for such a provision? *Sic semper est.*

Chapter 49

• • •

As the hands of the kitchen clock in Lucy push nearer and nearer to seven-thirty each evening, Sam and I begin concluding our day together. He will go out with friends or work awhile in his office or sometimes just sit an hour or two longer dozing in front of the television before he ends his day; but mine is done, and we say our early good nights before I climb the steps to our bedroom.

Observing the Divine Hours, as I have said, is to enter into a populous and communal space where both the words and their ordering are fixed in accord with the office's place in a day's rhythm and of each day's place within the larger rhythms of the Church's year. It is, indeed, this very fixedness that forges the communion of saints, both living and long since dead, within the hours' crystalline embrace. But such a regimen and observation in such a company was never intended to become a believer's only time of prayer nor to become a substitute for the language of an individual heart in either its ecstasies or its distress. From the very first, it never once occurred to me that the offices were my "private" prayer. They presented to me rather, as

I learned to observe them, like holy gifts to me as a creature. That I and others like me could stop and praise and enjoy was, and remains to this day, a kind of amazement to me. Within the course of each Divine Hour, a perfect jewel is burnished by us who, like children at play, shape and form and perform for a moment or two, and then, as if in response to some hidden signal, run away from one another and back to our other occupations.

Although I no longer close my fist to tally my prayers by kind, I still know, as do most believers, the full presence of adoration, confession, thanksgiving, supplication, and intercession in my prayer life; and I set aside three times each day for particular attention to those forms of engagement between my consciousness and God. In the morning before rising, in midafternoon after the office of Nones, and after I go upstairs each evening. Upstairs in the evening, I read a portion of scripture, sometimes a chapter, sometimes more and sometimes less, but always in sequence as I move through a particular book or Gospel or Epistle. Then, thus prepared, I pray. After that Compline. And after that . . . and after that the inexplicable. After that the gift of the tick or the gift of God by means of a tick.

Nobody can sleep ten hours each night, every night, or at least I can't. But neither have I ever, in all these years of trying, learned to watch television lying down flat on my back for very long. Sam has done everything humanly possible to facilitate the process for me; but regardless of what he does, the actors all look sideways or else so high up as to appear distorted. So he has now hit upon the scheme of taping for me the occasional shows or special productions that I need to watch for professional reasons or for personal pleasure; and we watch his tapes together before or just after supper. Sans television and barring narcolepsy, though, the things that one can do flat on one's back soon dwindle down to some form or another of reading.

One of the more annoying—or maybe just plain interesting—things about older bodies is that they get tired of being in one place for too long and even of being used in the same way for extended periods. Thus, after about an hour and a half of read-

ing in bed, it's a toss-up about whether it is my shoulders that refuse to hold a book up for another second or my eyes that rebel
over scanning another line. Sometimes I think it is my brain that
leads the protest chorus by refusing to engage another half-
baked thought. Whatever the mechanism of rebellion, the book
goes down, the light goes out, and there I am.

Never having lacked for imagination, I discovered early on
that I could turn out that light and go back into the day's events
to harvest what might—or sometimes might not—be useful in
something I was writing or studying or preparing an address
about. Within six months of my overlong bedtimes, I had come
to regard that mulling and editing and processing time as first a
boon and then a necessity. I wove that time into my workday
without even realizing it and without regard for the fact that I
technically was at rest. The thing about work, though, is that it
tends to offend us after a while . . . or perhaps we just tend to
want some other form of entertainment, like sleep. And sleep I
can do, passing thoughtlessly from writing or speaking in my
head on into dreaming in the same space, right up until that unknowable moment when the dreaming sends me through itself
and out into a quietness beyond which is voice by stillness.

Awake in a body that is asleep and aware without carapace
or agenda to confine awareness, I am and am not. Servant to the
speaker who shapes without speaking, I am consort and devotee
and no-thing until the dreaming draws me back again into itself,
and the body takes me back from the dreaming into itself.

It is this ineffable knowing that informs me now, and it is this
that holds me here, even as it draws me there. I can neither will
its coming nor by intention enter it, because the I constrains and
prevents me. But the I can tell of it, however opaquely; for it too
is prayer and the impossibility of its description is the nature of
prayer's opacity.

Memphis International

Chapter 50

• • •

Airports have probably informed my old age more than any other physical structure, a fact that at times strikes me as bizarre, and at other times as simply a bit peculiar. Either way, the situation is a self-imposed one. I love the places. Invariably, airport shops stock the most charming toys, the most outré kitsch, and the most innovative luggage of any place I know. Airports also have some of the most observable bars in Western civilization. Passing time with total strangers who are guaranteed by circumstance always to remain total strangers seems to loosen the human personality from its moorings in much the same way that an Internet chat room can, only with the added edge of happening in real time. The writer in me can pass hours in those bars, watching and eavesdropping. Not in a thousand years, however, would it ever have occurred to me deliberately to schedule a meeting with a stranger in an airport bar—not, that is, until a man named Bob Abernethy asked me to meet him in one. Admittedly, of course, he was not as much a stranger at that point as he was just a familiar face, the rest of whom I had never met.

Bob Abernethy is now so dear to my heart as a human being

and as a respected professional that my hesitancy over our first meeting seems ludicrous to me in retrospect. It probably would have seemed ludicrous to Bob right from the start, had he known about it. When, in April 1996, we met for drinks and lunch in the Cheers bar and grill at the head of the B Concourse of Memphis International, I had spoken to the man only one time in my life, but I had been watching and listening to him off and on for four decades as he covered the news, first from Washington and then from Los Angeles and, later, from London, for NBC News. More to the point, from 1989 right up through 1994, Sam and I had watched him almost nightly from Moscow as he covered the wind down of the Cold War and, in due time, the fall of the Kremlin itself.

Had anybody chanced to ask me, as 1996 began, whether or not I would ever meet Bob Abernethy in person, I would have shrugged off the question. "Whatever for?" would have been my immediate and ongoing reaction to such an idea. Our worlds, so far as I knew then, were continents apart personally as well as geographically. On the other hand, had anybody asked me to name the ten most urbane, sensible, and trustworthy American journalists of the day, Abernethy would have made the cut quite easily . . . which was why getting a phone call from him in early April had been an exercise first in incredulity and then in something I remember as being embarrassingly close to slowness of wit and, ultimately, in unresolved mystification.

He wanted, he said on that call, to speak to me about a project he had in mind and on which he thought I could be of some use, but he did not want to discuss the matter over the phone. Was I to be in the D.C. area anytime soon? No, I told him, my wings had been clipped for a few weeks by illness. He expressed the proper concern, and I reassured him that I was simply adjusting to a new drug that was taking care of the situation but required my staying fairly close to home for a month or two. Then, he said, could he come to me? It was at that point that the incredulity transmuted into confusion. What in the world could this man want?

I said certainly he could come to Lucy, if he felt that was better than a letter or phone call, but it was a long way to come with a question. I remember that he laughed then at the sharpness of my tone and made some remark to the effect that he had managed to spend a goodly portion of his life getting into and out of places that were a long way from anywhere. But he did it in a wry kind of way, and I gave up and laughed along with him. "Instead of Lucy, then, could you just meet me in the Memphis airport?" he said. "Maybe on the twenty-third? I have a break that day and could fly in, have lunch, and fly back to Washington before supper." I could, mainly because I was intrigued by that point. "Where?" he said, and all I could think of was Cheers.

"So be it," he said. "I'll e-mail you my flight times when I have them." And that had been the whole substance of our contact right up until the late morning of April 23, when I sat in Memphis International waiting for my familiar, but unknown, lunch companion to land and join me.

To say that Bob Abernethy is a handsome man would be to give him only half his due. He also has a presence that precedes and surrounds him and of which he seems totally unaware even when he is using it to project himself. It was a little like watching Moses part the waters, in other words, to sit there and watch him come down that concourse toward me. People, as if sensing his approach, turned their heads back, saw him, and then moved aside as he moved through them like a lion through its pride. As he got to the table where I was, he set his briefcase on the chair between us, shook my hand, and said, "I'm so glad you could make it. Thank you." And with that he proceeded to settle in as naturally as if we had known each other from dozens of previous encounters.

In 1984, Bob Abernethy had disappeared from public view — or at least from our television screens in Lucy — for almost a year. Sam and I had commented on his not being around anymore, but neither of us had given the matter much attention, especially since he showed up again later, and things at NBC News seemed to have returned to normal after all. What neither of us knew at the time was that Bob, an alumnus of Princeton on both the undergraduate and graduate levels, had gone back to school in 1984, but this time to Yale. To be exact, he had taken a leave of absence from the network for a year in order to study theology and social ethics at the Yale Divinity School. "This," he said that April day in Cheers, "I am telling you so you will understand that what I am about to propose has been a long time coming. It is not some recent idea, but one I have done everything I can to prepare for."

I listened, and as I listened, I began to see not only what Bob Abernethy saw, but also one of the most cockamamy concepts I had recently heard. Bob Abernethy, former Moscow bureau chief for a major network, had just resigned from NBC so that he could, of all unimaginable things, try to create, fund, produce, and host a weekly news show—each week, every week, no less— a news show that would deal only with religion and ethics in the world at large. "Not even halfway likely," I thought, but fortunately did not say.

He had a wish list of fellow travelers and a laundry list of needs and, as he pulled a clip of papers out of his briefcase, it was obvious that I was on both lists. There was no question that he was right about one thing: A sizable chunk of the action in religion in 1996 was in the book business; and a disproportionate and even more volatile area of reportable action was the number of conversations that religion books were evoking and informing in the general, as well as in the book-reading, populace. Given all that, what he needed first, he said, was for me to serve on his advisory board as he put a prospectus together to submit to a network.

That request, at least, was not an unprecedented one. I sat— and still sit—on a number of boards where, my ego would like to think anyway, both my own expertise and the stature and specialized range of *PW* can themselves grow, as well as be of benefit within the bounds of that association. I had no doubt, moreover, but that anything Bob Abernethy attempted, whether it ultimately succeeded or not, would be worth the energy and effort involved in the trying. That was no problem. Then, the issue of a board position having been resolved, he cocked his head at me and said that, in addition to a place on his board of advisers, what he needed even more was for me to help him contrive ways in which religion book news could be translated to, and incorporated in, a televised news format.

I don't remember what we ate or drank or how long we actually had together after that. I do know, however, that to this day I cannot pass a Cheers sign in any airport without experiencing a slight and involuntary lift to my shoulders and in my thoughts. Would I do these things? The man had to be crazy to have come all this way just to ask me that! Part of my job was doing the first thing he wanted, as we had already ascertained. As for the second part of his proposition? With no more than an e-mail of invitation, I would have thrown myself heart, soul, and head into the second part of his project just for the joy of seeing how such a thing might be done and of watching him do it. We shook hands, he left for his gate, and I left for Lucy, my mind already scurrying like the proverbial gerbil on its wheel.

Objectively speaking—by which I mean speaking in general, rather than deeply personal, terms—the most obvious result of my first afternoon with Bob Abernethy and of the dozens of other afternoons and evenings he had with dozens of other people around the country became, in September 1997, PBS's now much-acclaimed *Religion & Ethics NewsWeekly*. How he did it—how he persuaded a network to risk money on a weekly news show dealing solely with religion—no one except Bob himself will ever completely understand. Those of us who cheered him on and then helped when and as we could are probably as amazed as anyone else that first he dared the thing and then that he accomplished it. The show in and of itself, however, was not the sum of the experience for me. Rather, Bob Abernethy himself, certainly as an investigative journalist par excellence but also, later, as a trusted friend, was to become a formative agent and guide in my own, public progress toward the City of God.

Chapter 51

• • •

By January 1997, while Bob, with his advisory board in place, was spending all his time in putting together program concepts and a prospectus for potential funders, I was beginning to enjoy the good health that now sustains me. The dread of my own chest and its foibles had succumbed to my increasing faith in the magic of my new regimen, and I was back to work full-tilt. Daisy had been right; there was more than enough work to keep us all occupied—Robin, Henry, the two of us, and Lynn. Besides that, Robin's *Religion Marketing Newsletter* was continuing its own magic of seducing me with its possibilities.

In the last few days of November and just before the Thanksgiving break, I had prepared my column, now called "From Where I Sit," for the December 1996–January 1997 issue with a good deal of preholiday sangfroid and more even than my usual amount of pleasure in the doing of the thing. Some months earlier, a book by Terry Waite, entitled *Footfalls in Memory*, had been published in the United Kingdom, and I had received a review copy. *Taken on Trust*, Waite's memoir of his incarceration at the hands of Islamic extremists in Lebanon during the late eighties and early nineties, had been published two or three years earlier and had been an international best-seller. *Footfalls*, however, was a very different breed of cat, although it had its roots firmly planted in the same circumstances.

Footfalls is the story of all the books that Waite managed either to beg from his captors during his years in solitary confinement or, far more poignantly, to recall and then reconstruct for himself in his solitude. It is a book lover's book, a reader's book, a quiet, dear book, if ever there were one. And that is what I said in 1997's first issue of the *PW Religion Marketing Newsletter:*

> There is the dear book . . . the always-to-be-remembered-afterward, humble book . . . the book without hype but of such richness that it speaks fully to every part of one's being . . . the book that even in its imperfections stills for a brief while that constant, grinding hunger we all have for unconditional theology and a faith beyond the grasp of despair.

I wrote out of my own emotions in having engaged Waite's work, certainly; but I also wrote for my colleagues, for those who, like me, were born to look for and find God in words. It was not a surprise, then, that I got more than the usual number of responses to the piece . . . the e-mails, the notes, and the phone call or two. It was a phone call from Eric Major that was to have the repercussions, though.

In mid-1996 and just as he had said he would do, Tom Cahill had resigned his post as head of religion publishing at Doubleday in order to become the fiercely popular and able writer he is today. Before he left, however, he had done the other thing he had also said he hoped to do. He had gotten Eric Major to leave his publishing post in Britain and assume the leadership of religion publishing at Doubleday. I, like everyone else who knew him, had rejoiced at Eric's "jumping the pond," as Tom put it. I had even sent Eric a note to that effect; but we had not spoken since his coming to New York until the morning in mid-January when my office phone rang and it was Eric Major.

"I want to talk to you about this piece on Waite," he said. "I think it captures the spirit of the book better than anyone else has, and I want to use it as the foreword to the American edition when we publish it in the fall and then run part of it as the back jacket copy. Okay?"

All Major conversations are composed of racing sentences and most end in "okay?" I knew that already, but I really did not know how to respond to this particular one. Anyone on *PW*'s editorial staff is automatically proscribed, by that position, from blurbing books for very solid and obvious reasons. When a staff member's personal opinion is printed on the back of a book's jacket, that opinion can all too easily transfer in the public mind to being the opinion of the magazine itself. No publisher before Eric, however, so far as I know, had ever contrived a way around that proscription by asking a *PW* staff member to write a foreword with the stated intention before the fact of excerpting that foreword in order to, in effect, create a blurb on the back jacket.

I should say here that the Major scheme turned out to be so unimpugnable as a solution that I have now become something close to a mistress of the foreword, sometimes writing a half dozen or so of them a year and discovering, each time I do so, that I truly revel in furnishing forewords to good books. What I said to Eric originally, however, was a bit more cautious: "Hmmm . . . let me call Daisy on this one, and I'll get back to you."

I called Daisy, who laughed that great, deep chuckle that erupts when she is in the grip of genuine amusement. "My god," she said, "publishers will stoop to anything, won't they!" But then she also thought about it and finally said, "Sure. Why not. So far as I know there's no corporate rule against it; and if there's not one now, somebody can invent one later, if need be."

I called Eric back, and in September 1997 Doubleday published the American edition of *Footfalls in Memory* with sections from the foreword excerpted on its back jacket and looking for all the world like a blurb to me and anybody else who saw it. The whole episode had been perverse and delicious, and I loved it.

The episode had also been my first experience in working with Eric Major as one of his authors, however tenuously. I had enjoyed that, too; but unknown to me, he and Bob Abernethy, independently of each other and in unintentional concert, were about to change the coursings of my life completely.

Chapter 52

• • •

According to the rules of the writing craft, all good folktales and most fables must have three wise men or women as characters and/or commentators in them. Whether that rule always holds for autobiographies and histories, I do not know. I do know that as a principle, it is operative in this one. Bob Abernethy and Eric Major were two-thirds of a triad that was completed by a gentle, burly, don't-mess-with-me genius named Joe Durepos. Unlike Eric or Bob, however, Durepos can claim no innocence about his intentions or his methods. He was, is, and—pray God—will be my agent until death do us part. And at some point, still unknown to me and clearly never going to be revealed by Joe . . . at some point after Eric's January call and before July 1997, Joe contacted Eric with an idea; or Eric contacted Joe with an idea; or maybe they just had a casual conversation somewhere together and stumbled together upon an idea. I honestly do not know who said what to whom first. I do know that by late June 1997, Joe had begun calling me every few days with conversations that more or less followed the same narrative line each time he called:

I had to know, he would say . . . I had to know that confessing Americans—Jew and Christian alike—were beginning to grow weary of generic spirituality and, as a result, beginning to hunger for something more substantial on which to nourish their faith. I had to know this, because for the past year and a half I had been saying to publishers, clergy, and general audiences alike that such a shift was under way.

He was right. The focus of America's religious energy and investigative reading was shifting, by 1997, away from spirituality per se and more toward spirituality as a part of a faith tradition. Americans were, in other words, beginning to stuff the spirituality strand of the religion cable back into its place inside the mesh sleeve. Within American Christianity, the visible effect of that yearning toward home was indeed, as my friend Debra Farrington had so ironically observed, a "hastening toward to the third century." American Christians were looking to discover how things had been with our kind once upon a time before doctrine and schism and holy war had severed the body of Christ. What had our ancestors in the faith done and known and felt, particularly in caring for and exercising their spirits within the casing of the faith? Good Roman Catholic and former seminarian that he is, Joe Durepos knew the answer to that rhetorical question as well as I did. The early Church, first century as well as third, had brought three spiritual disciplines with them while wandering out of Judaism into the surprise of being Christian. Once that confessional distinction had become a wall by definition, the Christian faithful had held on to their three spiritual borrowings with ferocity. They had continued without interruption to practice, and rear their children in the practice of, the Passover or eucharistic meal, Sabbath observance, and fixed-hour prayer.

As Joe and I both very well knew, the Mass certainly did not lack for books about it and about tools for its appreciation. At the other end of the stick, most American Christians in 1997 saw church attendance as the sum total of Sabbath observance; and nothing was going to change that poverty of praxis for a few more years. Given both those extremes, it would seem that only fixed-hour prayer was lacking books and tools. Hmmmm . . .

Piety or piousness or religiosity—call it what you will—may

technically be the sin of religious pride; but in reality, it is the breathing embodiment of religious offensiveness. Always, in looking back over my own childhood, I can see a church congregation and a social landscape dotted with the disgustingly pious. Unfortunately, I can remember in excruciating detail three particular old codgers—two women and one man—who were so holy that they were the butt of our jokes as children just as their lives were the text for constant adult scrutiny. (A good dozen of the grown-ups of my acquaintance frequently and vociferously hoped to live long enough to expose the imperfection or secret sin that would bring the mighty down to earth among the rest of us.)

There is no accounting for the ways in which circumstance and experience write themselves upon the text of young lives, but somehow those holy coots writ large and dark upon mine. I would like to think that, as a devout observer, my abhorrence of them has been corrected in my own adulthood by an appreciation for humility as a spiritual virtue. I would like to think that, but I doubt it. I respect . . . indeed, even covet, paradoxical as that may be . . . the gift of true humility; but I just don't have it. Instead, I am the world's biggest show-off, given half an opportunity. No, what the pious of my childhood gave me was an abiding fear of ever, ever living the life of a religious caricature, of ever, ever becoming the butt of not-so-subtle, not-so-hidden jokes and scrutiny. To this day, every time I catch my public self getting too close to holy obsequiousness, I shut down like a lightning-struck generator.

That confession having been made, however, the truth also is that I really would rather spend the rest of my life in a hole somewhere as to do to young or even new Christians what the coots did to me. For years, the results of their religion were so repugnant as to drive me from the natural pursuits of my own. For that damage to another's soul in the service of one's own ego and self-approbation, there must be a special place in the prison chambers of Hell.

And beyond that abhorrence, and especially in the case of keeping the hours, there is a perfectly logical and natural assumption, I think, that the discipline should evidence itself over time in the life and conduct of the observant. My life as a show-off does not so evidence, and never will. Because of that, for the thirty-some years that stretched from the early 1960s to the summer of 1997, I had kept my mouth tightly shut about my observing of the Divine Offices. But mouths, of course, are hardly the only way we tell our deepest secrets.

"Eric Major," Joe said to me one afternoon, when he called, "is convinced that some way, somehow, it has to be possible to put together a book of hours that's accessible to everyone, even those who never heard of a breviary in their whole upbringing."

"Hmmmm . . . " I said again.

"He also thinks the time to start trying to see what such a thing would look like is right now."

"He's probably right about that part."

"He thinks you can do it."

The other shoe had dropped.

"Why would he think that?"

"Because from an outsider's point of view, you either pray the hours or else you have the best-trained bladder in the industry. Did you ever notice that every three hours you disappear from a meeting or a conversation? Nobody can go that often or that regularly."

He was right, of course. Yet being outed was still a long way from going public, and Joe knew that every bit as well as I did.

Chapter 53

• • •

Over our years of association, Bob Abernethy, Sam, and I have accumulated many memories, all happy ones for Sam and me, and hopefully for Bob as well. We tromped San Francisco one Sunday, the three of us, from services at Grace Cathedral to dim sum at Chinatown's best, to the Top of the Mark and back again for evening drinks, laughing like errant kids as we toasted our day. Sam and I spent a color-drenched New England weekend one autumn in the Abernethy mountain retreat, the three of us watching nature and talking of everything. I attended some powerful board meetings for *Religion & Ethics Newsweekly* and even made some flying trips to Washington to tape a show from time to time. My keenest memories, though, are of Bob in Lucy:

Bob, pulling his rental van off the county road and into the parking lot of a village church in Lucy for a quarter hour, so he could give his full attention to a theological discussion we were having and he intended to persuade me on. (He did.)

Bob standing at our kitchen sink washing dishes as we cleaned up together from a crew lunch. The man who, an hour earlier, had been on camera as interviewer and host would go back on camera as interviewer and host within another half hour. Meanwhile, he was washing dishes, so we could all get back to business. That somehow translated to me at the time, and still does, as what humility looks like when it is the real McCoy.

Bob going with me one afternoon to take the Eucharist to my shut-in friend and soul's sister Ruthe and her mother-in-law, Suzie. Being a United Church of Christ thoroughgoing Protestant, he had a considerable curiosity about what it meant for me to be a LEM, or lay eucharistic minister, licensed by the Episcopal Church to administer the elements to the sick and confined. Every Wednesday afternoon that I am not on the road, I drive from Lucy deeper into the countryside to celebrate the Eucharist with Ruthe; and Bob just itched to see what that looked like. I asked Ruthe's permission; and with it having been granted, Bob joined us in the service while his crew filmed in the background. What I remember best about that afternoon was how quiet he was, how clear he made it that among believers there is no playing to the camera, only the playing before God. In some ways, that afternoon became part of my working definition of holiness; and Ruthe and I still speak of it occasionally, even after so long a time.

The abiding memory—the central one around which all the others pivot—is none of these, however. The memory on which I myself pivoted is neither soft nor so easily captured. During the late 1990s, Bob and company made enough trips to The Farm In Lucy so that he knew Memphis International and Highway 51 about as well as any non-Memphian ever could. It was his first visit, though, that still matters the most.

It was the second week of August 1997. His dream of a religion news show was set to commence airing in less than six weeks, and he was in Lucy to put some footage in the can about a number of different subjects, footage he could store and draw down from as needed. He would shoot something, I would go change to a different outfit, and he would shoot again on a subject as distinct from the previous one as was my attire. We even shot a couple of segments outside, which in August in West Tennessee is a feat of human will over impossible circumstances.

Unable to persuade himself, much less the crew and me, that any further pursuit of the rural life and its spiritual ramifications was worth the human price, Bob moved us all back into the air-conditioning in order to shoot a segment down in the library. When used in regard to Lucy and our house, "library" is a euphemism looking for a place to land, if ever there were one. What we have is a fifty-year-old house on five levels, two of which are essentially at or below ground level. In southern heat, such an arrangement is as comfortable as it is fiscally prudent; but it nonetheless makes for some peculiarly nondescript domestic architecture, our "library" being one example of that consequence. Twenty-eight feet long and fourteen wide, the thing is only half below ground level, its windows opening right even with the turf of our front lawn. Its interior spaces, however, are the most generous in the house and lined by shelves, the shelves being themselves crammed full to the bursting with the books that are the tools of my trade. Thus the word "library," while hardly connoting elegance in our case, still does denote usage; and "library" it is.

As the crew set up, taped over the windows, and rearranged furniture, Bob and I chatted about what he wanted the next scenes to cover, some of the ideas he would be introducing, some of the new and forthcoming books he wanted me to discuss. It was all very ordinary and, as it was supposed to be, very relaxing and reassuring. Not for one minute do I think Bob Abernethy was dissembling as he prepared me that day for the cameras to go on. In fact, there's a part of me that thinks he was as surprised as I about what actually happened.

Once the cameras were running, he worked his way through the first two or three questions that he had told me to anticipate. And then, out of nowhere, he said, "Now, Phyllis, I know that you observe the daily offices. Tell us what living the Benedictine life does for your own spiritual life as a Christian."

Just for a flash of a second, I felt betrayed, set up, exposed. He obviously misread my reaction, for he tried to soothe me, not the situation: "It's all right. Just talk to me about what it's like to keep the hours, and we can edit you later."

Instead of telling him, I began to weep . . . not to burst into tears . . . not to heave with massive sobs . . . but to weep as one weeps when mourning. Something had just died for me, and while I could not name its name, I could feel its leaving.

"Cut," I heard him say. Then, to the crew, "Let's take a break, fellas." But he did not take a break. He sat there facing me in his host's chair, watched me struggle back to composure, gave me a handkerchief from his suit pocket, and said, "I am sorry. I had no idea." I believed him.

After that day, Bob came back a time or two to have that talk on fixed-hour prayer and even to film me as I observed it, in much the same way that he had filmed our Eucharist at Ruthe's, reverentially and accurately. In fact, since that August afternoon, film crews other than his have come into Lucy to film the same process and hear the same words of explanation; but they never would have, had Bob not asked his question . . . had Bob Abernethy not forced me to lay claim publicly to what I was . . . had Bob Abernethy not relieved me of a secretiveness that, I realize now, had itself become a form of spiritual pride.

He never ran that first footage, though I told him later that he should keep it; for I had never cried on tape before in my life and it is highly unlikely I ever will again. He had kept it, he said; and that was the end of that, except that I had been set free. A month later, in September, I signed, with both joy and gratitude, a contract with Eric Major and Doubleday for the first volume of the trilogy that would become *The Divine Hours*.

Chapter 54

• • •

During all the years from our marriage in 1955 right up until September 1997, I'd always said—and believed—that the seven little Tickles were what I had come to do. I have since changed that self-perception. *The Divine Hours* are what I came to do, though left to my own devices, I would never have discovered that.

Once Joe, Eric, and I had sealed our partnership, it became quite clear that Eric had far more than just a "notion" about what he wanted. The Major rhetorical form is not only run-on and sprightly; it is also quite direct and colorful. Whatever else I did in reconfiguring the breviary form, he said, I must first and foremost "get rid of all those goddamn ribbons, all right?" Since I had never quite got the hang of the ribbon system except at its crudest and most awkward level, I was immediately sympathetic to this imperative.

"Never forget," he would say from time to time, "that these books, whatever they turn out to be, have to work for the liturgically challenged," by which artless term he meant to include everyone not born and reared Roman Catholic. His other, very

British term for those of us not of his communion was "all you Proddies," as in "All you Proddies have it so easy"—this usually, of course, when he was on his way out his office door to daily Mass or a holy day of obligation.

And Eric was clear about two other things as well: No Latin or Latinate terms; and no preciousness. The Latin was pretentious (also, to his credit, "too Romanish") and the Latinate rubrics and directions were too daunting. As for no preciousness, that meant that whatever I assembled and we decided to go to press with had to end up looking like an ordinary novel and not a prayer book. "I want every man and woman who wants to, to be able to pray this thing on the train at nine o'clock in the morning without anybody else knowing what he's doing, okay?" It was more than okay. It was a passionate call to create the accessible within the inviolate constrictions of the traditional. After that, he let me have my head to run with the possibilities, an act of confidence that I could not have done justice to, as I now know, had I not had help.

Rebecca, our fourth daughter and seventh child, had been married only a year when she was devastated by chronic fatigue syndrome. Even after having watched her move through and beyond more than three years of that illness, I am still not convinced that CFS as such exists. Rather, I suspect CFS is a catchall label for one of the most vicious, ill-defined, and poorly differentiated complexes of illness presently afflicting us in this country. What had been a happy bride, a librarian, and an art student when illness overtook her gradually became a tragic vacancy that was in and out of pneumonia, in and out of pain, and in and out of hospital with some regularity and no sustained curative result.

By September 1997, however, Bec at last, and under the care of a superb specialist, had begun to recover. The bright mind was back, and the urge to work was surging again. I do not remember whether it was she who first said, "Please, can I help?" or I who first said, "Please, will you help?" It does not matter much now, for by October 1997 she had essentially moved herself into half of the farm's office space and within a week or two thereafter was almost as surrounded as I by stacks of papers, books, and notebooks.

There were still days when she could not come to work at all, sometimes even two or three of them in a row. The worst for me, though, were the mornings when she would come in the office door bright and smiling and then suddenly, an hour or two or three later, would visibly pale in front of my eyes, weaken, and only with great effort make it into the house itself and her father's recliner. Sometimes it would be hours before she could struggle back to her car and home. A time or two, she reluctantly let one of us drive her home. A time or two she did not even try that, spending the night instead with us. Yet I cannot think of *The Divine Hours* nor call to memory the almost two years she and I spent together in assembling those volumes without thinking as well of her physical struggle up, through, and eventually, now, out of illness. In part, I think, her courage infused the manuscript with some of itself, as if prayer had been added to prayer in a communion of pain as well as of the saints.

As it turned out, of course, there was no way I alone could have done what finally we did together. The task required a librarian's skills in some of its research and a librarian's bibliographic patience and training in almost all of its attendant paperwork. Beyond that, and somewhat to our mutual amazement upon discovering it, Rebecca had a reader's exquisite sensitivity to purely mechanical errors, catching almost effortlessly not only the obvious misspellings that all manuscripts contain, but also the misplaced or absent punctuation mark, the inappropriate indentation, the out-of-order rubric. It became so obvious to both of us that this was a mutually dependent piece of work we were engaged in that at one point in late 1998, when we at last knew what we doing and had relaxed into simply doing it, she said to me one afternoon, "We'd have been in one hell of a mess without the CFS."

To my astonishment, I heard myself agreeing with her: "Brother, wouldn't we!" We both stopped dead and looked at each other, a little appalled, I think, at what we had just acknowledged. I couldn't find anything to say, but she shrugged her shoulders. "Got to be a purpose for everything in this life" was all she said, leaving me to wonder how anyone could suffer into such grace in only twenty-three years.

Chapter 55

• • •

We ended up calling *The Divine Hours* "a manual for prayer," rather than a breviary, primarily because Eric thought the term "breviary" to be too freighted and because I thought it dishonest. The books are manuals, variations upon a theme, and an accommodation to the realities of contemporary Christian life . . . an accommodation, however, without much compromise in it.

Eric got his Latin- and Latinate-free rubrics of instruction. There is not an "Invitatory" on a single one of the almost two thousand pages that make up the three original volumes, but "The Request for Presence" appears on almost every third one of them. When push came to shove, Eric got overruled on his ribbons, and there is one lonely ribbon in each volume, which serves, unobtrusively, as a place marker. And most remarkable of all perhaps: A junior editor at Doubleday, aware of Eric's initial prerequisites, called me early one morning in 2000, less than a week after *Prayers for Summertime*, volume one of *The Divine Hours*, had been released, to say, with obvious excitement, "I'm on the train just now coming in to work, and there's this man across the aisle reading away so hard that I had to look to see what he was so engrossed in. Guess what . . ."

I did not have to guess. "He was praying the morning office," I said.

"Yes, yes, he was. He was praying our book, and I didn't even recognize it without its jacket!" Eric had succeeded in that, too; but there were other small victories and major graces that only he, Joe, Rebecca, and I were aware of.

Every tool for praying the hours, whether it is called a breviary or a manual or simply an abbey prayer book, must have some set cycle for incorporating the psalms into the daily offices. There was a time in the third and fourth centuries when the Desert Fathers had such a case of piety as to believe that the whole psalter had to be chanted or prayed each day. The practical limitations of that . . . one had to be celibate and cloistered just to have the time required . . . soon brought good Christian folk back to their senses; but that did not obviate the clear understanding that the psalms of the faith were to be raised in an orderly and consistent fashion and that the daily offices was how this was to be done.

Sitting in a converted garage in Lucy, Tennessee, with dozens of prayer books and hymnals and translations and collected writings of the saints strewn everywhere in stacks that exceeded even my penchant for stacks, I early stumbled across the hard truth that determining the cycle of psalms was the linchpin that made the rest work. At first, it was rather like a game of three-dimensional chess. Every time I moved a psalm, something else necessary got trumped or taken. Almost a month into trying every combination I could think of, I abruptly and almost accidentally hit upon the idea of a six-week cycle.

Why six weeks works and ten did not and five would not is beyond me now, just as it was then; but the truth of the thing is that once I began to drop psalms into place over a terrain of six weeks, or 126 Little Offices, the rest followed. It may not have fallen into place exactly, but the process of compiling transitioned into a marvelously absorbing puzzle. Whatever one chose to plug into the Gospel selection for each day's first office had to resonate with the psalm already assigned to that office, but it also had to adhere, insofar as possible and desirable, with the Church's lectionary selections for that day. So too did the hymns and the writings of the Church Fathers and the refrains and so on. Fascinating in the true and original sense of that word as bewitching, almost addicting.

Sometimes I would look up from a page trying to figure out why I suddenly could not see it very well, only to discover that the sun was going down outside and that Bec and I had been at our desks for ten hours straight without wearying of the work. At first, the sheer beauty of the sources we were dealing with and drawing from seemed to me to be the reason for my absorption. As the selecting and compiling progressed, however, and grew into something with discernible form and tone, I had a time of some several months when I thought that the beauty of the thing emerging in our hands was the force that drove us willingly through long hours and six-day weeks.

As we neared the end, however, and the first volume was in publishable form, the heady intoxication with beauty gave way in me to a kind of sweet quietness. It was almost done. What had begun as a challenge had ended up as a thing that wanted its own life and had needed us only to make passage for itself. Henceforth I could remember its gestation and rejoice in its birth and be eternally thankful for its having come, but I could not lay any claim to it. The volumes of *The Divine Hours* were not mine nor of me. They had merely come my way, and that was more than enough at the time.

Since 2000 and the turn of the millennium, *The Divine Hours* has grown, of course, and has spun off from itself other manuals, like *Christmastide* and *Eastertide*—manuals that are indeed ribbonless, much more slender than the larger volumes, softback, and clearly prayer books particularized to a holy season. In even so short a period as two or three years, the times have changed enough so that Christians no longer care much whether the cover of a fixed-hour prayer book looks like a novel or like what it actually is.

The Divine Hours is posted now on the Web throughout the day each day by some congregations for the use of all who want that mode of accessibility. In the same way, many other sites have sprung up using other compilations and breviaries as their texts for praying each day's offices. Besides that, other prayer books for observing the hours have also begun to flow in a small, but steady stream from monasteries and religious communities who have, from their beginnings, kept fixed-hour prayer and are just now finding a place and a time when the Christian laity is at last ready and eager to reclaim from its long exile the discipline that is their souls' heritage.

And through it all, the files in Lucy have become swollen with letters and e-mails . . . mostly e-mails . . . from fellow Christians, sometimes inquiring about some point of interest or the possibilities of some adaptation or other, but mainly just saying, "I'm doing it, and it's made all the difference." Besides their being in a ratio of two to one, men to women, the thing I treasure most about those growing piles of letters is that at a ratio, probably, of four to one, they are from Eric's "liturgically challenged," from men and women who were not born Roman Catholic or Orthodox or even Anglo-Catholic, but who, rather, were born Assemblies of God or Baptist or Presbyterian or whatever. It is the Presbyterians, though, that hold a special place in my heart.

Hail, fellow travelers of my natal family! Hail and well met! May God have mercy on all our times.

Chapter 56

· · ·

The months of compiling that stretched into the two plus years between September 1997 and the turn of the millennium were months of change as well as constancy. Even for prayer and its business, life apparently is not inclined to stop and make way. On May 1, 1998, Sam had triple-bypass surgery. Almost . . . almost . . . it was a relief to both of us. He had struggled with angina, with abject weariness, and with near narcolepsy for months and months. Like all too many other physicians, he had also insisted on treating himself with only an occasional on-the-elevator or in-the-parking-lot consultation with a colleague about what he should or should not be experimenting with. I would find the vials of nitroglycerin tablets in odd places — wedged into the cracks around the seat of his favorite recliner, tucked in the fruit basket on the kitchen counter, secreted behind a picture frame on the dresser in our bedroom — but his illness had become something we could not talk about . . . could not, in fact, even mention. And so it had grown like the notorious three-hundred-pound gorilla into a beast we could not reach each other around.

It was just after lunch on April 30 that the phone rang. It was Ralph Holyfield, a patient, friend, and now, but not then, business partner of Sam's. "He wouldn't let me call you," Ralph said, "but I just left Sam in the Emergency Room at Methodist. I found him walking down the street from his office trying to make it on his own."

By the time I got to the hospital, he was still on the gurney, but stabilized and more comfortable. He looked at me and said, "I didn't want you to know."

The idiocy of the remark was endearing and infuriating. Even in such extremes, he had to be the husband, the man, the one who protected. Then he said, "This is the one thing I always said I'd never let them do to me," and I knew he had spoken the other great truth of our immediate present. No one knows better than a physician—and no physician better than a heart/lung specialist—what the so beguilingly simple words "bypass surgery" can, and usually do, mean in human suffering. And his was to be an especially vicious recovery, or so it seemed to me helplessly watching as he worked his way through it.

He was back in the office for an hour or two within ten days; but the ankle-to-knee incision in his leg, through which the surgeons had had to remove arteries to replace the occluded ones in his chest, would not heal. We treated it for months, bathing it, dressing it, wrapping it in supports, everything. And the drugs he was taking made the weakness so intense that simple things like stirring coffee became chores. The farm withered and degenerated around us, and he could do nothing except watch. Now, alas, we could talk about his illness. The gorilla had embraced us, and there was no way not to talk about that morbid hug.

Eventually, the leg wound began to heal, and four months post-op, Sam declared the incision totally closed; but the muscle weakness continued, as did the abiding weariness . . . but then so too did the inventive mind and the gregarious nature of the man. It would take more than a compromised physical heart to damage those two things. In May 1999, almost a year to the day after his surgery, Ralph and Sam did what I now suspect Sam

Tickle had really wanted to do all along. They established Architectural MillWorks, Inc.

Ralph, before succumbing to the illness that had brought him to Sam in the first place, had been a craftsman building windows, fine custom doors, and elegant cabinetry out of a workshop on his farm in northern Mississippi. As he had begun to improve under Sam's care, two things had happened. The two had become fast friends; and Ralph had begun yearning to go back to work for himself again, but in a more substantive way. As, after his surgery, Sam became less and less able to sustain the rigors of private practice, I heard more and more in supper-table conversations about Ralph's need to get back to work and Sam's great idea. The great idea was that together they would establish a shop in Memphis itself, equip it, and see if custom windows, fine doors, and elegant cabinetry would play in the city and, of course, make its own way financially.

In the years after the children left us for their own homes, Sam and I had taken to doing what we could not do when they were with us and eternally clamoring to be fed. We would sit down at the kitchen table each night before we even started supper, have a drink together, and actually share in tranquillity what the day had been like for each of us. After May 1999, the tone of that new ritual changed from domestic tranquillity to scarcely veiled excitement . . .

. . . I should see the doors going into the Frazer house, doubled and arched, no less!

. . . I really had to go Sunday after we left church to see the plantation shutters and transoms the men had just delivered out in Glenover Forest. Magnificent!

. . . And he was going to take a couple of shots of the entertainment center that was going in downtown in one of those new condos on the river. I could see it while it was still in process that way. Incredible, all curved and carved, like that mantle they'd done for the Pendleton house, and so on . . .

On July 1, 2000, Sam Tickle, M.D., closed his medical office and officially retired from active practice. That did not mean that

I saw him any more frequently than in the past, just that he was dirtier when I did. The man whom I had always known as white-coated and stethoscope-yoked was now covered in construction-site mud and more sawdust than a chip pile holds. He who had never wavered from the pursuit of a medical detail now turned into an authority on fine woods and on where to procure them for how much, on which general contractors worked on what terms, and—most disconcerting of all to watch—on how to operate and maintain millworking equipment.

I now work in what has to be one of the most handsomely appointed offices I have ever seen . . . so handsome, in fact, that its presence on a farm in rural West Tennessee is an abiding incongruity. It is wall-to-wall—countertop to desk, filing cabinets to bookshelves—Sam Tickle. Both of us know, when we are in that space, that he is back, he is the man, he is the provider. If he is still not as strong as once he was—and he is not—then he is Sam in a different, but just as complete way. There are moments, however, when the vastness of the changes overwhelms me with a kind of ironic, if amused resignation. In those moments I tell him he is by way of becoming a character in his own life, which is true, but which seems to bother me more than him by a considerable margin.

PW was not in abeyance, of course, while or just because I was preoccupied with husbands and hearts, prayers and prayer manuals. Early in 1998, the magazine launched a fortnightly, slick-stock, full-color, newspaper-format ancillary publication called *Religion BookLine*. (In-house, we quickly came to refer to it simply as *RBL*, for obvious reasons.) Designed for professional religionists, whether in publishing or not, the thing was a joy to see and to read, but it was also expensive to produce. Lynn and Daisy were running it, and I was, at least on the masthead, an editor-at-large; but after six months, none of us really thought we could survive in such a costly format. After a year of trying, we ceased publication and converted to the electronic and still fortnightly *RBL*, which continues to show every sign of the fiscally responsible good health its progenitor lacked.

In addition to the struggle with the usual pressures of magazine work and of trying to expand our coverage into consumer venues like *RBL,* other changes had also been taking place. In March 1999, Robin was at last released from her agony and into the surcease of death. Even as we mourned her, we rejoiced for her that it was over. In typical Robin fashion, she had handpicked her own successor; and months before Robin actually slipped into the last terminal stages of her cancer, Sheri Malman had quietly, and without title, begun to assume the workload.

As the work in religion grew, so too did the team of us trying to cover it. The book-review process at last had to be split into the classic divisions of children and juvenile as opposed to adult titles; and Elizabeth Devereaux—shrewd, professional, deeply kind Elizabeth—became *PW*'s editor for children's religion books. Henry Carrigan left us that year as well to take up his post as publisher of Trinity Press International and, now, of T & T Clark. As he was preparing to leave, the rest of us were preparing to panic. Trying to find someone trained in American religion who is also an able writer, solid administrator, and willing to ply journalism as a trade is like trying to find a silver dollar in an ash heap. The chances of ever succeeding at it are very slim, but you will surely know it if you do. Lynn did and, believe me, we all knew.

She was Jana Reiss. She had a Ph.D. in nineteenth-century American religion; she wrote easy, lilting prose as almost no academic ever does; and she wanted to be a public, rather than a tenured, intellectual. Beyond that, like some kind of extra beneficence, she was an observant Mormon, a member of America's third-largest Christian communion and one that I'd often feared we might underserve out of sheer lack of staff expertise. Speaking now from the perspective of several years later, I don't think any of us, even Jana herself, could name a more welcome or blessed day than the one when she signed on as part of religion's editorial team.

And a team it has remained ever since, with one exception: In 2003, marriage and the need to try her hand at running her own consultancy took Sheri away from *PW.* During the three-plus years she was with us, though, she managed to meld herself into my affection every bit as much as Robin had said she would; and there I continue to hold her, knowing even as do so that I, presumably, will be the next to follow her in leave-taking. Age and religion itself now are drawing me there.

Chapter 57

• • •

My father, who was fifteenth in a family of sixteen children, had nine brothers, some of whom were dead long before I was born and one of whom was my absolute, no-holds-barred idol. Uncle Kay was a country doctor in the most Norman Rockwell sense of that term. His office, which was one flight up from Ridgely, Tennessee's, only drugstore, was filled with vials and concoctions and instruments that could only have inflicted torture in use, but in theory to me as a child were wonderfully shiny, ingeniously articulated toys. Doc Kay's hair was that thick, silver mane that one associates, for probably primitive reasons, with the truly gifted and truly able; and his figure was a duplicate of Santa Claus's. To some extent, so was his personality, which may have been another reason for my finding him the most compelling of the older men in my family.

Doc Kay has been dead now for over forty years, which means that while I still have a child's memories of him, his house, and his office, I have few memories of what he actually ever said or did in my presence. There is, however, one exception. There is one adage of his that will go with me to the grave. "You can always tell how bad off a patient is," he would say, "by how much noise he's making." Then he would add, as if in explanation, "It's the quiet ones you've got to scramble for. Anything making too much noise is not going to die in the next few minutes, but anything too quiet is already halfway there."

I don't know whether it was the apparent contradiction, to my child's mind anyway, in his observation that made it memorable, or whether it was simply the frequency of his saying it that engraved Doc Kay's wisdom on my understanding. Either way, I discovered over the years that his adage was applicable not only to his own patients, but also to Sam's, not to mention to most teenagers and the vast majority of wailing two-year-olds . . . which is a flip and deceptively lightweight way of going where next this story has to go if I am to write honestly of the years between 1999 and the present. Over and over again during those years, I have had to remind myself that anything making as much noise as religion in general and the Church in particular are currently making, has to be if not in perfect health, at least not in a state of eminent demise.

Sociologists talk about "wedge" issues. By that deceptively ordinary term, they mean to name the issues that one side or the other of a broad and/or public disagreement introduces over and over again into the common discussion, not so much in the hope of resolving the articles of conflict as in the hope of gaining new converts to its own, firmly ensconced, point of view. (Or, not infrequently, just of further inflaming some of the already persuaded who are deemed to lack a sufficiently militant fervor.) Such issues become "wedges" in that they distance, often beyond all hope of repair, the opposing stances of each side, one from another. But more subtly—and more disastrously—the wedge issues often devolve from being precepts and practices worthy of debate into becoming little more than playing pieces in a deadly game. They cease to be themselves, in other words, and become instead tools for probing and prodding the larger, less tangible, more abstract, but far more central point or points of dissension. Abortion, now and for the last half century, has been a wedge issue in America.

Destructive of life and fanatically, often biblically, addressed by the extremists on both sides, abortion is a conflict within the cable of religion. By definition, however, it is a moral, not a spiritual or corporeal issue. That is to say that the abortion debate pivots, instead, on a question that is foundational to morality: What is life? What constitutes it, in other words? And on the subtext question of What is the role of our species in it? There have been several periods in history during which humanity enjoyed a working definition of life. Ours, unfortunately, just does not happen to be one of those times. One of the characteristics of post-Enlightenment society, in fact, is that, thanks to the advances of physical science during the twentieth century, we are awash in a veritable sea of many possibilities for adapting, tailoring, producing, manipulating, editing, ending, and generally redefining human life . . .

Or is it life, if it comes from a bottle?

Or does it have a soul if it is cloned?

Or does it have life when it has no consciousness?

Or . . .

The questions that flow from our confusion and lack of necessary ethical definitions are almost without number. Just thinking of them staggers our common imagination, even as more and more possibilities for engineering speciel change proceed to flow, without mercy, out from laboratories and juried periodicals onto the pages of slick-papered newsweeklies and upscale newspapers. Because we do not presently know what life is . . . have not known for almost a century, in fact . . . we cannot resolve our disagreements about it.

But abortion, being the only time-tested way we have of mechanically exercising our values on life as an abstract, constitutes our most accessible, least esoteric basis for fighting among ourselves about what life is . . . and, of course, about what the relative or moral value of each life is within the vaster concept of life itself. As the oldest and most familiar tool available to the majority of us for discussion, abortion by the mid-twentieth century had already begun to morph into a wedge, a pawn—a puck, even—in the struggle among ourselves to understand and do-

mesticate what we know and what—God, have mercy on us—
we know we can never again unknow. In arguing abortion, we
argue and inflame each other over a whole roll call of untamed
demons for which it is both surrogate and sibling. Nor can there
be much question that morality will be the strand in religion's
three-stranded rope that will come to occupy the later decades of
this century as totally and relentlessly as the strand of spirituality preoccupied and commanded much of the last century, or as
brutally and obdurately as corporeality presently occupies this
time and place of my writing.

As that part of religion which is concerned with the "body,"
or physical presence of religion, corporeality translates, at an
everyday level, to the visible evidences of "church" such as budgets and real estate, scriptures and clergy, creeds and social-
outreach programs, so forth and so on. Any working, thinking
adult would have had to have passed the closing years of the
twentieth century and the opening ones of the twenty-first in total isolation not to have developed at least some opinions about
two or three of those areas of religion's corporeality.

What are the proper sources of funding for social-outreach
programs? What are the margins between Church and State?
What causes sex scandals among our ordained clergy, and who
or what is to blame? Those, and a baker's dozen other questions
like them, are all matters arising from, and evidencing, religion's
physical presence among us. They are not, however, wedge issues. That is to say that, aside from the presence of religious ar-
tifacts in governmental or public space, they are still subject to
discussion and, hopefully, to bloodless resolution.

No, the central debate within corporeality is, and has been
for most of Euro-American history, that of the authority and/or
acceptable interpretation of scripture. Just as the business of
defining life and our responsibility to it is at the core of morality,
so the defining of scriptural authority and the subtext question of
determining whose interpretation thereof may or may not be received is foundational to corporeality within the Abrahamic
faiths. As with life, there have been eras in our history when the

authority of scripture was unchallenged within the populace at large and when its interpretation rested secure in the hands of an ordained, established order. Once again, ours is just not such a time. In our time and place, moreover, the fury of the debate has taken the form of discerning from scripture and creeds who is in and who is out of God's range of acceptance and favor. Whom shall we, in the name of God, scorn? Whom, in our fervor, shall we cast out?

And as the years of irresolution have dragged on, the debate has become ever and ever more tendentious and the wedge issues it has spawned more and more searingly hot. Deciding . . . always deciding . . . who is in and who is out of God's creedally patrolled State of Grace. Few, if any, of us have failed to feel that heat.

Chapter 58

• • •

Late in 2003, Professor Israel Knohl of the Hebrew University in Jerusalem published a most remarkable book, *The Divine Symphony: The Bible's Many Voices*. What is remarkable about the book is not so much how well it did or did not do in the marketplace or even how many prestigious reviews it did or did not garner. What is remarkable is its thesis and Professor Knohl's defense thereof.

In essence, from the subtitle of his book on, Knohl assumes the presence, in the composition of the texts foundational to both Judaism and Christianity, of many authorial hands other than the stated and/or apparent ones. Since that notion has long since been established as fact, the involvement of "many voices" is hardly a point of rousing interest. What is rousing is Knohl's assumption that the many unknown voices, with their many competing parts and their tonal contradictions and their atonal paradoxes, compose in aggregate a symphony, and that it is the symphony itself that is divine. What he takes as a working thesis, in other words, is that the God of Abraham, Isaac, David, Jesus, and Paul is in the music and not the parts. And this he begins to prove, in good midrashic fashion, straight out of the sacred text itself by quoting Psalm 62, verse 12 and going from there:

One thing God has spoken;
Two things have I heard:
that might belongs to God.

Knohl's is the first lyrical defense I have heard of the inspired use of many ways of hearing as the means of leading humanity to the singularity of one conclusion: God. In lo these many years of desperate listening, his is the first lyrical defense I have heard — and I was brought to tears by its promise. Wedges and the bitter clashes that foist them cannot retain their necessary heat in a time of lyricism. The lyric belongs to springtime, and its coming is both herald and proof of winter's end . . . though God knows that the winter which still, even as I write, holds us in its last throes — this most recent winter of our discontent — has been a bitter one.

When Sam and I began, in 1997, to attend and then, by 1998, to become congregants of Holy Trinity Community Church, we were not only asking for a place within a new spiritual family, but we were also walking straight into a maelstrom. Holy Trinity is all-inclusive, which, there as elsewhere, means that every spectrum of God's rainbow, sexually, racially, and ethnically, has received, or could upon confession of faith receive, the same kind of family acceptance we have.

We went to Holy Trinity because of one man, Tim Meadows, the senior pastor and himself gay. We went because of some two hundred or so other people who, in aggregate, rock the nave of Holy Trinity several times a week with their enthusiasm for God as they have found Him and been accepted by Him in Jesus, the Christ. Such energy is not only hard to ignore, but participating in it is also addicting. We went because of a smaller coterie of people within the two hundred plus who, in addition to welcoming us, shared with us the common ground of years of living with media, communications technology, and the arts as means of religious perception and exercise. We also went assuming that while the Episcopal Church in the United States of America would not ordain gay priests in 1997, it most certainly would do so momentarily, allowing Tim Meadows to stand for holy orders in ECUSA and allowing Holy Trinity to follow him into full membership as a parish within the Episcopal Church.

Whatever one thinks about homosexuality can be defended by scripture. I can argue any one of about five distinct and incompatible positions with impeccable exegesis. Indeed, anyone who accuses an opponent on this issue of being ascriptural is too uninformed to be in the debate in the first place. As the comparative religionist Huston Smith suggests, the opponents employing wedge issues like homosexuality are almost all absolutists nowadays—almost all believers in the authority of scripture and the absolute necessity laid upon every believer to adhere to it. The problem is not in God's one statement, in other words, but in the hearers' receipt of disjointed messages . . . or perhaps, as Knohl knows, the inability of human ears to hear the integrated harmony.

In becoming congregants of Holy Trinity, Sam and I did what we did not out of any desire to take up a position on one side or the other of a well-wedged issue. Rather, we did what we did out of the sure knowledge that we were at last where we belonged, the sure knowledge that we had found our place in the larger kingdom of God; and we have not looked back since. For one or two of our children and for two or three of our children's spouses, ours has been a painful, compromising, embarrassing move; and I would be less than a mother if there was not a sorrow in that for me. Of even greater sorrow is the fact that we as their parents cannot speak easily, if at all, to some of them about the activities, discoveries, and friendships that are central to our own, ongoing experience of the faith we profess.

Despite the elevation of an openly gay man to our episcopacy in 2003, a similar mourning afflicts me when I am among fellow Episcopalians who, continuing to believe that I am a sinner because I keep spiritual company with sinners, must either challenge or avoid me. They will not have me, despite the fact that I am still one of them. While Sam eventually changed his status from congregant of Holy Trinity to that of full member, I have remained as congregant of Holy Trinity with full membership in an Episcopal parish in Memphis. My license to serve as both a lector in the Church and as a lay eucharistic minister is Episcopalian in authority, and without it, I would be bereft of that small part of my life that so enriches the whole. Unable to read the sacred texts before the assembled church, unable to carry the elements to the sick and especially to Ruthe, unable to speak the occasional homily, I would be, inside my own life, as a cripple inside a prison.

I know this to be true, because once, just briefly, I experienced that bereavement. We had been attending Holy Trinity for almost a year when the senior warden of our Episcopal parish in Lucy, himself a good friend, came knocking on my office door to say . . . quietly, awkwardly, even perhaps apologetically . . . that inasmuch as we had transferred our attention and attendance, though not our membership or all our giving, to Holy Trinity, it would no longer be possible for St. Anne's vestry to recommend to the Bishop the renewal of my licenses. Given that we were now part of "that church," things could not be otherwise, he said.

During the subsequent month or so that it took me to find and join a parish that would recommend my licenses for renewal, I suffered. I also learned just how exquisitely the question of biblical authority and interpretation can scorch when one touches the wedge of homosexuality. Shortly thereafter, I was to make a similar discovery about scriptural and doctrinal certitude's other great wedge issue, that of religious tolerance . . . or religious intolerance in the name of God, as the case may be. I was to do so by the simple process, unlikely as such may seem, of accepting a position on another board of advisers for another start-up enterprise of enormous worth and potential.

With pleasure and a genuine sense of having been complimented, I accepted, late in 1999, the request of the Christian Science Church that I serve as a member of its inaugural board of advisers for a proposed library. To be housed in Boston, more or less across the Church's immense public plaza from the mother church of First Church of Christ, Scientist, and contiguous with the editorial offices of the *Christian Science Monitor*, that library was to become two things: first, a repository for the collected papers of Mary Baker Eddy that would be archival and, second, a center for the study of female leaders in nineteenth-century American religion. Its lower floors would be open to all who wished to come; its upper floors of archival collections, open and available to all credentialed scholars. It was brilliant and breathtaking as a concept, and The Mary Baker Eddy Library for the Betterment of Humanity is now, in reality, all that which was envisioned and more.

I am not a Christian Scientist, nor will I ever be. As I have several times remarked to my hosts and colleagues at that Church, I stoutly disagree with several of the scriptural assumptions or interpretations on which Christian Science and its practices rest. That does not mean, though, that I disagree with the importance of a great library or with that library's perfect right to expect from me whatever I can bring to its furtherance. The sorrow—not the regret, never the regret—the sorrow in that for me and the price to be paid for it are the assaults upon my own beliefs that it has provoked. Sometimes more intellectual challenges than attacks and, once or twice over the past few years, more vicious screeds than assaults, those inquisitions have come, usually, from the most unexpected places: from fellow journalists who should know better and who, at least in the popular imagination, would be assumed to care less; from fellow Episcopalians; even from perfect strangers reaching in to me through the Internet. Yet in every one of them there is a consistent text or subtext: To be in fellowship with sinners is to encourage and be guilty of their sin, "sin" and "sinners" having both been clearly defined by the Bible, if only I would look at section Abc or Xyz, for instance. The only humor in the thing is that the citations of Abc are themselves almost always subject to various interpretative renderings among the inquisitors and those of Xyz almost always vary in the combinations, emphases, and conclusions as-signed to them.

None of us can withstand attack, I suspect, without some pain. Moreover, anyone who has an ounce of human empathy cannot suffer attack without some sorrowing over the ferocity of the need that drives us to afflict each other. An anxiety that can be allayed only if one feels within himself or herself right about God and where we have positioned Him in our living is a damna-tion most devoutly to be feared. And few of us can suffer the loss of intimacy or even of goodwill without grieving for what is gone. Certainly I cannot and have not. What one does, instead, is continue to ask if the task is worth the cost and, finding the an-swer to be yes, then to push on. Certainly, The Mary Baker Eddy Library and continuing to serve on its board of advisers were more than worthy of the price . . . which was why Sam and I were ticketed to fly out of Memphis International for Boston's Logan airport early on Friday morning, September 14, 2001.

We did not make that trip.

Chapter 59

• • •

Sam and I are from the same small town in East Tennessee and grew up there together. We have, in fact, known each other since infancy. We came, however, from very different stock. My parents, although Tennesseans their whole lives through, were born and reared in the Delta-like farmlands of West Tennessee and, as such, were adult transplants to the high hill country of Appalachia. Sam's mother, on the other hand, was a seventh-generation East Tennessean, her Grandfather Witcher's land at the time of his death still being registered at the county courthouse under an original bill of grant signed by King George III of England.

Mamaw — it was the only name by which any of us ever called her — Mamaw was, in other words, a Witcher in a place where that name meant something. But she was also a disciplined woman, and she taught her descendants — our children especially, for they came last in the progression of her grandchildren — to lay responsible claim to the blood they carried and to the heritage they enjoyed. That is undoubtedly part — a large part, in fact — of the reason for their absorption even today, in their own adulthood, with everything Witcher, including the roadside marker on the south side of the Limestone Cove Highway just a bit east by southeast of the little town of Unicoi, Tennessee.

Put there by Tennessee's State Historical Commission, the thick metal sign marks the turn-in to a nineteenth-century cemetery. Still used from time to time for burials and still maintained in a more or less informal way by the community around it, the graveyard is like almost every other country graveyard you have ever seen . . . treed, cool, and silent. It is, in fact, unremarkable in every way save for the sign just outside its entrance and the commanding mound of a communal grave at its front, northernmost corner.

The Historical Commission's marker, with its black letters raised high and sharp off its silvered surface, says, succinctly: "Here are buried the eight civilians killed at the home of Dr. David Bell in November 1863. En route to Kentucky to join Federal forces, they were found by a detachment of Col. W. A. Witcher's Confederate cavalry, while waiting for breakfast. They were: B. Blackburn, Calvin Cantrel, Elijah Gentry, Jacob Lyons, Wiley Royal, John Sparks and two unknown. Buried nearby is Dr. Bell's brother, James, killed at the same time." The events of that November morning almost a century and a half ago are still referred to locally either as the Limestone Cove Tragedy or as Witcher's Massacre. What the roadside marker does not say, however—what it simply assumes every visitor will know—is that the slayers and the slain of Limestone Cove were all southerners, probably most of them even kin, who were caught in a conflict of such clashing values, opposing moral directions, and variant scriptural interpretations as could only be resolved by war.

In point of actual fact, the W. A. Witcher who was a colonel of the Confederate cavalry was not Mamaw's forebear, though common sense and mountain isolation make it almost inconceivable that he was not related at some degree of proximity or remove. But kin by an establishable relationship or not, for all the years of our own youngsters' childhood, when we would be in eastern Tennessee visiting Mamaw and decide to take her out for a family ride, she as often as not would say to Sam, "Let's stop by the cemetery and show the children the marker."

This was not a macabre gesture on her part. Indeed, it was quite the opposite; for once we were there, she would read our children first the marker itself and then the gravestone on the common grave mound: "They were: B. Blackburn, Calvin Cantrel, Elijah Gentry, Jacob Lyons, Wiley Royal, John Sparks, and two unknown." Almost, I can say the litany of their names without having to read them after so many years of hearing them.

But after the reading, our children, and we with them, would turn aside. They went running off as children almost always do when they are set loose in the open spaces of a cemetery; and Sam and I simply wandered away in order to distance ourselves from Mamaw. We wandered, that is, so as to not intrude on what was to follow.

Always, Mamaw would bend down and pick up some ob-ject . . . a leaf, a twig, a bit of grass, a fallen acorn shell the squir-rels had left. She would toy for a minute or two with whatever she had chosen, fingering it as one does with the beads of a prayer chain. Then her fingers would grow quiet, the chosen ob-ject sometimes even dropping from them, and her eyes would fill . . . so full sometimes that the tears welled over and down into the slack of her cheeks; but there were never any words after that. When she was done, she would call to us, saying that we needed to get home for supper, and then begin fussing over the children, brushing leaves off one or spit-scrubbing dirt off the hands of another with her handkerchief. It was all over once again.

There are, of course, a number of things that one can con-clude from Witcher's Massacre and the roadside sign that marks the burial site of its victims. The first and most obvious is that ideas are always more powerful than the commonality of either blood or place. They always have been and presumably always will be.

The second is that had the South won the War Between the

States, the roadside marker would announce "The Site of Witcher's Victory" and history would talk about "The Rout at Limestone Cove." Cynical as such a statement may sound, we human beings deny the irony of it to our own peril. None of us can afford ever to forget that the tale pivots in accord with who the victor is.

The third possible conclusion is gentler and nearer to compassion than to survival. It is the understanding that in war there is never a right or a wrong that does not have its other and opposite side. Only with the passage of time do the issues involved in any war come to seem unadulterated, inherent, and clear.

As an old woman—one almost as old now as Mamaw was then—I can also say that death always buys something. In the case of Limestone Cove, both the heroes and the antagonists, by their actions and their dying, tore away the mores, beliefs, and patterns of one way of life and thereby brought about a more moral, more equitable, more just way of being for more people, themselves as well as their opponents. This was true in their case not necessarily because they as individuals wanted to pursue a course of massacre and violation as such. I would wager a considerable sum, in fact, that most of the men under Colonel Witcher's command no more wanted to kill for the sake of killing than the dead wanted to be killed. Rather, every one of them, victor and vanquished, on that November morning was part of an epoch and an outmoded human social construct that had run their courses.

As a kind of footnote, the sometime journalist in me must also add to my list of conclusions the observation that bits of the quotidian like "killed waiting for breakfast" are always worthy of fierce respect. Juxtaposed to copy one way, they are morally suspect because they prejudice by their selective use of a minor fact; positioned in another, they become the keys to that noble construct which is good copy.

But having said all of that, I must hasten to say that not for one minute do I think—nor did Sam or I ever think—that Mamaw was preoccupied with any of these thoughts as she stood in front of the burial mound at Limestone Cove and wept so sound-lessly. What she was doing instead—and what we understood at the time she was doing—was stopping awhile before a void into which no words can go. Created by violence, the cemetery at Limestone Cove was, and remains, a deceptively bucolic pas-sageway into an eternal interruption that is beyond interrup-tion . . . which is itself complete. It was this and this alone before which I always thought my mother-in-law stood and wept; or I did until the day she said to me, "It is good to be here."

Chapter 60

• • •

The cemetery at Limestone Cove is the smallest and hum-
blest of all small and humble historical sites, so much so in
fact that I am amazed when I occasionally discover that some
non–east Tennessee, nonhistory buff acquaintance has even
heard of it. And as for Witcher's Massacre, I have to assume that
it was the very smallest and least revered of all the bloody engagements that made the War Between the States the bloodiest
and most deadly war in American history.

Today we in this country have another cemetery. We call it
now by the name of Ground Zero, for we were given it like a
wound to our bodies in mid-September 2001. The two sites —
Limestone Cove and Ground Zero — could not be more dissimi-
lar. The nineteenth-century one is small, rural, infrequently seen,
completely resolved; the twenty-first-century one, huge beyond
our imagining, exquisitely urban, quietly but constantly visited
even after sunset, and years, perhaps even decades, from resolution. Eventually, of course, when we come to post the list of those
who were interrupted at Ground Zero, our list, like that of Limestone Cove's, will contain the names of men and women who

were made into heroes one fall morning simply because they stopped too long, or not long enough, in waiting for their breakfast. But far more than violence and some caprice of diurnal timing have bound the two burial sites together in my mind over the days and weeks and months and, now, years since 9/11.

Like many Americans, Sam and I did not travel for over a month after the Al Qaeda attacks. We were not afraid to pick up our normal schedule of trips and meetings; or at least I have no memory of personal fear during those weeks. There is no question, of course, but that we were stayed by, first, the impossibility of finding readily accessible flights during those weeks and, second, by the enormous inconvenience of trying to get onto a flight once it was booked. Beyond those obstacles, however, and far more effectually, a great quiet held us in Lucy . . . a quiet of grief not just for those who had died, but also for an order and a way of being on the earth that had died with them. We needed time.

By mid-October, though, as the world beyond Lucy began to shake itself from its stupor, we too had to shake off our mourning lassitude. For several months, I had been scheduled to spend the entire day of Friday, October 19, doing some archival research in the library at *PW*; and I could neither cancel nor reschedule that trip. To make it, however, was to make our first trip into Manhattan since the attacks. More difficultly, for me it would be to make my first trip into our offices since the deaths of 9/11. The two young men who had, every fortnight, put *Religion BookLine* up on the Web had been on their way to Los Angeles in the plane that took down the south tower. I did not know them . . . had never even met them personally, in fact . . . but those whom I love in that New York office had known them; had worked with them; had, as our librarian told me so quietly, stood at the office windows and watched as they burned to death.

Because I could not bear the thought—perhaps, the presumption even—of taking my sorrow-at-a-remove into that grieving office without some more physical sense of what it had been, and will always be, for those who stood and watched, Sam and I flew into La Guardia a day early; and on that Thursday afternoon, we made our first pilgrimage to Ground Zero. At first the cabbie we hailed refused to take us, until Sam thought to change our destination by saying that if he would take us down the FDR Drive toward the Battery and then maybe just back up as near to Rector Street? Somehow that adjustment eased the driver's reservations; and within twenty minutes thereafter, we were getting out of our cab and making our way north toward Trinity Wall Street Episcopal Church and its now-fabled chapel of St. Paul's.

The barricades that at that time cordoned off the acres of destruction wrapped around the southeastern corner of Trinity's churchyard, and we began walking them there, walking slowly northward, walking with dozens and dozens of other sorrow-filled people. Ash and debris were everywhere, the odor of smoke from the burning buildings pervasive; but so too was the silence. There was little sound . . . no street traffic, no commerce, certainly, but more tellingly, there was no conversation among us who walked save for an occasional "Excuse me" or "Can you see around me?" Men and women alike were crying, but crying as soundlessly and unguardedly as once I had watched Mamaw cry.

As Sam and I got a bit more than halfway up the barricades, the odor of smoke grew sharper, and we could hear the occasional disturbance of a jackhammer working in the rubble. We could also feel the rain . . . except that it was not raining. The day, like so many days in that memorable October, was almost preternaturally cloudless. There was, nonetheless, a light mist falling both inside and just along the outer edges of the barriers. Like everyone else moving along the cordons, I stopped and looked up in confusion only to determine first that indeed there was no rain and then to discover the source of the falling mist.

Three or four teams of workmen were cleaning the buildings of Ground Zero. Twenty, perhaps twenty-five or even thirty stories above our heads, a dozen or so men were hosing the windows and exterior facings of buildings that, while still structurally usable, were nonetheless too cloaked in ash and soot to be habitable.

Almost immediately, however, my attention was drawn away from watching the hoses above me and back to the people around me. Some of them, as they perceived what was happening above us, began to edge quietly forward and lean, one after another, ever so gently, into the ashy mist, receiving it like a baptism upon outstretched hands and upturned faces. And as they did so, I heard Mamaw's voice saying across the years, "It is good to be here."

Ground Zero and Limestone Cove, though they differ sharply in size, are places of aggregate, orchestrated death. Both are testimonies in mounded earth and tortured steel to the insult of civilian deaths in the name of war; both are testimonies to the irony of abrupt deaths caught forever, like freeze-frames, in a surround of normalcy. The experience of being in one is, in many ways, very like the experience of being in the other: Neither our minds, with their imaginations and endless chattering, nor our bodies, with their mortal fears and necessities, can survive for long in these or any other place of so many and such deliberate interruptions. Human bloodshed and the violence done to our sense of fair expectations still draw us to try, however . . . still dare us, even, to stop awhile and stare at this rip in the curtain of our understanding, this enervating rupture in the stabilizing shell of our minds' perceptions and our bodies' dimensions.

And like those October mourners in whose company once I stood, I still find myself needing, from time to time, to lean closer into the rifts of both Limestone Cove and the World Trade Center — to lean forward until my awareness slips, bereft of my will, into them, and I stand gazing awhile into the dark . . . the luminous, all-receiving dark. I stand in thought and prayer, as once upon another time my mother-in-law used to do, at the margin between the worlds, and, like her, I gaze in upon the enormity of life when it is measured by the sum of its losses.

Chapter 61

• • •

As was true of the parsing of Limestone Cove when I and mine were infrequent visitors there many years ago, so too now with my parsing of Ground Zero. That is to say that, as with Limestone Cove, there are a number of things that may be said of Ground Zero: Ideas, now as then, are still more powerful than the commonalities of a shared humanity. Clearly, at least in the short term, they are more potent even than the expedient charity and enlightened self-interest that logically should appertain in a shrinking world. It is also true that now, just as then, violence born of ideas is purer before itself and in its own eyes than is violence born of patent greed or ambition or arrogance. As a result, it must be addressed differently and feared more.

I can say with surety of our own time, as I do of Witcher's Massacre, that the tale of 9/11, when told a century and a half from now, will pivot on who the victor is—not militarily, but morally—and if we forget that fact, we do so to our own detriment; for now as then, in no war is there ever a right or a wrong that does not have its other and opposite side. Only with the passage of time do the issues involved come to seem unadulterated, inherent, and clear.

I can say—indeed, I must say, because I am so keenly convicted of it—I can say that war and mass death always buy something for someone. They always destroy . . . break away . . . level out . . . the old, former ways. It is the lot of the dead to suffer that ending, but it is the duty of the living to redeem the newness such death has brought. For those who survived Witcher's Massacre and lived to maintain and attend their souls while maintaining and attending their dead, the result has been a better life for all of us in this country regardless of our color or culture. Yet all of us know as well that elsewhere there are other mass grave sites that have not been so redeemed and that will forever tarnish the lives and souls of our kind . . . which brings me, and probably most Americans, full circle to the question of consequence: How then must we live with these dead and this grave?

It is a preemptive question, embracing as it does all the realities and vicissitudes of body, spirit, and mind as they labor together to sculpt a soul. Beyond preemptive, however, it was also ubiquitous as a question in the months after 9/11, which is the reason that on April 5, 2002, not quite seven months after the Al Qaeda attacks, I was once more at Trinity Wall Street Episcopal Church. This time, however, Sam and I were not there to walk the barricades (although we did do that two days later), but for me to be one of four keynote speakers for a gathering of the Church at large. The nave of that great building was itself full, while in Episcopal parish halls and diocesan houses around the country, hundreds who could not be physically present joined the consultation by satellite and open phone lines. The question to be addressed by the thus assembled Church was, "How Then Must We Live?"

I had spoken before at Trinity—had spoken, in fact, as a keynoter for what is known within the Episcopal Church as a Trinity Institute. In title and logistics, the April 2002 conference was another Trinity Institute, albeit a more hastily titled and modified one than would otherwise have been true; and preparing for it had been for me like a slow rousing from a dark winter's sleep.

During the days, weeks, and then half year immediately after 9/11, I had remained largely silent about Ground Zero, both in print and on the air. To talk—to say anything—seemed to me to diminish and indeed to demean the magnitude of what had happened. Even when colleagues, trolling for quotable commentary, called and asked for something, anything, they could run, I could not furnish it. Quite literally, I had nothing to say. Thus it was that as the April institute drew nearer and nearer, I found myself moving like a sleepwalker through the world of words, picking up a phrase here and throwing it back down there until, finally, I stood in the chancel of Trinity Church and did the only thing I knew how to do. I told the story of Limestone Cove.

Because I am old, or near to it—and perhaps because of Limestone Cove—I found it both easy and truthful to say that day that there is one overarching answer to the lament of "How Then Must We Live?," one answer that, for me, takes primacy of place every time I approach it: We first must live within the long lens of history and the longer perspective of eternity. We are not alone here. Rather, we stand where other human beings have stood innumerable times before; and it is through our sorrow and our sense of insult and offense that we join them—those ancestors and ancient kin—who suffered in their time the outrage of human circumstance and then went on to celebrate the indestructibility of the human spirit even when it is slaughtered by its own hand.

Beyond that fact lies another, namely that the ancients, from the most aesthete Hindu sadhu to the shrewd Christian who masqueraded for years as my mother-in-law, have always understood that death is philosophy's dark gift to the human spirit's formation. All things can pale before its hegemony; and all things, if we live long enough, do come to be measured in terms of its inevitability. The sages of every age have always known and understood as well that rituals like baptism are religion's sweet gifts to the heart's surcease as surely as ecstasy and prayer are the cordial mentors that consciousness assigns us. They are tools bequeathed to all of us equally by virtue of our god-given humanness and transmitted to us by a great company of human witnesses. We would be poor stewards of those gifts if we were so foolish or so arrogant as to not employ them.

Experience and reverence urge upon me the daily remembrance of another commonality as well. The psalmist of Judaism's tradition—and of mine and of Islam's—captured that commonality best in the song that vows, "We will open our mouths in a parable; we will declare the mysteries of ancient times. That which we have heard and known, and what our forefathers have told us, we will not hide from our children . . . that the generations to come might know, and the children yet unborn; and that they in turn might tell it to their children."

What the psalmist understood and many men and women since him have articulated so well is that there were blessings in Limestone Cove for my children. For them as children, there was the blessing of identity. In their maturity, there was the blessing of a belonging bought and sealed, visible and solid—a belonging forged by a common and remembered sorrow. And there was indeed, coming from that place, the blessing of a richer, fuller, more generous life for them and for all of those caught, as they were and are, alive, together, and vulnerable, on this globe. Those blessings were recognized by my children because one grandmother made of one mass grave site a treasury or tabernacle for such riches of the heart. Knowing that as intimately and personally as I do, I can do no less than she, in her time, taught me to do; I must assume a holy responsibility to 9/11's story—to its truth, to its consecration, and to its reverent transmittal.

I could, and did, say all of these things at Trinity, just as I could say, and have said, them all several times since. As observations or commentary, they do not trouble me any more now than they troubled me when, standing in front of my fellow Christians in April 2002, I spoke them publicly. What troubled me at Trinity was what I had not said—what, indeed, it seemed to me none of us had said.

We—speakers and participants and distance callers alike—we had all talked about 9/11 because it could and can be "talked" about. It is an event and, as such, subject to analysis and therefore to a form of knowing. That is, as an event it can be reported upon and reacted to with words, those untrustworthy, narrow-gauge cars within whose maws we transport the ore from its hiding place out to our necessity. But what of the darkness? What of the center beyond the words and beyond even their miners? September 11 may surround the tomb, but what lies interior to it? What of the difference between 9/11 and Ground Zero?

I left Trinity feeling like a charlatan and, worse, I left knowing I had proved myself to myself as inept and a coward. Ground Zero—by which I mean the indissoluble silence, and not necessarily the place—Ground Zero mocks our dreadful obsession with knowing. An interruption without words and railcar tracks, it holds back an obscuring curtain and lets some portion of not-knowing show itself, like God passing before a largely cosseted Moses.

No, what every part of me cried out to say at Trinity was not the words of an address or even a story of family truth; what I wanted only to speak were the opening lines of a borrowed but sublime song: "My soul doth magnify the Lord and rejoice in God, my Savior" and then after them, to say nothing.

Such a thing would have been offensive, of course, not only to my hearers, but also to me . . . offensive because I could not express—was totally unequipped to express, even to myself—the surety that connected my mourning and our country's terror with awe and my need to praise. Job, whose faith redeemed his private anguish, is well remembered for his "Though He slay me, yet will I trust Him," but scarcely not at all for his later psalms of amazement: "I have uttered what I did not understand, things too wonderful for me, which I did not know . . . I had heard of you by the hearing of the ear, and now my eye sees you; therefore I despise myself, and repent in dust and ashes." Such a forgetfulness is probably as it should be; for Job, although possessed of faith from the beginning, had arrived at his humility and awe only after he had talked with God and been directly persuaded by both word and example. But Mary's Magnificat had been before the fact. She had spoken it at the commencement of her sorrow and with more than constancy. She had rejoiced in being before God, whatever the horror and however great the confusion; and her praise had been the transparency through which we came to realize God among us. Now we stood at that moment when the choice between being Mary and being Job was to be made.

Yet fear of censure, of accusations of insensitivity, and even of abrogating to myself what was another's sorrow prevented me from probing my own confusion through to such conclusions. I held my tongue and kept my own counsel and thus, I also left Trinity tired almost to sickness . . . tired of myself, tired of words, tired of living on the outside of life.

Chapter 62

• • •

Each year for many years, Oxford University Press and the New York Public Library have cosponsored what is called the Lectures in the Humanities Series. A paper on an assigned theme or subject is written by an invited guest, delivered first as a public lecture in the library, and then, after modification and expansion, published as a book by Oxford. In early 2001, sensing an increasing desire for greater substance and theological depth in popular god-talk, the Library and Oxford had decided to give the fall 2002–spring 2003 lecture season over to sin and evil. To effect this, they had decided to focus upon the seven deadly sins in particular, commissioning a lecture and resultant book on each of them.

When Oxford's call of invitation came, I had been more incredulous than flattered at first (though I recovered shortly thereafter). Being a watcher and chronicler of religion as it interacts with popular culture, or even as it articulates within itself, is not theology. If it is any one, clear thing at all, it really is a form of sociology. Sin and evil, on the other hand, as the Library and Oxford knew so well, are theology. To speak and write upon

them . . . especially to speak and write upon one of the seven
deadly sins . . . within so visible, well-vetted, and influential a
venue as the New York Public and/or Oxford University Press
would be to do theology in the most public and vulnerable way.
During my years at *PW*, I had learned to exchange academic
carefulness for journalistic carefulness; and while both are ad-
mirable standards, they are not identical ways of working and
certainly they are not identical ways of framing the pertinent
questions. More to the point, over the years since 1971 when I
had left the academy for publishing, I had learned to exchange
focused research for predictive instinct and a kind of informed
market savvy. Editorial boards and marketing meetings had become my juries and my peer reviews. Above and beyond all this
even, there was also the sobering fact that I had never formally
studied theology in my whole life. What theology I might lay
claim to, I had gained as an autodidact, rarely the world's most
secure platform for doing public business.

Nevertheless and moreover, as they say . . . nevertheless, a
contract had been proffered and, if memory serves, I had hesitated not at all about signing it. Joe Durepos negotiated a time
extension on some contracts that I had already signed. Then he
negotiated the Oxford contract; and by midspring 2002, I had
Greed sitting firmly in place on my desk, looking at me with
amusement, and saying, "Now, what are you going to do with
me, Darlin'?" It was Greed, then, and all her progeny that were
placidly and coyly waiting for me and my world-weariness of
soul when Sam and I got back from Trinity on April 8.

I still speak of Greed with a capital letter, for she became a
living thing to me over our year or so of time together. She also
became deeply feminine or, more accurately, deeply Amazonian;
and when, in mid-October, I stood at the podium of the Library
to deliver my lecture on her, I'd titled it "Greed: Matriarch of a
Deadly Clan."

I have no idea now why I had ever thought that an engagement with a sin—any sin—would be an exercise only in academic theology. Nor, for that matter, do I have the slightest idea

why I was ever so naive as to assume that theology, academic or otherwise, would remain a matter of my head and my less than freshly honed intellect. Not so. And as a result, like a lovely chimera of many hues and golden-green eyes, Greed insinuated herself everywhere that summer, sliding soundless as a dream into all the nooks and crannies of my awareness.

I amassed books and essays and published lectures about her until my office was half-buried in them, yet none of those learned things could contain the sum of her. I began to see her in the art I loved and sense her in the conversations I overheard. I even began to discern her placidly watching me from the shoreline in the prayers I offered. In time, I came to love her as one loves the lightning's wildfire or the tornado's funnel . . . with fascination and horror, respect and appreciation. She was indeed the matriarch of the Devil's kingdom; she was the mother of More . . . more food, more sex, more wealth, more prestige, more leisure, more power, more control, more self-regard. But she was also magnificent, the agent of God, the subtle seductress; and telling her story had become a personal matter between the two of us.

Like Rip Van Winkle awakened from his long snooze, I lumbered about disoriented and inept for months, at times thinking that I would never reduce so much raw material to a publishable coherence and, at other times, doubting that I had ever possessed the skills required to organize sources into a thesis in the first place. There were days at a time during the summer of 2002 when I despaired of ever caging Greed long enough to snapshot her history, much less describe her uses or prophesy her future. And she laughed at me. Over and over again she laughed at me . . . laughed about how many parts of me she had occupied over the years, about how many times I had fed her well with the substance of my life, about how many times she had snatched me back from love in order to restore me to her houseboy, Ego.

Then, just as I lost all hope of reducing so roiling a half year of research and introspection into anything cohesive, she lay down like a lover beside me one afternoon and submitted. I might not have her piniored for all time or even piniored as any other of her more agile chroniclers would pinion her, but I at last understood her in relation to what I understood life to be. Like the angel wrestling Jacob, she had wounded me; but she had given way at last, and I could let her go.

When I write of all this now, I realize of course that I invite the charge of inflation. That is, I run the risk of seeming to over-state the dreadful and delicious process that was my April to October 2002, and then my October 2002 through spring 2003. But there is no exaggeration here. Things were as I have said; and my time with Greed had been pivotal. It had been like a cure for me or, perhaps better, like an extended stay in a house of recovery. In wrestling with Greed, I had rediscovered something I had forgotten over the years, namely how much I love to study. I had also discovered, somewhat to my surprise, how little I actually know about the doctrine, history, and thinkers of the Church. But mainly she had pushed me in—almost—to the place where the tracks stop, and I had seen—almost—the faraway borders of the place where the magnificence begins.

Chapter 63

• • •

In March 2003, three days after my sixty-ninth birthday
and at the end of the second week of Lent, Daisy came to
Lucy for a visit. There was to be no work, no business talk, no
agenda except time together. Once her plans were made, and to
add to the celebratory sense of things, she, Sam, and I all coerced
two other friends, Joel Fotinos and Alan Stevenson, to take the
same flight in from La Guardia and share the weekend. Joel is
head of Tarcher Publishing, a division of Penguin Putnam, and
Alan is a documentary filmmaker, so it was a bit disingenuous to
say that there was to be no shoptalk; but our mutual pledge was
to hold it to a minimum.

The three of them arrived on Friday at lunchtime, each coming off the plane loaded with the maximum allowable number of
bundles . . . which was as nothing compared to what the five of
us toted out of baggage claim a few minutes later and to our waiting cars. The agreement had been that Daisy would bring kosher
dinner with her from New York so that we could celebrate Shabbat together that night in Lucy. What no one could have anticipated was, first, how much food Daisy would think five people

needed in order to survive a weekend and, second, how many different insulated cartons a Manhattan deli could manage to use in packing her largess. As a benign fortune would have it, the idea all along had been for Sam and me to drive two cars to Memphis International so that I could take Daisy, Joel, and Alan sightseeing while he took supper and their luggage to Lucy. Had things been otherwise, Joel, Alan, and I would undoubtedly still have been standing in that garage at sundown, surrounded by luggage, if not by Sam, food, or Daisy. As it was, Sam went north with supper, and the rest of us went south to Graceland, Elvis Presley's home being the one thing Daisy truly wanted to see this time around.

Whether one is an Elvis aficionado or not is almost immaterial to conversations about Graceland. It is a shrine in its own right now. Like Medjagore or Guadalupe, it has been made holy by the affection of the humble and the candid. To walk through the garish and tastelessly opulent rooms, to wander the corridors of platinum records and shrieking photographs, even to stand in front of the family grave sites and see the King buried just a few feet away from the twin brother who died at birth and whom he strove always to replace and compensate for . . . to do these things is to touch the naked power of one man's music in the anguish and glory of a small life written large by fate.

The sightseers who enter Graceland are usually a lively bunch, jostling, humming the lyrics of favorite songs, chatting. When they exit Graceland, they almost all go quietly. Certainly we did, Daisy especially being more still within herself than is usual with her. And because the mood upon us was both sweet and sad, we decided to make our way home without more looking and roaming.

In preparation for Daisy's coming and our observant weekend together in a Christian and very non-kosher house, Sam had bought enough rolls of sheet plastic to drape all of our cooking and eating surfaces. (Actually, he had bought enough sheet plastic to drape the whole farm, but excess is Sam's middle name; and since we all knew that, nobody fretted.) By the time the four of us got home from Graceland, he had the rolls all out and waiting in the kitchen, along with paper plates and plastic silverware and two or three new pots and pans with the stickers still in them, not to mention all the deli food still sealed in its insulated boxes and waiting on the countertops. Manhattan clearly had come to The Farm In Lucy; and the minute she saw it all, Daisy's mood lifted. The chuckle was back, the energy, the bustling to unpack and the interruptions to tell another story or hear someone else's. In truth, had sundown come a minute sooner, I have no doubt that we would never have been ready. As it was, we just barely made it.

Joel and Alan draped tables and counters, while Daisy unpacked food and Sam poured drinks into plastic tumblers and then carried what she handed him from kitchen to dining room. In her haste to pack the night before, she had forgotten her prayer book; so I was dispatched to scratch around in the library for a siddur that would more or less cover the bases of having Hebrew for her and a parallel English text for the four goyim among us. At almost the last minute, Daisy ran up to her room for the small, folding, silver candleholder she had brought with her. Then, as sundown came, we held hands around the table, Daisy sang the prayers, and we lit the candles. The Sabbath had begun.

I truly do not know what we ate that night, there was so much of it. Nor do I know how long the others sat around the table and talked. When I and my heart had to leave them for bed, they were hardly into the middle of their conversation, I suspect. They were certainly still at it two and a half hours later, anyway, when I laid down my book and drifted off to sleep on the lilt of their voices.

The next morning, Daisy slept in. Because it was the Sabbath, she could go nowhere and do nothing anyway, save rest and read and dream. The men, on the other hand, were not so restricted, and they headed out early for whatever it is that men do when they are together in relaxed company. The only limitation on their freedom was Daisy's imperative of the previous afternoon that whatever else they did, they had jolly well better be back in Lucy and ready to roll the minute sundown came, because she was going to spend Saturday night on Beale Street or know the reason why.

About one-thirty, I heard her stirring about upstairs and set down the book I was reading. In a few minutes she came down, we fell into easy conversation about not much of anything, and then the two of us shared a light lunch of Sabbath leftovers at the kitchen table. When we were done, Daisy wandered into the dining room. The little candlestick holder was still there, of course, and the prayer book was still sitting in a side chair where she had set it the night before. Otherwise the room looked very much as it always does—homey, a little crowded, and a lot battered from years of hard use.

The dining room is my favorite room of the house, probably because of all the odds and ends we have filled it with; or perhaps we have filled it with treasures because I love it as a space. Who's to say? Either way, it is full . . . two Victorian side chairs that were my mother's and another armed one that was my father's favorite bedroom chair; a pedestal made from the nineteenth-century newel post a friend had rescued at the last minute from a Memphis wrecking crew; an eighteenth-century sheep-nosed clock my father had found in a little shop near the Tower of London and brought home with him. Having ticktocked its way through all the days of my childhood and then through all the days of our children's growing up, it is especially dear.

There are canvases I garnered from the trash bin at the College of Art, each of them a remembrance of a beloved student, or now, juxtaposed to them, the canvases and art of two of our own children. There's the wall of windows with their solid run of three-quarter-length curtains. I had made those curtains from lace I hauled all the way home from Germany in my lap lest it should become crimped in my suitcase. And beneath the windows, there is the handsome, glass-sided box that Sam made as housing, hot bed, and display box for his orchids.

In the center, looking almost apologetic because of its normalcy, sits the dining room table surrounded by its matching, but now wobbly chairs. Sam and I started housekeeping with that table, except that originally it was circular, not oblong, and seated four, not a battalion. As the years have gone by and our family has grown, he has added first one leaf and then another and then another, so that the present table bears as little resemblance to our original as Great-grandpa does to his progeny. As Sam has added leaves, he has also had to adjust for the obvious difference between the scuffed-up and distressed original table and the pristine surfaces of the new inserts. The first time I found him in the driveway, pitchfork in hand, thrashing a new table leaf for all it was worth, I briefly doubted him. When he was through, however, there was no discernible difference between the leaf he had battered and the original table in the shaping of whose character we had all had a hand.

Daisy was, in fact, touching one of the leaves of the table when she turned and said to me, "This is your best room."

"I know," I said. "I love it too."

"Tell me about this," she said and she patted the table. So I told her about it, including the story of Sam and his pitchfork. She nodded, but she didn't respond the way she usually does to one of my stories. Instead she said, "And the clock?"

I told her about that, about how my father had brought it home from graduate study in England, about how many times Sam had had to repair it, about the stickers on its interior walls where other clockmakers from as long ago as 1756 had mended it, about how the kids were already fighting over who gets it when we are gone, about all of that. She only nodded.

"This chair?" And I told her about my father and how he had always sat in that chair to put on or take off his hosiery and about how, even though it was too fragile now to sit in, I could not bear to lose it lest I lose some part of him, some remembrance of him as he looked to me in the dusk of dawn or evening, sitting there to pull his socks on or off.

"These?"

"My mother's," I said. "Sentinels from her front room parlor where no one ever sat, but everyone laid their coats."

She didn't say anything for a few seconds, then looked up at me, shook her head just slightly, and said, "We have no things, you know."

It was as matter-of-fact and as devoid of self-pity as her "I thought you knew" had been a decade earlier in the Holocaust museum. At first, I did not understand and then, of course, I did.

"Oh," she said, as if oblivious to what she had just shown me. "Oh, there's a 1928 gaudy bed-and-dresser set that I'll get when my mother dies. It was so god-awful that the family who sponsored us here was glad to get rid of it, but I can remember my parents sleeping in it . . ." And she chatted on; but I could not follow what she was saying.

"We have no things, you know."

There it was again, the tear in the curtain, the tesseract.

When, a decade earlier, Daisy Maryles had laid her hand on my arm and said, "And that, Tickle, is why you and I cannot . . . must not . . . fail in what we have set out to do," she had picked my life up, turned it a quarter turn, and then set it back upon its foundations to face in a different direction. When, in March 2003, Daisy Maryles stood in my dining room and, shaking her head, observed one of the, to her, mundane facts of her life — We have no things — she did not change my angle of vision. She simply released me from the presumption of a borrowed one. In effect, and however unintentionally, she reminded me again that the soul which would not be slothful must risk its own landscape.

Terra Incognita

Chapter 64

• • •

"And all shall be well and all manner of thing shall be well."
The words are from *The Cloud of Unknowing*, but the poet
T. S. Eliot quotes them in the closing lines of his meditation on
the abandoned and moldering abbey at Little Gidding in England. And this shall be, he says . . . this inviolate pledge shall be
realized . . . when the rose and the fire are one.

I do not know where the rose and the fire are one nor, I suspect, does anyone else. I do know that they are. I understand as
well—and probably always have—that so long as I have breath,
I must seek, though never know, their unity. If there is nothing
new in that vocation, there certainly is nothing unique or particular in it either. Stories of questing for the holy are as ubiquitous
as humanity itself, just as human yearning for the divine dates
from as long ago and far away as the act of creation that separated us from it in the first place. What is particular almost to the
point of seeming to have been customized to each of us, though,
is how the definition of that which we seek changes both within
the course of our own years and within the course of history. If
divinity does not evolve—and I assume it does not—we at least

mature, both as individual souls and as an order of creation. Like children growing toward parenthood, we understand ourselves and that which bore us in ways that change and then gain focus in proportion to, and as we approach, our own fullness and our function.

None of us ever recognizes, of course, much less can name, the moment of final change, of the shift that is to be the last one in our present maturing. That moment has not occurred—cannot occur—until the time required for recognizing it is no longer holding us. But if we can never declare as final any shift in who we are, most of us can and do recognize a shift as having occurred. Certainly I knew by March 2003 that one had occurred in me.

In April and less than a full month after Daisy, Joel, and Alan had been with us in Lucy, Sam and I were back on the road, this time to Camp Allen, Texas. Located just outside the small town of Navasota and within easy driving distance of Houston, Camp Allen is not only one of the Episcopal Church's larger and more beautiful conference and retreat centers, but also one of its more sophisticated. We had never been before and so, though I was there to speak, we were also there to enjoy some free time and explore new surroundings as well as to listen and learn.

One of Camp Allen's really solid benefits is a substantial book-gifts-necessities store, where the stock is broad—especially in books—and the pricing is sympathetic. Since cruising bookstores is an occupational hazard for people in my line of work, I had glanced in two or three times during the week, though I had found nothing I wanted to buy. On Thursday, the day before we were to leave, Sam and I were in front of the store when a friend of his came up and the two of them fell to talking. I slipped away, more out of disinterest than anything else, and went back into the store. The manager waved, I commented on a piece of especially handsome ceramic work hanging on the wall, and she invited me into her office to see some work she had just received from the same artist but had not yet processed for display.

Like most book-and-gift store offices, hers was far more interesting than was the shop itself. A hodgepodge of treasures both coming and going, it was as much a study in stacks as my own office in Lucy often is. "Help yourself," she said with a grin and a kind of half wave of her hand to bless the whole of her mess. "Every single thing in here is for sale one way or another, even that tray of rings on their way out of here, if I can just get time to take them off the inventory."

And she was as good as her word. She went off to wait on a customer while I plowed around in her boxes and piles. Again finding nothing I either wanted or needed, I was turning to go back into the store when I saw the tray of rejected rings sitting on the pulled-out drawer of her desk. I rifled through it with my forefinger, unearthing in the process a clunky kind of ring that looked, for all the world, as if it had been fashioned from aluminum or some similar, if harder alloy. The thing was at least a half inch in width, solid enough to function like a miniature brass knuckle, and totally without scrolling or decoration. Rather, there was, dead center of the band's front, a cross cut out in the metal . . . and I grinned the minute I realized what I had.

Pilgrim's crosses are not very popular in lay use these days, but that was what this one was, a pilgrim's cross. And regardless of the substance or worth or lack of inherent beauty in the ring, I wanted that cross on my finger. Like every writer, I spend hours every day of my life in looking down at my hands as they move across the keyboard in front of me . . . or as they drive the red pen across the drafts of half-done manuscripts I usually wish were not in front of me. I would never have thought of a ring as symbol and talisman for me. In fact, I would never have thought of jewelry for me in any context at all, for I own very little of it and wear even less. But a pilgrim's cross constantly in my line of sight, a ring too heavy to ever be entirely comfortable, a band so wide it would callus both one's palm and one's finger . . . ah, there is such branding as the soul seeks when the question has changed and the ground shifted.

I bought the ring—it turned out to be silver after all, just tarnished and badly shopworn—and I have worn it every day since

I bought it, save for the two required for a jeweler to size it to my much smaller finger. It is the first thing I put on in the morning and the last thing I take off at night. I think, however, that I wear it not so much as the mnemonic I had first thought I was buying, but as the best picture I can offer, either to myself or to anyone else, of the tesseract, the receiving rift, the tear in the curtain.

By definition, the arms, head, and post of a pilgrim's cross are stark in line and sharply angular. The arms are slightly narrower than the head and base; but all four are turned, like unforgiving triangles, with their flared bases to the exterior and their apices to the center . . .

. . . to a center that, in an incised pilgrim's cross, is there only by absence

. . . a center that is a mystery of geometry, an openness for which there is no known definition

. . . a center somewhere inside of, and beyond which, is the union of the fire and the rose.

We shall have word of one another, no doubt, over the years ahead, you and I; but meanwhile I bid you adieu and ask Godspeed on all our journeys.

PHYLLIS TICKLE

The Farm In Lucy
Epiphany 2004